UNDER THE SHADOW OF WEIMAR

Under the Shadow of Weimar

Democracy, Law, and Racial Incitement in Six Countries

EDITED BY
Louis Greenspan
and
Cyril Levitt

Westport, Connecticut
London

Library of Congress Cataloging-in-Publication Data

Under the shadow of Weimar : democracy, law, and racial incitement in
  six countries / edited by Louis Greenspan and Cyril Levitt.
      p. cm.
    Includes bibliographical references and index.
    ISBN 0-275-94055-1 (alk. paper)
      1. Hate crimes. 2. Racism. 3. Hate crimes—Germany—History.
    4. Racism—Germany—History. I. Greenspan, Louis I., 1934– .
    II. Levitt, Cyril.
    K5274.U53 1993
    342'.0873—dc20
    [342.2873]   92-23062

British Library Cataloguing in Publication Data is available.

Library of Congress Catalog Card Number: 92-23062
ISBN: 0-275-94055-1

First published in 1993

Praeger Publishers, 88 Post Road West, Westport, CT 06881
An imprint of Greenwood Publishing Group, Inc.

Printed in the United States of America

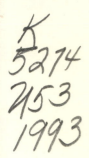

The paper used in this book complies with the Permanent
Paper Standard issued by the National Information Standards
Organization (Z39.48-1984).

10 9 8 7 6 5 4 3 2 1

*To the Forgotten Democratic Jurists
of the Weimar Republic*

Contents

Acknowledgments

The editors would like to thank the Arts Research Board of McMaster University for its financial support for the early stages of research for this volume.

We are also grateful to the following for their advice and support: Dr. Alan Borovoy, Dr. Howard Brotz, Ms. Arlene Duncan, Mr. Gabe Glazer, Mr. Ben Kayfetz, Dr. David Kretzmer, Mr. Manuel Prutschi, Dr. Richard Rempel, Dr. Stephen Roth.

UNDER THE SHADOW OF WEIMAR

Introduction

The chapters in this volume address one of the great questions facing democracies in the modern world. Should they defend themselves against racist political agitation by passing laws that will curb freedom of speech? A similar question is at the heart of controversies concerning laws against pornography. The racial agitation discussed in the chapters of this volume is especially blatant and usually comes to popular attention through provocative incidents that seem calculated to outrage the public. In France, for example, vandals have desecrated Jewish cemeteries, opened coffins, and placed corpses in obscene poses. In Israel the Kach Party has recommended a program of discrimination against Arabs that is reminiscent of the Nürnberg Laws of September 15, 1935. In the United States uniformed Nazis have marched through Jewish suburbs, and in other democratic countries political agitators have gained large followings by calling for the expulsion of immigrants from Asia and Africa.

This volume was conceived by the editors during one such shocking episode—the trial of Ernst Zundel in Toronto in 1984. Zundel, a German national who had been living in Canada since the late 1950s, was indicted for distributing pamphlets that pronounced the holocaust a hoax. These pamphlets offered their readers updated versions of the *Protocols of the Learned Elders of Zion* with accusations of Jewish conspiracies linked to supposed threats to European culture by immigrants from Asia and Africa.

The requirements of the law called for procedures that created a kind of theater of the absurd in the courtroom. Zundel was charged under an archaic law prohibiting the spreading of "false news" (see Chapter 7).[1] This law required the prosecuting attorney to demonstrate the falsity of the claims of the accused; that is, the prosecution was required to "prove" that the holocaust had actually occurred and that the accused did not believe his own propaganda. For the onlookers the proceedings seemed to have been devised by a master of fantasy, for they created the illusion that the very credibility of the holocaust depended on the outcome of the trial. The witnesses assembled in Toronto by the defense enhanced the atmosphere of the absurd. These international superstars of holocaust denial—literary figures, chemists, former concentration camp guards—testified that postwar confessions of Nazis had been extorted by torture; that the diary of Anne Frank was a forgery; that most of the Jews of Europe were still alive; and so on. One witness, a former concentration camp guard, described Auschwitz as a haven from the rigors of war. When he was asked, under cross-examination, why there was barbed wire around the camp, he replied that barbed wire was necessary to keep people out. It was no wonder that Canadians were divided as to whether they had borne witness to a horror or a farce.

In the immediate aftermath it was difficult for Canadians, Canadian Jews included, to come to a consensus concerning the significance of the trial. Many, especially holocaust survivors, believed that the fight to convict Zundel had shown the kind of determination to combat racism that had been lacking in Germany and Europe during the inter-war period. Others, however, saw this revival of an elemental, outspoken, and unabashed racism as an aberration. For them racism in extreme forms persisted but was in disrepute. Beginning with the destruction of Nazism and the revulsion against anti-Semitism as an ideology, continuing with the passage of the civil rights laws that destroyed the system of racism in the American South, and continuing on in our own day to the dismantling of apartheid in South Africa, the tides of history were sweeping away the racist anachronism. For them Zundel and his associates were about as significant as the occasional case of smallpox.

Even those who disputed this optimistic account of contemporary history as a saga about the end of racism could dismiss these neo-racists as a throwback from a bygone era. They argued that racism was alive and well, but in disguised forms. They called attention to "systemic racism," "sublimated racism." For them the enemy was the suave, liberal administrator who spoke the language of egalitarianism but supported structures of employment and reward that maintained the disadvantages of racial minorities. For them the outspoken racism of the holocaust denial was a diversion from a subtle, more menacing and widespread form of racism.

But though no one would deny the achievements of democratic pressure against racism and no one would deny the reality of sublimated and disguised forms of racism, even though one might argue about its extent, it is not possible to ignore the growth of elemental racist political agitation and the reappearance in the public realm of racist political parties and agitators whose appeal is to the most visceral racist sentiments. Since the first Zundel trial in 1984, political parties with avowedly racist programs have made important gains in France, Germany, and Israel. In the United States an ex-wizard of the Ku Klux Klan gained over one-half the white vote in a gubernatorial race in Louisiana. Racism is one of the growing isms of the 1990s. What is the nature of the challenge of racism to democracy?

This volume grew out of the debates provoked by the Zundel trial over the role of the law in the fight against racist agitation. In Canada the trials of Zundel and later of Jim Keegstra raised three distinct but interrelated questions. First, did the phenomenon of open racist agitation warrant special provision in the criminal law? This, after all, gave the agitators publicity and indeed the dignity of public exposure in the courts of law. Second, can democratic governments formulate laws that will curb racist speech without undermining the fundamental democratic commitment to freedom of speech? Finally, if laws directed against racist agitation can be so formulated, is criminal legislation effective as a weapon against racism?

Though we, the editors, are students of social and political theory, we decided to address these questions in the light of practical experience. A number of democratic countries have been struggling with these issues—in the legislatures, in the courts, and in the press. What have they done? What have they accomplished? In the absence of material that provided an international perspective on this subject, we asked authors from different nations to provide accounts of their countries' attempts to formulate laws against racial invective. We solicited accounts of the genesis of existing laws, of the political and legal cultures in which these laws were formulated, and of the efficacy of these laws in checking racist expression. Our material provides an account of democracy versus racism in selected countries mainly since the end of World War II. We say "mainly" because the reference point of these discussions, the reality that haunts all the deliberations, is the experience of the Weimar Republic—a democracy that was overwhelmed by the forces of racism, whose fate has been seen as a warning and an example to all others. Accordingly, we begin with a chapter on the often unsung and underestimated struggle of that democracy's ill-fated attempt to defend itself.

The questions that we pose regarding the significance of neo-racist politics, the compatibility of curbs against racist expression and democracy, and the effectiveness of the law against racist political parties must be viewed in the context of the history of neo-racism after World War II. A sketch of that history can be gleaned from the chapters in this volume, and it suggests a disquieting pattern of growth in primal, elemental racism. This, at the very least, affects the question of significance not because the major western democracies are about to be overwhelmed by racially motivated parties but because they are facing vigorous racial challenges in the political realm. It is true that democracy has made great gains since World War II, and we can hope that we are in a period of democratic ascendancy. But as the garden of democracy grows and spreads its fragrance, there is a disquieting proliferation of the weeds of intolerance. How great is the threat to the garden from the weeds? How effective or dangerous is the herbicide? Must democracy redefine itself by becoming less democratic?

The chapters herein indicate that the growth of racist agitation was not incremental but occurred in a series of spurts. At the end of World War II the United Nations (UN) included the concept of "fundamental human rights" in its charter[2] and authorized the Human Rights Commission and the International Legal Commission to prepare the Universal Declaration of Human Rights. Previous statements were included in the American Declaration of Independence and in the Declaration of the Rights of Man after the French Revolution; and, early in the twentieth century, American legal scholars took steps to introduce the concept of human rights into international law. In March 1948, the Declaration was adopted as a General Assembly resolution; it included twenty-eight rights and ten duties, which influenced subsequent conventions on human rights.[3] Though these resolutions were recognized by member nations and were included in a number of peace treaties at the end of the war, it is characteristic of this period that most nations did not perceive any need to draft legislation directed specifically against racist agitation. Although existing legislation had, on occasion, been used in cases of racial incitement (e.g., the Public Order Act in the United Kingdom during the 1930s—see Chapter 3), there was no legislation that had been specifically targeted to the problems of racial incitement or racist expression. A clear exception to this is Germany, where the Allies in 1945 imposed, at least for a time, a process of de-Nazification. Prior to the Nazi assumption of power, the Weimar democracy had laws that, like those in England, could be used for this purpose. The political elites that founded the Federal Republic in 1949 believed it was necessary to go beyond the legislation of the Weimar era; hence they adopted Article 139 of the Basic Law, which stated that nothing in the Basic Law could interfere with the "liberation of the German people from National Socialism and militarism" (see Chapter 4). Other democracies developed educational plans to combat ethnic and racial prejudice. In Holland, for example, authorities sponsored an educational program in the fine arts as a way of creating a personality type that would be immune to the appeal of fascism. In Canada, a coalition of the Jewish community, organized Labour, and many Christian churches began to campaign for legislation (but not for criminal legislation against racial incitement) that could expose and destroy the edifice of "gentlemen's agreements" that sustained an effective structure of discrimination. Even Hollywood was enlisted: Films such as *Crossfire* (1947) and *Gentlemen's Agreement* (1947) exposed anti-Semitism in the United States.

From 1945 to the 1960s these efforts seemed effective in keeping racist extremism beyond the pale of legitimate public discourse. Racist groups continued to exist, and racist demagogues continued to be active. In Germany and France unrepentant fascists continued to disturb the public realm. But racism was perceived by the public as a nightmare from which the world had awakened. Special interest groups such as the Canadian Jewish Congress (CJC) found that their policy of "quarantining" racist agitators was effective. The CJC explored legal means to combat racism and anti-Semitism, but few thought it necessary to introduce legislation to curb an ideology whose time had passed.[4]

The second advance of neo-racism began in the late 1950s and early 1960s. In North America and in Europe racist agitators began to act with an impunity that had not been seen for decades and in some countries racist parties began to register modest electoral successes. They never gained a large public following, but they did challenge the so-called quarantine that had been in effect since the end of World War II by capturing the attention of the media. In the Federal Republic of Germany, Adolph Von Thadden and the Neudemokratische Partei Deutschlands (NPD) achieved a small but unexpected electoral success. Other neo-Nazi parties appeared in the United States and Canada. George Lincoln Rockwell, self-proclaimed führer of the American Nazi Party, toured college campuses in the United States. An agitator named David Stanley and Canadian Nazi Party founder John Beattie achieved notoriety through skillful use of modern public relations techniques. In Europe, the waves of immigration from Asia and Africa created the basis for a new and potent phase of racist agitation in societies that needed the immigrants for their economic survival but feared the dilution of their homogeneous cultures and populations. One of the early parties to raise race as a political issue was the National Front, which was formed in England in 1968. Racists received decisive support from a prominent, mainline Conservative, Enoch Powell, who announced in 1968 that "like the Romans, I seem to see 'the River Tiber flowing with much blood'."[5] In spite of the fact that Enoch Powell was dismissed from his position in Edward Heath's shadow cabinet, he remained before the public eye.

This new racism called forth a new response. Democratic governments began to explore remedies available through the criminal law. Most sought new legislation. The United States was an exception, holding fast to the First Amendment (see Chapter 5). Earlier, the government of Britain introduced the Race Relations Act of 1965, and France, responding to similar problems, passed laws against racism in 1972. In Canada in 1965 the problem of racist agitation was perceived to be serious enough that the government formed a special committee led by Maxwell Cohen, dean of the Law School at McGill University, which contained distinguished members including future prime minister Pierre Eliott Trudeau and future justice minister Mark McQuigan. The Cohen Committee recommended the adoption of anti-hate laws in the Criminal Code of Canada. Finally, the United Nations adopted a convention on the elimination of all forms of racial discrimination. On December 18, 1968, the United Nations adopted Resolution 2233/XXII condemning all ideologies based on intolerance and called upon nations to act to prevent racial discrimination.

This phase of racist agitation was short-lived. Some of the movements, such as that of David Stanley in Canada, simply evaporated; others met with determined resistance from the local population. Thus, an outraged citizenry of Nuremberg held demonstrations to prevent Adolph Von Thadden from holding a rally for his party in that city of so many bitter memories. Enoch Powell's movement faded and neo-Nazism seemed to have had its brief day.

The significance of the wave of agitation from the late 1950s to the mid-1970s was that it spawned a new generation of racist leaders and followers and even new tactics such as the skillful use of television. These were not the has-beens of the 1940s. The new and younger generation of racists had come to the fore and had acted with impunity, raising new issues such as nonwhite immigration. In that sense they had broken through the immune barrier created in the aftermath of the war. Democratic governments had to contemplate legal measures to eliminate or contain the threat from racist agitators. However, this new push by racist groups proved to have limited strength. Part of the reason for this was that the spirit of the times was clearly out of phase with the racist ethos. The civil rights movement in the United States had captured the attention of the world as the time-honored doctrine of "separate but equal" was struck down by the Supreme Court. Congress enacted the Civil Rights Bill in 1965. Racism's hour had not struck.

But an intense debate was initiated on the limits of the law as a weapon against racism. The proposed legislation and other special measures against Nazism created vigorous controversy from the very beginning. One of the early manifestations of the agony of liberal democracies in the face of open racist provocation could be seen in the controversy surrounding the Nazi march in Skokie.[6] Skokie, Illinois, a suburb of Chicago with a large number of holocaust survivors, had been chosen by the American Nazi Party as the location for a march. Storm troopers were to parade publicly in full uniform replete with swastika emblems. The Jewish community and its supporters argued that such a march would undermine democracy by inciting violence. The American Civil Liberties Union countered that to suppress the march would be tantamount to giving a "heckler's veto"—that is, a mandate to the audience to disrupt and silence a speaker and thus disrupt free and peaceful demonstrations in a democracy. The courts ruled in favor of permitting the march. However, the controversy surrounding this incident was but a microcosm of the general debate surrounding special measures against racist agitation. The debate raised a gripping and as yet unresolved controversy between those who believe that democracy might be undermined by failure to deter racist parties in their infancy and others who argue that democracy might be undermined by special laws limiting freedom of expression.

Those who favor a strategy in criminal law against racist expression point to the generally recognized view that freedom of expression is not an absolute right. Expression that directly incites and causes physical harm is neither countenanced by law nor protected by constitutions. It is not the limitation on freedom of expression per se that is at issue; rather, the circumstances under which and the ways in which it is to be limited are the subject of debate. The use of the criminal law is justified, according to these authorities, on three general grounds.

1. Democracy, a system of government based on law, has a right to use the law against those who would subvert it. The Weimar Republic, it has been argued, failed to defend itself in this way and the world paid a terrible price.

2. Freedom of expression must yield *some* ground before the right of minorities to live in dignity as members of the general community free

from harassment by racist groups. This right is highlighted in the case of those who have suffered under and survived brutal racist regimes.

3. Laws can be crafted with care to limit (if not entirely eliminate) the incursion upon legitimate nonracist expression. The small sacrifice would be worth the gain of stopping racist movements in their tracks.

Civil libertarians accept the view that freedom of expression is not an absolute principle, but they question extending the curb upon expression beyond the incitement to immediate physical harm. Can democracy remain vibrant if it is only prepared to tolerate opinions that are acceptable to the majority? Is freedom of speech not threatened for all if it is taken away from the few, even the malicious few? Are the sensitivities of survivors protected when racist demagogues are given a platform in the courts, and subsequently in the media, day after day for weeks or months during trials and appeals? Perhaps most important, the civil libertarian asks whether these legal measures, for which we are asked to sacrifice some of our freedom, are an appropriate and effective weapon in democracy's arsenal, or whether we are being asked to trade freedom for legal snake oil. Is there reason to believe that legislation limiting freedom of speech can be drafted with such surgical precision that racist malignancy can be removed but healthy controversy protected?

Stephen Roth discusses these issues fully in his comprehensive summary chapter at the end of this book; indeed, he comes to the heart of the problem. He reaffirms the central role of freedom of expression as the strategic prerequisite of democratic societies but observes that this must be tempered by the necessity to contain and thwart racist attacks. However, as he himself notes, we have no evidence that the laws are effective in containing racist agitation, and we do have some evidence to show that such laws have a chilling effect on the freedoms they are designed to protect. But in Roth's view, a view shared by many but not all contributors to this volume, there is a greater risk in not having these laws on the books.

The complexity of the issue will be evident to every reader who considers that the different authors in this volume come to different conclusions, not only about the effectiveness of the law as an instrument against racist agitation in general, but about the excessiveness of the use of the law against different manifestations of racism. Thus, some authors might approve laws against group libel but oppose judicial interference in historical questions concerning the facts of the holocaust. The U.S. Supreme Court fears the chilling effect on free speech more than it fears racist agitators. Others take a different view. France, Germany, and Canada have decided that laws against racial incitement are legitimate limitations to democratic freedoms. Thus, many of the chapters herein give valuable insights into the complex deliberations of the legislative bodies and of the courts on these matters. Their very complexity raises questions about their effectiveness, for the distinctions that are called for require a highly refined legal scholasticism. In Germany, for example, it is not a crime to dispute the number of Jews killed in the holocaust, but it is a crime to say that the myth of the holocaust is perpetrated by a Jewish conspiracy.

In the 1980s a new wave of racist agitation began to gather force. These racist groups have succeeded where their predecessors have failed, for they have managed to gain a place for themselves in the legitimate political arena of a number of democratic societies. Not all racist groups, to be sure, have gained political respectability, and David Duke in the United States can muster votes only by playing down his overtly racist past and promoting his new "legitimate" conservatism. But the new racism has many different manifestations. Some groups, such as the Aryan Nations, are connected to terrorism and call for violence. These are portrayed in a number of films that depict bands of white supremacists in the United States who are prepared to commit acts of violence.[7] But however great the problems such racists pose to law enforcement may be, such groups pose no new challenges to lawmakers. Since violence and direct incitement to violence are part of their political strategy, they already violate universally accepted norms of public order. But we are specifically concerned with groups that are far more sophisticated—and therefore far less vulnerable to legal action.

One of these tendencies was the movement toward holocaust denial that began in the last days of the Third Reich, as the perpetrators made systematic attempts to eliminate the evidence of their crimes. Immediately after the war some isolated fascists issued denials, but the movement came into public view only in the late 1970s and 1980s. By that time it had published a number of texts such as Arthur Butz's *The Hoax of the Twentieth Century*, and it began to organize much of the trappings associated with academic enterprises. This included the establishment of the *Journal of Historical Review*, the organization of conferences, and the founding of a speaker's bureau. The organization gave its views a mantle of respectability. The connection between holocaust denial and other forms of racism has become more evident over the years. "Holocaust denial" has been adopted by racist parties whose prime energies are directed against Africans and Asians. Its text is that the holocaust is a lie. Its subtext is that if the holocaust can be discredited, all is permitted.

This movement had branches in Canada, the United States, France, and Germany. In Germany it was connected to attempts to resurrect Nazism, but in many other countries it was directed at giving other forms of racism greater legitimacy. The connection between holocaust denial and racism against Asians and Africans is evident from the pamphlets that were published in England and circulated by Zundel in Canada. Most racist parties (the notable exception being the one that arose in Israel) paid homage to holocaust denial, and they still do. Holocaust denial, the new form of anti-Semitism built on the old charges of a world Jewish conspiracy, constitutes the highest level of abstraction, racism's theoretical physics of hate. Racists see holocaust denial as an important project, for the holocaust had given racism a bad name.

But the most disquieting breakthrough of the 1980s and 1990s is the rise of political parties in democratic polities with carefully worded racist programs that have attracted a not insignificant following among the electorate. Such parties emerged most dramatically in Israel (the Kach Party of Rabbi Kahane), in France (the National Front of Jean Marie Le Pen), and in Germany (the Republicans of Franz Schönhuber). These racists of the 1980s and 1990s are more potent than the racists of the 1960s in their ability to articulate resentments and fears within the body politic that respectable conservatives are hesitant to face. The Kahane movement calls for the expulsion of Arabs, drawing its strength from propositions shared by all Zionists. Le Pen's call for expulsion of Arabs from France draws on French xenophobia and economic fears that both feed on and contribute to the xenophobia. The German Republicans have preyed on the widespread fear of massive immigration, especially in the former German Democratic Republic.

The Kahane movement spread more rapidly than the public or the authorities assumed that it would, and it was perceived as a menace by all shades of opinion in Israel. The significance of the movement lies in its attempt to justify its racist contentions as logical consequences of mainstream Zionist ideology and, for that matter, of Judaism itself (see Chapter 6).

In France, the National Front became so successful with the electorate that racism became a legitimate ism within the political spectrum. Perhaps Karl Marx was correct about the crowing of the Gallic cock. In 1988 Le Pen was reported to have said that "racism in France today is patriotism."[8] Much of the public must have agreed, as Le Pen achieved the support of over 20 percent of the electorate in some areas. The rise of his party is significant because it occurred in a country that had supposedly immunized itself through laws against racist agitation and, as we see in Chapter 2, has passed new ones.

Thus, in this recent stage in the evolution of racism after World War II, a new set of problems has emerged. These first public discussions on racism and democracy in which racism has moved beyond the fringe into the mainstream of politics focusing on proposed legislation, give new urgency to the tensions between laws banning racial incitement and the commitment of every democracy to freedom of expression. Although these questions have not lost any of their urgency, the new circumstances raise questions about the effectiveness of racist legislation in achieving its goals. The Kahane movement seems to have been checked. Le Pen's movement and Schönhuber's party have established themselves in spite of the efforts of legislators. All have been effective enough to force other right-wing parties in both of these societies to adopt parts of their programs.

Recent headlines concerning neo-Nazi violence against immigrants and asylum-seekers in Germany reflect the anger of many former citizens of the German Democratic Republic (GDR) over their material plight. The "respectable" racists like Schönhuber have capitalized on this sentiment, which is not strictly confined to areas of the former GDR, yet as we see in Chapter 4, Germany today has some of the toughest anti-hate legislation in the world.

The reach for respectability shows alarming signs of success, although it is difficult to predict whether this initial thrust into the political mainstream can be sustained. There are several reasons for the successful forward momentum of racist parties. First, the serious-minded among their leadership have recognized that the aura of violence surrounding racist groups in the past has shut them out of significant politics. With slogans such as "Hitler was right—he gassed the Jews" promoted by the American Nazi Party in the 1960s, the racist right could make no headway in the general population. Second, mainstream conservative groups have been unwilling or unable to cross the ideological divide in order to co-opt substantial fears in western societies arising from unemployment, economic crisis, a falling standard of living, and immigration. Most moderate right-wing parties have successfully purged the racists from their midst and adopted "liberal" attitudes toward immigrant populations. In France and Germany, where there has been some evidence to show that the parties in power have moved to appease the fears of a significant portion of the electorate by tightening strictures on immigration and moving in the direction of repatriation of visible minorities, the response has generally been one of too little, too late. The momentum here may lie to the right of the general consensus.[9]

We have not intended in this survey to announce the end of democracy or the imminent triumph of racism. Our present world can be best understood as a maelstrom in which several powerful currents are swirling. There is the current of democracy, a current that brought an end to colonialism, to the racial structures just cited; there is the current of sophisticated disputes about racism such as those connected with affirmative action; and there is also the current of visceral racism that appeared at the Zundel trials. In this work we will isolate the latter and the problems connected with it.

Many of the chapters are concerned with holocaust denial, which would seem to give priority to anti-Semitism rather than other forms of racism. We are accustomed to placing the holocaust in a class and dimension all its own. But one of the results of present-day racist agitation is to give holocaust denial a standing within the strategy of other forms of racism. Le Pen is concerned very little with Jews but has been charged with holocaust denial. This theme has also emerged in the speeches of David Duke.

The question that initially motivated us to undertake the task of preparing this volume was that of conflicting rights in democratic states, the fundamental right of free expression, and the right of democracies to protect themselves and their citizens against racist incitement. We hoped that by examining the legal theories and practices in various countries and by presenting the arguments on both sides of the issue, we would be able to clarify the problem and allow the reader to follow the more compelling argument, for or against anti-hate laws. We were especially hopeful that the investigation into the situation in the Weimar Republic would point the way to a solution for the modern democracies. But we made the interesting discovery that both defenders of anti-hate laws and civil libertarians opposed to such laws found the material on Weimar supportive of their respective positions. We were unable to realize our goal of providing a clear answer to the problem of the clash of freedoms and rights involved in this question. The issues are too complex and case-specific for an inclusive and definitive direction to be recommended. However, we have provided the reader with an overview of existing approaches in international perspective and a thorough airing of the issues involved. The lack of a definitive answer to the main question is a result not of a paucity of information but of the inherent complexity that racial incitement poses to modern democracies.

NOTES

1. This law was struck down by the Supreme Court of Canada on August 27, 1992.

2. The preamble to the United Nations Charter adopted in 1945 reads in part:

> We the Peoples of the United Nations determined to save succeeding generations from the scourge of war . . . and to reaffirm faith in fundamental human rights, in the dignity and worth of the human person, in the equal

rights of men and women and nations large and small, and . . . to practice tolerance and live together in peace with one another as good neighbors . . .

3. Examples include: The Convention on the Prevention and Prosecution of the Crime of Genocide (1948); The Convention on the Status of Refugees (1951); The Supplementary Convention on the Elimination of Slavery (1956); The Convention on the Elimination of All Forms of Racial Discrimination (1965).

4. Unlike American Jewish organizations such as the American Jewish Congress or the American Jewish Committee, which make no claim to represent all Jews or Jewish organizations in the United States, the Canadian Jewish Congress was conceived to be an umbrella organization that speaks for Canada's Jewish communities.

5. Arthur Warwick, *British Society since 1945* (Harmondsworth: Penguin, 1982), 169.

6. Donald Alexander Downs, *Nazis in Skokie: Freedom, Community, and the First Amendment* (Notre Dame: University of Notre Dame Press, 1985).

7. Examples of such films are Costa Gravas's *Betrayed* (1988) and *Dead Bang* (1989).

8. *Facts on File* (New York: Facts on File, 1988), 364.

9. This was written before the recent waves of violence in Germany.

1

Under the Shadow of Weimar: What Are the Lessons for the Modern Democracies?

Cyril Levitt

INTRODUCTION

The growth of a human rights consciousness in the international community during the second half of the twentieth century can be understood, in part, as a reaction to the genocidal horrors of the holocaust. The United Nations fought the racist powers in World War II, and they stitched this anti-racism into the very cornerstone of their charter. When lawmakers in the postwar liberal democracies faced the problem of racial incitement within their borders, they had in the back of their minds the image of the Weimar Republic, a fledgling democratic state that was overwhelmed by a politically organized racist movement. For this reason alone it would be desirable to review the legal record of the first German republic, to outline the legislation in effect at the time, to examine the application of existing laws by the police and the courts, and to assess the role of law in preventing (or failing to prevent) the political success of racist organizations.

In the introduction to his book on Spinoza, Leo Strauss (1965:1–3) maintains that the unwillingness of the Weimar democracy to wield the sword of justice in legitimate self-defense was to blame for the calamity that befell it. Others agree with this assessment. One often hears people demand that government pass tough laws against hate groups, that it prosecute them without mercy because the failure to legislate and the failure to prosecute these fringe groups had such tragic consequences for the Weimar Republic. Indeed, large numbers of people have argued that Hitler could have been stopped. They believe he began with a handful of marginal characters in 1920 and by means of his diabolical talent for mesmerizing large crowds was able to lead his party to power a scant thirteen years later. They are convinced that anti-hate laws, if they existed at all, were either too weak or ignored by the authorities. So when our civil libertarians argue that the purveyors of hate in our society are pathetic and marginal, when they suggest that laws against them will either not be effective or are too dangerous for a democratic society to enact, many people respond: "Hitler and his gang were also pathetic purveyors of hate in 1920, and look what happened as a result of the inaction of a democracy."

There are two fundamental difficulties with this position. The first betrays a lack of understanding of the specifics of the Weimar situation. Hitler's group may have been small at first, but it existed alongside many other *völkisch*, extreme nationalist and anti-Semitic groups whose members numbered well into the hundreds of thousands and whose sympathizers could be counted in the millions. Hitler's evil genius was not responsible for creating anti-Semitism but for unifying it and giving it a political direction. The second problem arises from a lack of knowledge of anti-hate laws in the Weimar Republic; of the ways in which they were used by individuals, organized groups, the police, and prosecuting attorneys; of how they were interpreted by the courts; of the conduct and outcome of trials and their effectiveness in the struggle against racist expression. In what follows two misperceptions are clearly dispelled: (1) Weimar Germany had few and feeble laws to protect itself against the racist onslaught, and (2) Jews didn't have the will to make use of whatever legal remedies existed. Both perceptions, as we will see, are misleading.

The following are the laws under which most of the criminal law prosecutions[1] of anti-Semitic expression were conducted in the Weimar Republic:

1. Incitement to Class Struggle (Paragraph 130, Criminal Code):

Whoever publicly incites different classes of the population to violent actions against one another in a way that jeopardizes the public peace will be punished with a fine of 600 marks or with a prison term of up to two years.

2. Religious Insult (Paragraph 166, Criminal Code):

Whoever blasphemes God in that he causes annoyance in public by expressions of abuse, or whoever publicly insults one of the Christian churches or another existing religious society with rights of corporation in the federal jurisdiction, its institutions, or customs; likewise whoever commits insulting mischief in a church or in another specific place that is specified for religious gatherings, will be punished with a prison term of up to three years.

3. Insult (Paragraphs 185–187, 189, 190, 192–196, Criminal Code):

(186) Whoever asserts or spreads a fact in relation to another person that serves to make the other contemptible or demeaned in the public view will, if this fact is not demonstrably true, be punished with a fine or with arrest or with prison up to one year, and, if this insult is done publicly or through the spread of literature, pictures, or representations, with a fine or prison term of up to two years.

(187) Whoever against his better knowledge asserts or spreads a fact in relation to another person that makes him contemptible in the public view or that serves to threaten his credit will be punished with prison for a term of up to two years on account of defamatory insult, or if the defamation is done publicly or through the spreading of literature, pictures, or representations, with prison for not under one month. If extenuating circumstances are present, the penalty can be reduced to one day in prison or a fine.

(189) Whoever insults the memory of a deceased individual in that he asserts or spreads an untrue fact, which would have served to make the deceased contemptible or demeaned in the public view in his lifetime, will be punished with imprisonment of up to six months. If extenuating circumstances are present, this can be reduced to a fine. Prosecution occurs only upon request of the parents, the children, or the spouse of the deceased.

(193) Rebukeful judgments of scientific, artistic, or occupational performance, as well as utterances that are made for the execution or defense of rights or for the protection of legitimate interests, as well as reproaches and reprimands of superiors against their subordinates, employment reports, or judgments on the part of a civil servant and similar cases are only punishable when the presence of an insult arises from the form of the expression or from the circumstances under which it occurred.

THE CASES

The major Jewish organization concerned with combating anti-Semitism during the Weimar Republic was Der Central-Verein deutscher Staatsbürger jüdischen Glaubens—the Central Union of German Citizens of the Jewish Faith (hereafter CV)—founded in 1893.[2] The best available record of criminal prosecutions of anti-Semitic incitement is found in the publications of the CV, especially in its weekly newspaper, the *C.V. Zeitung*. The following material is based largely on this and other CV sources. It should be noted that the CV was often very critical of the courts and more often than not called attention to cases that it thought had been mishandled.

It is true, as Niewyk (1975) and Beer (1986, 1988:149–176) argue, that the overwhelming majority of cases that went to trial were adjudicated fairly, that is, according to the wording of the law. Nevertheless, there were sufficient numbers of clearly biased verdicts to cause serious alarm in democratic circles in general and in the Jewish community in particular.[3] The examples that follow have been selected because they are representative of those cases in which the rulings either were not in accord with the law—in which case they present the bias of the courts against Jews—or point out the weakness of legislation itself from the point of view of the protection of Jewish interests. These cases are extremely important in spite of their atypical character because racists were emboldened and encouraged by them, and because Jewish organizations were guided in their actions by them. The perception of a crisis of trust in the law created an atmosphere of suspicion, uncertainty, and, perhaps, fear. We can imagine what the effect of only half a dozen clearly anti-Jewish rulings in the Canadian or American judicial systems would have on popular opinion, to say nothing of the effect on the Jewish community, in spite of the thousands of cases adjudicated fairly at the same time.

The crisis of law in the eyes of Germany's Jews was founded on the following considerations: (1) the unequal treatment of Jews from time to time by the justice system, (2) the acceptance by the courts at times of unreasonable arguments advanced by anti-Semites and/or the rejection of reasonable arguments made by Jewish plaintiffs, (3) unusually narrow interpretations of the law in a number of cases involving Jews, (4) the free reign accorded prominent anti-Semites in some court proceedings (e.g., haranguing and badgering their accusers), and (5) the occasional directly anti-Semitic remark made by a court clerk, prosecuting attorney, or judge during a trial.

Incitement to Class Hatred

In its issue of 8 October 1926 under the heading: "Is there actually equal protection of all citizens?" the *C.V. Zeitung* describes the case involving two articles, "Der Blutbund" (The Blood League) and "Synagoguenjude Schlesinger" (Synagogue-Jew Schlesinger), that appeared in *Der Stürmer*. The first article contained a cartoon depicting caricatures of Jewish males sucking the blood out of a naked "Aryan" woman. The sketch was fitted with a descriptive commentary. The local CV group in Nuremberg laid a criminal complaint against this incitement under paragraph 130 of the Criminal Code (incitement to class hatred) and demanded the confiscation of the newspaper. *Der Stürmer* was brought to trial, but the judge ruled as follows:

The incitement which the plaintiff sees in the two articles "The Blood League" and "Synagogue-Jew Schlesinger" must, in order to satisfy the condition [*Tatbestand*] of paragraph 130 of the Criminal Code, be an incitement not only to hate or to contempt or to political opposition, but rather an incitement to violent actions. An incitement whose aim is violent actions cannot, however, be inferred from the content of the contested issue [of *Der Stürmer*]. Even if one were to assume this [to be the case], the further factual legal requirement would be absent, that is, that this incitement be likely objectively to threaten the public peace, namely, by calling forth the danger of the outbreak of violent activities against Jewry. That the author or the publisher reckoned with such an effect is even less demonstrable. ("Wirklich gleicher Schutz allen Staatsbürgern?" *C.V. Zeitung*, 8 October 1926, p. 535)

The author of the report in the *C.V. Zeitung* lamented this narrow interpretation of incitement in arguing that the judge would have ruled against *Der Stürmer* only if Jews had been beaten to a bloody pulp on the streets of Nuremberg. Foerder (1924:7–8) had already dealt with this issue in his pamphlet when he wrote:

The Supreme Court, moreover, decided in Volume 34, page 268, that the instigation of violent acts against Jews fulfills this requirement when a corresponding fear in the Jews is subjectively called forth; it doesn't matter if the invitation is objectively likely to cause violent acts to occur. This decision is frequently ignored. Even if it [the Supreme Court interpretation] didn't exist, we should think that the public singing of the song with the refrain: "kill the Jews" is sufficient grounds to disrupt the public peace.

There was in fact a great variation in interpretation of the incitement law among the German courts, although the tendency to accept a broader view

seems to have been growing. In the case of *völkisch* agitator Berengar El-
sner von Gronow before a court of assessors in Göttingen in January
1927, a broad interpretation of paragraph 130 by the court led to a conviction. Gronow placed a picture of a ritual murder scene in the window of a
völkisch bookstore beside one depicting the murder of Saint Rudolph,
along with a note telling parents to beware of this *Kulturschande*—this
"cultural defilement." The prosecuting attorney (who was about to retire)
refused to prosecute, arguing that the juxtaposition of the pictures "did not
go beyond the limits of the conflict of opinion protected under the laws"
and that the implicit critique was of an old Israelite custom that had no impact upon the Jewish community of the present. But the case was taken up
by the new state attorney, who prosecuted vigorously and got a conviction
that brought with it a jail term of three weeks or a fine of 300 marks and
the removal of the offensive picture. This verdict produced a favorable
reaction in the *C.V. Zeitung*:

The decision is significant: it exposes the disseminators of this kind of
shameful pictures as political agitators and takes from them the aura of
"enlighteners of the people," with which they so gladly surround themselves. It, rightly, doesn't cling formalistically to an interpretation that sees
the condition [*Tatbestand*] of paragraph 130 of the Criminal Code (the so-
called incitement to class hatred) as given, when violent acts are provoked
expressis verbis; rather, it renews the view expressed long ago by the
Supreme Court that the concept of "incitement" doesn't require a direct
provocation but rather the *indirect* influence suffices, e.g., through illustrations without a text. ("Krankhafte Instinkte," *C.V. Zeitung*, 27 January
1928, p. 40)

One legal trick that anti-Semites used to get around the provisions of
this law (it was also used to escape the clutches of the law against religious libel, as we will see) was the claim that the incitement was directed
at the Jewish race, not at the stirring up of class hatred. Foerder, for
example, cites the case involving a student club at a high school in Silesia
whose members ambled through the town of Frankenstein singing a song
with the refrain:

> Grease the guillotine with Jew-fat,
> Blood must flow, Jew-blood!

Charges could not be laid in this connection under paragraph 130, according to a prosecuting attorney who was also a member of a *völkisch*
organization, since:

According to the recent position advocated by the courts Germans and Jews
within the German Reich don't constitute different classes, but different

races. Even if one wants to see an incitement in the criticized refrain, only the race antagonisms could be seen to be intensified, but not a provocation to class struggle.

In fact, as Foerder (1924:8) points out, the Supreme Court expressly ruled that Jews are afforded protection under paragraph 130. He adds that the failure of this law to extend its protection beyond the narrow definition of social class would essentially lead to an open season on minorities living on German soil. The authorities would stand helpless before the incitement to murder directed against members of the Rumanian or Polish populations living within the borders of the *Reich*.

Finally, he argued that what the law meant by "threatening the public peace" was unclear. Did it refer to the *objective* disruption of the peace and order, or would the merely *subjective* feeling of a threat to peace and security suffice for the law to be broken? Once again there were different interpretations by the courts.

In order to put teeth into the law and to clarify its provisions, the CV supported a revision of the law with the wording, "Whoever publicly incites to a criminal action or to violent activities against a person or things will be punished with two years' imprisonment or a fine." Writing in the *C.V. Zeitung* in 1926, Dr. J. Picard of Cologne assesses the proposed revision as follows:

First, the concept of class is absent here. . . . Moreover, in place of the word "incitement" [*anreizen*] stands the verb "provoke" [*auffordern*], about which the official reason is that "it refers to every expression that according to the intention of the perpetrator is supposed to have the effect of inspiring in the other the decision to take violent action."—The ambiguous nature of the disruption of the public peace is entirely missing from here. And above all the stipulation punishes violent activities against things just as it does against persons. It is also clear that precisely this extension of the old state of affairs would be valuable to us; for until now, when troublemakers in the mood for a pogrom during brawls provoke the destruction of Jewish display windows and stores, they could hardly be touched by the criminal law, if it didn't come to violent actions.[4]

Revisions of the criminal law were severely hampered by the political stalemate throughout the course of the Weimar Republic. This law was not revised.

Religious Insult

The law against religious insult was another weapon in the arsenal of the German justice system that was used against anti-Semitic attacks upon

the Jewish religion and Jewish institutions. In many cases in which
charges were laid and prosecutions pursued, convictions were obtained.
One example is the case of Georg Quindel of Hanover. In 1924 he published an article in his *völkisch* newspaper *Der Sturm* entitled "Der Juden-
gott Jahwe" (The Jew-God Yahweh) in which he contended that there
were two Yahwehs. "Yahweh" was the unutterable name for the god of
the ancient Hebrews; the second was a secret, devilish god worshipped in
secret by the Jews. Rabbi Dr. Freund, who bore witness for the prosecution, was able to make short shrift of Quindel's theological speculations.
The court found Quindel guilty and sentenced him to a fine of 150 marks.
The court took note that Quindel had read many books, but, in the court's
view, he lacked the mental capacity to digest them ("Quindel wegen
Gotteslästerung bestraft: Mildernde Umstände: geistige Unfähigkeit,"
C.V. Zeitung, 12 October 1924, p. 623).

But there were a number of tricks used by the anti-Semites to get
around the provisions of this law as well. Theodor Fritsch, perhaps the
most prolific of the hate mongers in both Imperial Germany and the Weimar Republic and a man who did much to fertilize the ground for National
Socialism, sought to convince the courts that his attacks on the god of the
Jews were directed against the old deity of the ancient Hebrews but not
the modern Jewish concept, which had been influenced by the prophets
and above all by Christianity. He had some limited success in this.

Foerder (1924:9) points out a charge laid under paragraph 166 against a
newspaper that carried a report of a visit of a family of Russian Jews to a
synagogue. This report stated: "They offered thanks to their bloodthirsty
and hate-filled God, for having given them the power to live without
effort from the labor dripping with the sweat of the stupid, good-natured
'Goyims' [sic, non-Jews]." The court found the newspaper not guilty,
arguing that the words "bloodthirsty" and "hate-filled" could not be construed as a "raw insult" given "the general ferment and nervousness of
the present time." Furthermore, the court found no blasphemy in the article suggesting that, at most, the Russian-Jewish family, perhaps Russian-
Jewish families in general, were libeled by it. The prosecution appealed
and the Supreme Court overturned the not guilty verdict, arguing that in
portraying this Russian-Jewish family (and in not distinguishing it from
other Jewish families) giving thanks to their god for advancing their unethical cause, the newspaper not only cast aspersions on the character of
the family but also upon its god. As far as the issue of the ferment and
nervousness of the times is concerned, the High Court ruled that this
could not be the basis for determining whether an expression was libelous
or not. The existing conditions can at most provide a basis for determining
the extent of the penalty to be assessed.

Two other possibilities of getting around the provisions of this law were used by defendants who had been charged under it. The first of these was similar to the defense raised in connection with paragraph 130 concerning incitement to class hatred. Many defense lawyers argued that the insult (which was not denied) was not directed against the Jewish religion but against the Jewish race. This tactic gained importance as the older Christian anti-Semitism was yielding to the modern racist view. Foerder (1924:11) cites the case of a private tutor named Knobel who was charged under paragraph 166 for leading a group of twelve- to fourteen-year-old *völkisch* youth in spitting three times in front of a Jewish cemetery. Upon his apprehension the tutor claimed that he hadn't intended to show disrespect to the Jewish dead: only to the Jewish race. The provincial court of Glogau accepted this explanation.

Another loophole used by anti-Semites charged under this paragraph of the Criminal Code centered on the specific teachings of the Jewish religion. According to the wording of the law, these were not protected. Specific Christian doctrines such as that of the trinity, on the other hand, were defined as part of the religious institution or community.

One case, in which we see a prosecuting attorney accepting the *völkisch* claims, concerns the publication of an anti-Semitic piece in the *völkisch* paper *Die Flamme*, which referred to:

Jewish pigs, who, faithful to their religious law texts, the Talmud and Shulchan Aruch, defile non-Jewish women and girls. The rabbinical teaching makes these acts of these pig-priests into a *duty* and elevates them to a *religious law*, when it states: "The defilement of non-Jewish women is not a sin. Sanhedrin 52."

The CV lodged a complaint with the office of the state attorney in Bamberg. The response of the state attorney to the complaint is enlightening:

The article that is objected to in No. 23 of the *Flamme* advances the assertion "the rabbinical teaching makes the defilement of non-Jewish women and girls into a duty and into a religious law." Thus it contains an attack on the teaching of the Jewish religious community. Paragraph 166, however, according to its wording and origin, wishes to protect not the teaching of the religious communities, but only the society itself and its institutions against insulting attacks. According to the established administration of justice the teaching is not to be considered as an institution in the sense of this regulation. An attack against a doctrine is, therefore, not an infraction of paragraph 166. . . . Moreover, the article is not directed, as is shown in the wording, against the Jewish *religious community*, but rather "against the Jewish race"; an insult from this direction is not to be deemed a transgression against religion, but at most as libel. The prosecution of such can be pursued by means of a private action. Thus, the prosecution on account of a transgression against a religion was terminated. ("Gleicher Schutz allen Staatsbürgen!" *C.V. Zeitung*, 17 September 1926, pp. 499–500)

Difficulties, in the view of the CV, in prosecuting these cases would have been lessened with the adoption of two new draft laws that would replace paragraph 166 in a revised Criminal Code. In draft paragraph 167, religious *teachings* would also be covered. Furthermore, according to this draft, actual suffering would not have to be established, nor would the concept of god have to be involved in the action. Under this law both Fritsch's and Knobel's attempts at avoiding a conviction would have been impossible.

The proposed paragraph 168 would cover the disruption of religious services no matter where they occur. This is an improvement over existing legislation, according to which the services must be taking place in a recognized house of worship. But since Jews can pray anywhere, they were not accorded full protection under the law.

Insult, Libel, Slander

The Weimar Republic was notorious for the large number of libel cases that involved men of high office. They would be regularly libeled in order to force them to press charges. Once in court, the libeler would use the opportunity to minutely examine the private life of the plaintiff in order to discredit him.[5] Perhaps the most spectacular of these court cases was initiated by the first president of the Republic, Friedrich Ebert. Late in World War I, Ebert joined a strike committee of munitions workers who had put down their tools in spite of the difficult situation on the front. He was accused of treason by Dr. Emil Gansser, a member of one of the *völkisch* parties. Gansser's accusation, contained in an open letter to Ebert, was printed by Erwin Rothardt, assistant editor of the Mitteldeutsche Presse. Ebert brought suit against Gansser and Rothardt, but the former first fled the country and later received parliamentary immunity from prosecution when he was elected to the Reichstag. Rothardt, however, was tried, convicted, and sentenced to three months in jail. Even though the court agreed that Ebert had acted in the national interest by joining the strike committee in order to bring the strike to a swift conclusion, he was nevertheless found guilty of treason in a technical, legal sense. This is precisely the result that Gansser and Rothardt wanted to achieve. It was a tactic that was used time and again in the Weimar Republic to discredit public figures. The courts were thus used as forums for casting aspersions upon the character of leading personalities. Ebert was continually hounded by such charges, and some historians suggest that the constant battles in the courts that he fought in order to clear his name caused his early death.[6]

These libel trials often had a so-called Jewish connection, even when the target of the libel or slander was not Jewish and had no connection to the Jewish community. Such was the case of Albert Grzesinski, president of the Berlin Police Department and Prussian minister of the interior (SPD). Grzesinski was hounded continually by the Nazis in speech and in print and he took his tormentors to court one hundred times, although, as T. Rasehorn points out, this represents only a fraction of the number of attacks that he suffered. The Nazis defamed him as a "Jew-Bastard," supposedly the illegitimate progeny of a Jewish farmer named Cohn and a woman who worked for him. (In fact, both his mother and father came from respectable middle-class, non-Jewish, German families.) Grzesinski's personal life was also dragged through the mud. The Nazis put a great deal of effort into provoking Grzesinski to bring charges of libel against them even though it was easy to prove that all these allegations were untrue.[7]

Rasehorn (1985:209) explains why they were so anxious to be taken to court:

But the courts often didn't protect the person here, but rather harmed him. The administration of justice in the trials initiated by Ebert and the then federal chancellor Marx (*Zentrum*) was continued here. Marx, who was himself a judge for a long while, let it be known in a speech to the Reichstag on 17 February 1926 that he would no longer lay criminal charges for defamation and insult.

At times, Grzesinski didn't even have the satisfaction of winning the case against his defamers. In one trial, the judge found the claim that someone was an illegitimate child with one Jewish parent not libelous even if it was not true.[8] But even when Grzesinski was successful in achieving a "victory" in court, the Nazis had achieved a huge propaganda triumph in exchange for the small fine of 300–500 reichsmarks in each case.

Every simple propaganda film, every leaflet, or every kind of other propaganda costs more and doesn't have nearly the lasting and impressive effect as this kind of agitation that appeals to the lowest instincts.[9]

Certainly non-Jews were subject to this abuse, but Jewish officials and public figures a fortiori had to reckon with this kind of hounding constantly. The feisty nemesis of Göbbels, Bernhard Weiss, vice-president of

the Berlin Police Department, went to court on a regular basis to contest
the libel and slander directed at him by his arch-enemies. Göbbels never
referred to Weiss by name but by the Jewish-sounding "Isidor." For this
Weiss dragged the Nazi propagandist to court again and again. And even
though Weiss won his cases, Bering (1985:328) suggests that he was in
fact the loser:

Weiss won all his trials, from the juridical point of view, but he was,
nevertheless, always the loser. These supposedly harmless jokes and word
games, which had as their object a change of name, were not at all harmless,
because they always affected the identity of the person.

In light of this Bering (1985:321) wonders "whether the police vice-president would not have been better advised, in spite of everything, to simply
allow the reproaches of the Nazis to reverberate in silence."

There were many other such cases of libel throughout the course of the
Weimar Republic. The famous libel trial of Theodor Fritsch initiated by
Max Warburg went to five appeals and continued over several years.[10]
But there were also many instances of libel contested in the courts by less
illustrious persons. Among these were cases of group libel brought by
Jewish groups, notwithstanding the fact that the "crime" of group libel
was not clearly defined in the Criminal Code, as we will soon see. This
absence of a clearly defined group libel remedy in the law was the subject
of concern by the leaders of the CV (Holländer 1923:1), who supported
such a law in the new draft of the Criminal Code ("Kollektivbeleidigung,"
C.V. Zeitung, 19 November 1926, p. 609). Historians of the *Ab-
wehrtätigkeit* in the Weimar Republic have also suggested that a law
against group libel would have considerably strengthened the defensive
arsenal of anti-racist forces (see, for example, Paucker 1968:78).

Although many paragraphs in the Criminal Code relating to the laws of
insult specified who may bring charges and under which conditions, as
Alfred Hirschberg (1929:9–34) points out in a study that was published
by the CV, the juridical understanding of "insult" was something that was
hotly contested.

Here is an example reported by the *C.V. Zeitung* of a court case involving only two individuals: A physician sent a note to three neighbors who
declined to use his services. Instead they called upon another doctor for
their medical needs. The physician in question inquired whether his nationalist activities—he was the local leader of a *völkisch* group—constituted the reason for their not calling on him or whether they simply
preferred the services of a "Jewish physician" (the popular colleague in
question was a Christian from a mixed marriage). The latter charged the

former before an *Ehrengericht* (court of honor). But the note sender was found not guilty. This caused the CV to cynically write: *"Geht es um die Kasse, benutzt man auch die Rasse!"* (If it's a question of money, race is used as well!) ("Neugierige Fragen an einen Gutsbesitzer: eine Ehrengerichtliche Entscheidung," *C.V. Zeitung*, 17 July 1924, p. 431).

Another case involved repeated insults hurled at his Jewish landlord by a French tenant. The latter was in the habit of calling the former a "German pig." The Jewish landlord initiated proceedings against the tenant. But the judge in the Berlin court argued that no insult had occurred since the landlord was Jewish and it was commonly understood that Jews were not true Germans even though they may possess German citizenship. E. Eyck (1926:23) points out in this connection that the judge is incapable of feeling just how upsetting such insults are to members of the Jewish community.[11]

Many cases of insult were leveled not at individual Jews but at Jews as a group. No explicit law existed in the Criminal Code that offered the Jewish community protection from such collective attacks. Foerder suggested that the Jews would have a better chance in the courts if charges were brought by an organization that represented all of Germany's Jews. (The Verband der Deutscher Juden, which had been an umbrella organization representing most German Jews, had ceased to exist in 1922.) In the absence of such an organization, charges would have to be brought by individuals or smaller organizations. This left an opening for anti-Semites to claim that the plaintiffs were not the Jews meant as the object of attack. According to a decision of the Supreme Court in 1881 (which actually concerned a case of collective defamation of Jews), it is necessary to prove that the defendant meant to insult certain persons and to specify which persons were meant to be insulted (Foerder 1924:13). It wasn't so much the lack of an effective legal remedy that bothered Jewish jurists, but the inconsistency of the courts in applying the law differently according to which groups were being libeled. Foerder suggests that broader interpretations of the law were made, but not when it concerned the Jews. In 1880, for example, a journalist was charged with libel for writing an article in which he asserted that there were a large number of unprincipled careerists among Prussian judges. The Supreme Court found that an insult could be seen here against each individual Prussian judge, even though only an unidentified portion of them was actually attacked. In fact, it was precisely on account of this indeterminateness that every member of the class had grounds for action against libel. Foerder (1924:13) points out that similar decisions were reached in relation to landed proprietors and Prussian officers. Beer (1986:233) adds the following groups who received group protection in this fashion: the officer corps of a garrison,

German noncommissioned officers, army trainers, German officers, German troops that fought in Belgium, the conservative majority of an electoral meeting, the big landowners of a specific province, all clerics of the Christian religion, Germans living among Poles in areas of mixed composition, the members of a general synod, detectives who were on duty at a specific place during a specific time. In fact, the only group that was excluded from this kind of protection was the Jews.

Erich Eyck, writing in the *C.V. Zeitung*, reviewed the problem of group defamation from the point of view of Jewish interests. In the eyes of the law, only an individual can be libeled. A corporation or juridical person cannot. But a plurality of natural individuals who are conceptualized under a collective designation can be libeled, as in the case of officers of a garrison or judges of a certain district. This is true if the libel applies to every individual who falls under this specific collective designation. The libel doesn't have to refer to any particular individual(s); the libeler doesn't even have to know of the existence of the individual(s) in question. Eyck goes on to say that there are a number of subjective elements at work here. Whether or not the general defamatory assertion can be seen to apply to the person bringing the charge is a matter that had not been consistently decided in juridical practice. Sometimes the law drew the definition of the group of offended persons narrowly, sometimes much more broadly. In the case involving the defamation of Germans by a Pole in an area of mixed ethnic composition, the court ruled:

The broad extent of the plurality of individuals who are affected by a collective defamation is not in itself in opposition to the fact that all those individual persons without exception can be conceived to be defamed if it can be assumed that this result is circumscribed by the intention of the defamer. ("Um die Frage der Kollektivbeleidigung: Eine juristische Untersuchung von Rechtsanwalt Dr. Erich Eyck," *C.V. Zeitung*, 26 February 1926, 101–102)

Eyck also called attention to a 1926 decision that promised the Jews similar legal redress. A leaflet of the Völkische Partei, insulting to Jews, was distributed in Bretten (Baden) in relation to the elections on 4 May 1924. Five young lads were fined 150 marks. They appealed the fine, arguing that the contents of the leaflet did not apply to the Jews in Bretten. The local judge agreed with them and they were acquitted. The Amtsgericht (Petty Court)[12] in Bretten justified the acquittal on 9 January 1925 on traditional grounds that "the defamations were not directed at a specific, limited circle of persons, since Jewry in its entirety is affected." But on further appeal the Oberlandsgericht (State or Provincial Court of

Appeals) at Karlsruhe ruled that "the defamation, with regard to its contents, is directed against every single member of the Israelites living in Bretten." The acquittal was overturned and the matter referred to a new hearing at the Amtsgericht in Pforzheim (28 January 1926). This court found the defendants guilty and leveled fines between 50 and 120 marks and costs. Within two months the judgment had to be published in the *Süddeutschen Volksblatt*, the paper of the local Deutschnationale Volkspartei (DNVP), and the *Brettener Zeitung* (*C.V. Zeitung,* 19 February 1926, p. 88).

According to Eyck, this decision is important insofar as it breaks with the argument laid down by the Supreme Court in 1881 according to which libelous statements about Jews as a group cannot be prosecuted. Nevertheless, this new ruling does not relate to defamations of Jews everywhere. The circle of Jews affected is limited to Jews of Bretten, speaking a peculiar dialect, on a certain day.

There were yet other problems facing complainants in cases of defamation. One of the protections of free expression that stood in the way of prosecuting libel or slander was the "protection of legitimate interests" guaranteed in paragraph 193 of the Criminal Code. Foerder (1924:13) points out that second only to extreme intoxication, the protection of legitimate interests was the most popular grounds adopted by anti-Semites at their defamation trials. He also points out that this legitimate protection of free expression was often abused in that it was sometimes successfully employed as a cover to unjustly accuse Jews of unethical or criminal behavior. In one such example, the chairman of the Breslau section of the *völkisch* Deutscher Schutz- und Trutzbund was taken to court by the Central-Verein for declaring before an audience of 3,000 that the CV maintained a "murder central" in the Saxon town of Halle that had offered a reward for the murder of a local *völkisch* leader. The court found the defendant not guilty on the grounds that he had a justifiable interest in making the charge to a meeting that was called by invitation only to protect the *völkisch* leadership from attacks by the CV. On appeal an assessor court overturned the verdict and found him guilty, but in a second appeal he was again found innocent.

In another case cited by Foerder (1924:14–15) and repeated by Beer (1986:235–236), a *völkisch* doctor was found innocent of defaming a Jewish colleague in a professional journal. He accused him of giving false testimony for the benefit of a fellow Jewish physician in a dispute between that physician and a Christian patient. The assessor court found him guilty of libel by insinuating that the judgment of the Jewish doctor was clouded by his religious affiliation. But the appeal court reversed the decision, arguing that the accused did not intend to libel his Jewish colleague. The main issue for the court was the motive for the false attestation attributed to the plaintiff by the accused. The accused believed that the Jewish religion demands that one Jew support a fellow Jew even if this requires immoral or illegal action. Whether or not such an ethical command exists for the Jewish faith is irrelevant in the eyes of the court. It is sufficient that the accused *believed* that such a postulate exists. In other words, the defendant attributed a lofty motive to what the *völkisch* doctor considered bearing false witness on the part of the plaintiff, who after all did not lie out of self-interest. Whether or not the Jewish colleague made false statements under oath is also irrelevant in the eyes of the court. The accused believed it to be true.

Foerder (1924:15–16) goes on to suggest that the defamer may act to protect a legitimate interest when recourse to defamation in the only alternative left to the individual. In the case of anti-Semitic attacks it has often been the avenue of first choice.

In both of the above cases one cannot speak of the defamer being *forced* to give their Jew-hatred the free reign that they did. The leader of the meeting did in no way have to accuse the regional group of the Central-Verein in Halle of instigating murder, in order to cloak the supposed fearfulness of the German Schutz- und Trutzbund in *Breslau*. The doctor could have practiced the sharpest professional criticism without at all touching upon the religious affiliation of his colleague.

Jewish complaints were not only directed at the failures of the system of justice to protect Jewish rights and interests, they were also voiced in regard to what was widely perceived as a double standard in applying the law. One area of deep concern involved the response of prosecuting attorneys to Jewish complaints. It was the prerogative of the state attorneys in cases of delicts concerning libel, coercion, threats, and bodily harm to recognize a public interest in the prosecution. Very often, Jewish complainants were told that there was no public interest in the case, hence they were advised either to pursue the charges by means of a private action or simply to drop the matter. Foerder (1924:15–16) describes the advantages in having a case prosecuted by the state attorney:

The practical consequences of these different treatments is shown above all in the fact that the aggrieved is a party in the private action [and] thus cannot be called as a witness, therefore under certain circumstances in relation to the denials of the accused and in the absence of other witnesses cannot offer any proof for the substance of his denunciation. In addition he must pay certain costs in advance. Moreover, when he must prosecute the case himself, he has no access to the state attorney, the organs of the police for, say, the necessary investigations. But beyond this an entirely different moral effect is, of course, worked upon the delinquent when he sees that the state attorney's office immediately takes the part of the aggrieved and helps him to achieve satisfaction.

Here are several examples of cases rejected by state attorneys for not being of public interest:

A Jewish woman who was hit over the head with a walking stick by a leading anti-Semite without provocation so that she suffered a severe nervous shock.

An old Jewish man who was cursed in the crudest way and threatened with death by a young overseer at the Kurplatz in Salzbrunn.

A young Jewish man who was attacked and beaten up by five anti-Semitic rowdies on a public street at night.

A Jewish salesman whose display windows were smashed by a member of a respectable student organization. The student declared upon his being questioned by the police: "When I smash the windows of a Semite, that does no harm."

Foerder (1924:15–16) goes on to say that the rejection by the state attorneys in these cases was appealed and in some cases went all the way to the Ministry of Justice. But the state attorneys seemed to have no problem in seeing a public interest in the prosecution of cases brought by anti-Semites against Jews for forcibly removing their swastika pins. Sometimes these cases were treated as theft. Erich Eyck (1926:53) also criticized this double standard when he wrote: "that the same ideas that show themselves to be insufficient to count as libel of Jews, in another case go so far that it comes to criminal prosecution." Ludwig Holländer, director of the CV, pointed out on many occasions that the public outcry would be extremely intense should a Jewish author libel the Christian religion in ways that are repeatedly done by anti-Semites in relation to the Jewish religion.

THE LESSONS OF THE WEIMAR EXPERIENCE

Let us examine these experiences of the Weimar Republic with an eye to the current debate between proponents of tough legislation against racist expression and civil libertarians who oppose it. What does each group of protagonists learn from the historical record we have briefly reviewed here? Those who urge legislation argue that the criminal laws were neither tough enough nor consistently and ruthlessly applied by police, state prosecutors, or the courts. The politicized character of the civil service and judiciary, which leaned heavily to the right, helped take the sting out of the law. Only in a strong and flourishing democracy can the laws be made to work as they were intended. But the Weimar Republic was a "democracy without democrats" (see, for example, Loebe 1954:95), and this prevented the law from acting as a proper bulwark against racist expression.

The lack of laws with teeth is also attributable to the political situation of the Weimar Republic. Proponents of legislation will argue that the greatest single lacuna in the criminal law of Germany at the time was the absence of a clear group libel law that was broad enough to prevent racist slurs. (The failure to extend the protection of existing legislation to the Jews generally, as had in fact been done for other groups, was yet another example of a biased judiciary.) The CV tried for years to get the Reichstag to revise existing legislation that had been formulated during the Imperial period.[13] But the stalemate occasioned by the chronic split between left and right political parties in the Reichstag made agreement upon revision impossible.[14]

The civil libertarian accepts the portrayal of political conditions in the Weimar Republic but adopts a diametrically opposed view with regard to their significance for the current situation. If ever a case could be made for having laws against racist expression, it is precisely in an embattled democracy. When all the stops have been pulled and the country teeters on the brink of civil war, all but the most doctrinaire of civil libertarians would support laws or any other instrument of political power to save the democratic form of rule. In the case of the Weimar Republic, the *general* defense of democracy failed. But in a thriving democracy such laws are simply unnecessary because a racist movement cannot subvert a strong democratic polity. Laws that curb freedom of expression to choke racist groups may in fact do a great deal of harm. The best prophylaxis for a democratic state in the face of racist attacks can in the long run only be its commitment to basic freedoms. Foremost among these freedoms is the freedom of expression. It is impossible, according to this point of view, to devise a law so finely tuned as to catch only racists within its net. There is a constant danger that what most people conceive to be legitimate expression will also be subject to legal control. Even if no legitimate expression is in fact curtailed by the law, the very existence of the law may exert a chilling effect upon speech, writing, and other forms of expression. If freedom of expression means anything, as John Stuart and Harriet Mill pointed out almost a century and a half ago, it means the freedom to express disagreeable, unpopular, and disturbing views. Laws aimed at suppressing freedom of expression are either ineffective (in the case of Weimar) or unnecessary (in the case of the modern democracies).

Furthermore, there is some evidence to show that even in the Weimar Republic the use of the criminal law had a negative impact upon the general struggle against political racism. Was the Weimar democracy well served by having criminal trials for racist expression? That Jewish leaders themselves were cautious in this regard can be seen from the record. As early as 1919, Alfred Wiener suggested that the decision to press charges be carefully considered on a case-by-case basis and that only serious cases be pursued. He wrote:

We create martyrs for little money and the real wire-pullers of the movement remain untouched. And then it is not in the character of our times *expressis verbis* for one to hide behind the state attorney and policeman at every trifle. *Enlightenment, that is the solution.* (Wiener 1919:299)

That the Nazis not only welcomed show trials but actually tried to provoke them is common knowledge. Julius Streicher, editor of the infamous *Der Stürmer* in Nuremberg, was particularly adept at redirecting the course of his trials. Instead of focusing on the libelous attacks he made on the Jewish religion, Streicher managed to turn the proceedings in such a way as to place the Talmud on trial. He and other Nazis were able to harangue the court for hours and to have expert witnesses dismissed for being in the "pay" of Jewish interests. Between 1923 and 1933 *Der Stürmer* was either confiscated or taken to court thirty-six times. R. L. Bytwerk (1975:48) reports that during a single eleven-day period in 1928, five suits were pressed against members of *Der Stürmer* staff.

The description in the *C.V. Zeitung* of the famous Talmud trial of November 1929 involving Streicher and his co-worker Holz is accurately rendered by Bytwerk. If we change the word "Talmud" to the word "holocaust" we can see how close the strategy of current holocaust deniers is to the one adopted by the Nazis:

The trial received national publicity, again adding to Streicher's reputation. The audience was once more strongly partisan. The *C.V. Zeitung* noted that Streicher and Holz addressed the court as if it were a mass meeting, which indeed is how they probably viewed it. The courtroom was a platform from which they could reach an enormous audience. The atmosphere in the courtroom is suggested by the audience's response to the State Attorney's call of eight months for Streicher and ten for Holz: the audience burst out in laughter. Streicher called upon the full reserves of showmanship. Expert witnesses were called, the Talmud in a multi-volume Hebrew edition was produced, and spectacular tales of Jewish misdeeds were reported. Streicher, when questioned about the reliability of such stories, replied that they must have been true, otherwise they would not have been printed. (Bytwerk 1975:48; cf. *C.V. Zeitung*, 1, 8, and 29 November 1929)

The benefits that the Nazi Party reaped from Streicher's courtroom antics were paid for by Streicher and the Party, and at times the fines that he was required to pay and the additional costs incurred forced him to appeal for money. But whatever the cost to Streicher and the Party, they could not have purchased on the open market the publicity the trials received. It is worthwhile to cite Bytwerk (1975:54–56) at length in this connection:

What were the rhetorical advantages of Streicher's trials? First, they gave him and the NSDAP large amounts of publicity, and to the NSDAP the difference between fame and obscurity was more important than the difference between love and hate. Joseph Göbbels, writing of his early struggles in Berlin, claimed that the most important thing was to be known; only then could one win supporters. Streicher's trials certainly accomplished the goal of making the NSDAP known. The trials further provided Streicher not only with the prominence that made of him a sought-after speaker, but also the material to speak upon. Audiences were eager to hear Streicher's account of what happened at his most recent trial. His convictions were used to support his case. "When one visits a courtroom these days," he once told a meeting, "it is just like walking into a synagogue." Naturally, an anti-Semite could not expect a fair trial from a courtroom filled with Jews; his convictions were entirely explainable. He told another meeting, "I doubt that there is still a court in this nation or in this state that has the courage to announce a German verdict." Guilt was therefore transformed into innocence; convictions of anti-Semites were held to be un-German. Trials also enabled Streicher to claim he was more important than he in truth was. In 1928, for example, *Der Stürmer* claimed that each new issue was studied in the offices of a hundred Jewish lawyers, in the hope of finding something amiss. This claim was certainly untrue, but it was also plausible to a Nuremberger who constantly read accounts of Streicher's trials in the newspapers. Those trials that ended with jail terms gave opportunity for Streicher to portray himself as a martyr in truth's cause. . . . When Streicher began his jail terms, he was often accompanied to prison by hundreds of his followers, making a celebration out of temporary defeat. While he was in jail, he sometimes wrote articles for *Der Stürmer*. Protest meetings were often held, demanding his release. His release became a cause for celebration. Six hundred people came to meet him in 1926; several thousands, including Adolf Hitler, in 1930. Streicher nearly always addressed a crowded public meeting on the evening of his release. In short, a jail term was a fruitful well of propaganda. Since his followers were convinced of his innocence, trials became evidence of his persecution. Ironically, the more Streicher was brought to court, the more highly his followers thought of him. They attended trials not to determine whether Streicher was guilty, but to see a battle between truth and error, their selective perception filtering out information damaging to Streicher. The courts were an important element in Streicher's rhetorical campaign. Every effort was made to secure extensive publicity. To the Jewish organizations, conviction was first seen as a victory; to the Nazis, the benefits of a trial more than outweighed the costs. Paucker, for example, observes that though the 1929 Talmud trial was hailed as a Jewish victory, it was in truth a victory for the NSDAP.

Yet the Central-Verein learned from such spectacles and avoided giving the Nazis these kinds of platforms. As Paucker (1968:81–82) points out, the CV countered propaganda by means of injunctions against newspapers and by hitting the centers of distribution with threats of court action.

Which interpretation of the significance of the Weimar experience for the problems facing current democratic states should be adopted? Clearly, no automatic course of action suggests itself to modern liberal governments vis-à-vis the use of the law as a weapon against racist incitement. Nevertheless, all can agree that the law alone cannot contain a growing social movement. At best it can be used as part of a larger strategy. Whether limiting freedom of expression by means of criminal law serves to strengthen the general defense of democracy or weaken it is a difficult question that democracies have been forced to confront. What follows in this book is an attempt to show how this has been done and to assess the different approaches adopted in specific countries.

ACKNOWLEDGMENTS

The author would like to thank the following for their assistance: Alan Borovoy, Gerry Chaple, Irwin Cotler, Bruce Elman, Louis Greenspan, Ben Kayfetz, David Kretzmer, Michael Marrus, Arnold Paucker, David Schneiderman, William Shaffir, and Alan Zysblat. I would also like to thank Shlomo Mayer, Director of the Leo Baeck Institute in Jerusalem, and Ruth Sauer, Librarian at the Wiener Library in Tel Aviv, for their help in tracing sources.

Sections of this chapter are reproduced with the permission of Thomson Canada Limited from Cyril Levitt, "Racial Incitement and the Law: The Case of the Weimar Republic," in David Schneiderman, ed., *Freedom of Expression and the Charter* (Toronto: Thomson, 1991), pp. 211–242.

Material from "Julius Streicher: The Rhetoric of an Anti-Semite," by Randall Lee Bytwerk (Ph.D. diss., Northwestern University, 1975), pp. 48, 54–56, has been reproduced by permission of Randall Lee Bytwerk.

NOTES

1. For attempts to use the civil law to defend against anti-Semitic attacks, see Paucker (1968:74–84), Beer (1986:255–269), and Morgenthaler (1991).

2. There is a sizeable body of research on the defense against anti-Semitic attacks mounted by the CV during the Weimar Republic. See, for example, Hearst (1960:10ff), Levitt (1991a:151–167; 1991b:211–242), and Paucker (1966:405–499; 1968:74–84). On the history of this discussion, see Paucker (1986:55–65).

3. See my critique of the position of Niewyk and Beer in Levitt (1991a).

4. Picard is not completely accepting of the proposed revision here since it doesn't eliminate the possibility of leveling a mere fine in such a serious matter. See Picard (1926:393–395).

5. The practice of maligning an opponent to the point that he brings suit in order to use the court proceedings to ask embarrassingly personal questions and raise doubts in the public mind as to his moral qualities was also used *against* anti-Semites. One of the most poignant examples of this concerns the libel suit by Pastor Münchmeyer of the North Sea island of Borkum against several Jewish and non-Jewish authors, publishers, and distributors of a pamphlet directed against him entitled, "The False Priest, or the Chief of the Cannibals of the North Sea Islanders." Borkum had a national reputation for being a resort at which Jews were not welcome. It had a sort of unofficial anti-Semitic anthem—the Borkum song—that was played by the band at a popular spa and sung regularly by the guests. The CV had a difficult time in getting the singing of the song and the playing of the music stopped. Münchmeyer was one of the leaders of the anti-Semitic movement on the island. Forced to press charges at the circulation of the pamphlet, Münchmeyer was discredited in court and put out of business even though the defendants lost the case and paid a nominal fine. Compare Hirschberg (1926a:217–272; 1926b:283), Weil (1926:297–298), Niewyk (1975:111).

6. Another famous example is that of Karl Helferich, former *Staatsekretär* (state secretary), who accused the first minister of finance, Matthias Erzberger, of being corrupt and thus a liability to Germany in a story in the *Kreuzzeitung* entitled, *"Fort mit Erzberger"* (Erzberger Be Gone). Helferich, who became a leading figure in the DNVP, openly declared that he made his allegations in order to get Erzberger into court, where he could use the "truth defense" to pull Erzberger through the mud in public. Even though Helferich was fined 300 reichsmarks, Erzberger's career was ruined and he resigned. (Erzberger had raised the ire of the nationalist right with his peace resolution in the Reichstag in July 1917. On 26 August 1921 Erzberger was murdered by two former members of the Erhardt Brigade.) See Petersen (1988:57).

7. Nazi member of the Prussian Landtag, Kube, in a letter wrote: "I have requested our Gauleiter for East Hanover, Mr. Telschow, to employ the entire labour power of the local group of the National Socialist German Worker's Party for this politically altogether extraordinarily important trial." See Rasehorn (1985:208).

8. See "Calumniare audacter" (author anonymous), *Die Justiz* 8 (1932–1933): 106–121. Compare Rasehorn (1985:173–174, 209).

9. "Calumniare," p. 121; compare Rasehorn (1985:210).

10. "Fritsch drei Monaten Gefängnis verurteilt: Die endgültige Erledigung einer Verleumdung," *C.V. Zeitung,* 19 December 1924, p. 815; "Der Warburg-Fritsch-Prozess: Vor der Urteilsverkündung in Hamburg," *C.V. Zeitung,* 22 January 1926, p. 41; "Der Ausgang des Warburg-Fritsch Prozesses: Fritsch zu 1000 Mark Geldstrafe

verurteilt," *C.V. Zeitung,* 29 January 1926, p. 52; "Aufhebung eines Fehlurteils. Das Revisionsurteil in Sachen Warburg-Fritsch," *C.V. Zeitung,* 23 April 1926, pp. 229–230; "Zur Neuauflage des Warburg-Fritsch-Prozesses," *C.V. Zeitung,* 22 October 1926, p. 560; "Fritsch zu 4 Monaten Gefängnis verurteilt," *C.V. Zeitung,* 29 October 1926, p. 573; "Das Urteil im Prozess Warburg-Fritsch bestätigt," *C.V. Zeitung,* 1 April 1927, p. 164.

11.   A reference to the same case is found in "Offener Brief an Herrn Dr. Otto Liebmann, Herausgeber der Deutschen Juristen-Zeitung. Von Reichsjustizminister a.D. Dr. Gustav Radbruch, ordentl. Professor der Rechte an der Universität Kiel," *Die Justiz* 1 (1925–1926):196. Compare Rasehorn (1985:169).

12.   "It functions as a trial court with a jurisdiction that is limited to the less serious cases, both civil and criminal." Detlev Vagts, "Introduction," in Müller (1991:x).

13.   For a presentation of the amendments and proposals of the CV and others in relation to this aspect of criminal law, see Beer (1986:307–327). The laws that were used against anti-Semites in the Weimar Republic were developed during the Imperial period and were designed to mitigate the rise of socialism (incitement to class struggle) or to blunt the violence of the Kulturkampf.

14.   A powerful argument used by proponents of legislation does not relate directly to the Weimar experience. They suggest that freedom of expression must yield in this case to the right of survivors of Nazi persecution and their families to live without having to confront Nazi or Nazi-inspired groups, propaganda, and symbols. When they are confronted with this argument, civil libertarians suggest that democracy demands this level of tolerance. The only expression that may be limited is that which presents a clear and present danger of instigating violent action.

2

French Law and Racial Incitement:
On the Necessity and Limits of the Legal Responses

Roger Errera

THE SITUATION PRIOR TO 1945

In France, in the late 1930s anti-Semitism had reached an intensity unknown since the Dreyfus affair.[1] Authors such as Maurras, Celine, Rebatet, Brasiach, or Daudet had become so violent that their works called for incitement to murder. By the spring of 1939 the government felt compelled to respond and introduced the concept of group libel into French law. Until then libel, both a tort and an offense under French law,[2] applied only to individuals.

On 19 March 1939 the government introduced a statute[3] (*décret-loi* of 21 April 1939) in which incitement to hatred between citizens because of race[4] or religion could be punished by imprisonment from one month to a year or a fine from 500 to 10,000 francs.

This early legislation was too little and too late. Its wording made it difficult for private parties or the state to prosecute racist authors effectively. Thus, it was rarely used.[5] On 27 August 1940, in one of its first

acts (Marrus and Paxton 1981), the Vichy government repealed this legislation. A few weeks later the government adopted its first measures
against the Jews.

THE PERIOD 1945–1972

After the war ended, it seemed that revulsion against the horrors of the
concentration camps and the crimes of the Vichy government against the
Jews was so deeply rooted that racial incitement and anti-Semitism had
vanished. The virtual extinction of the extreme right from the political
arena was especially encouraging. But in a few years anti-Semitism began
to make a comeback. First, the surviving elements of the pro-Vichy right
were emboldened to incitement against the Jews. Later, in the early
1950s, the anti-Semitism in Soviet Russia and in most of the satellites—as
manifested in the notorious "doctor's plot" and in the Prague Trials of
1952, when "cosmopolitanism" and "Zionism" became phrases of
calumny—found an echo within the French Communist Party and its
writers.[6]

After the Six Day War of 1967 a new dimension of anti-Semitism disguised as anti-Zionism made a lasting appearance in France as elsewhere.

Under these circumstances the statute of 1939 was put to the test but
was found lacking in several areas: wording, procedural limitations, and
limitations of the courts.

There were four problems with the wording of the statute. (1) Racist
libel was an offense if the intent of the libel was to incite hatred between
groups. This is the opposite of normal libel actions in which the intent is
presumed and the onus is on the accused to establish that he acted in good
faith. In the legislation under consideration, the burden of proof falls on
the plaintiff. (2) The statute covers persons belonging to a race or religion
but omits mention of nationality or other categories of group. (3) Since
discrimination on the grounds of race or religion was not unlawful, advocacy of such discrimination was not an offense. (4) As stated earlier, libel
is by definition confined to allegations of facts.

The most important problem in the area of procedural limitations was
the question of who had authority to initiate prosecutions. The state prosecutor was entrusted with this authority but as a branch of the Ministry of
Justice was little inclined to initiate any appropriate legal actions. Individuals were not authorized to initiate suits against group libel unless they
were named as individuals. The case prohibited civil liberties groups from
initiating prosecutions unless they themselves were defamed in the case.

   In terms of limitations of the courts, a few cases will illustrate the fact
that the courts themselves were reluctant to enforce the statutes even after
the full horror of the Nazi camps had been revealed.

   • In October 1947 a rightist Paris daily published a series of articles denouncing the invasion of French medicine by foreigners. (This tactic had
been successful in the 1930s and brought about a restrictive statute in
1933.) The articles alleged that such "foreigners" (meaning Jews and
Bessarabians) specialized in abortions, swindles, false certificates, and
forged documents. Dr. Rosenwald, the editor of a well-known directory
of doctors, and his associates were personally attacked. Several actions
were initiated but all were ruled inadmissible. One association of
physicians was refused standing because it had been created after the
publication of the articles. Another was refused because none of its
members were named specifically. The court ruled that either the members
be named specifically or the group be so small that they can be deemed to
have been named. Since the latter was not the case here, the court awarded
symbolic carnage only to Dr. Rosenwald, but it specified that the award
was based on "normal libel." The editor had to pay a fine but was
acquitted on the charge of group libel. The aim of the statute, the court
ruled, was to punish "incitement to hatred," that is, the unleashing of
passions creating troubles, social and racial disorders, and agitation—in a
word, violence. The court ruled that none of this applied here.[7]

   • In 1948–1949 a Royalist weekly published a series of anti-Semitic
articles. Three associations of Jewish veterans and concentration camp
inmates sued the editor and three other persons on the grounds of group
libel. The Court of Appeal declared the action inadmissible, since the
complainants could not prove that they had been directly and personally
harmed. But in this case the state prosecutor initiated an action and the
editor was ultimately convicted and sentenced.[8]

   • Some courts came to very strange decisions. For example, in one case
a Mr. R. was sued and convicted for group libel because of his anti-
Semitic writings. The lower court, however, neglected to say whether the
intent of the author of the writings had been to incite hatred. The Court of
Appeal filled this gap in a highly prejudicial fashion. It noted that the
author had merely invited the readers to a "sound distrust of Jews,"
pointing out that they were "foreigners." He had advocated "anti-Semitism
in the French style," a "measured and reasonable anti-Semitism" with "fair
and necessary statutes" that appealed to reason rather than to passion. The
court emphasized that the author opposed the "ignoble German racist
oppression" and on these very dubious grounds acquitted him.[9]

The only legislative reform occurred on 29 November 1954 through the amendment of a statute of 1949. The 1949 statute had prohibited publications directed to young people from presenting lying, theft, laziness, hatred, debauchery, or any such material that might undermine the morality of young people. The 1954 reform added the phrase, "or to inspire or foster ethnic prejudice." If such legislation seems anachronistic or unnecessary, it should be noted that the commission in charge of overseeing the enforcement of this statute found a good deal of disquieting material. It noted: "In publications addressed to young people, one does not find material that can be characterized as anti-Semitic, but we do find Arabs, Indians (from India), East Asians, and especially Japanese depicted as treacherous and cruel, and Blacks are depicted either as savages or naive and childish." The commission also complained that drawings caricatured racial characteristics.

THE 1972 STATUTE AND SUBSEQUENT REFORMS

By the late 1960s and early 1970s the time seemed ripe for reform. Groups concerned with civil liberties were dissatisfied with the laws and with the record of enforcement. Civil rights associations and political parties were active in proposing new draft legislation. Four private members' bills were pending in Parliament.[10] Finally, the growing severity of the courts, the readiness in many cases to use the legal instruments or call for their reform, indicated a growing awareness of the issue and a growing sense of urgency.[11] A number of disturbing events in France aroused the government to move in this area.

There was a rapid development of racial incitement against foreign workers. By this time there were three million workers in France, mainly from North Africa. The incitement consisted of a campaign against their presence. The campaign focused on security (as when the press gave special prominence to crimes in which the accused was a North African) and on public health and finances (as when the press accused foreigners of "invading" public hospitals, "at our cost"). The overall aim of this campaign was to spread distrust and fear (Mesnil 1966:744). Even gypsies were targeted whenever they were involved in an incident, however minor. The fact that they were French citizens was irrelevant.

In 1971 France ratified the UN 1965 Convention (UNTS 213) on the elimination of all forms of racial discrimination (Schwelb 1966:996; Buergenthal 1977:187; Lerner 1980, 1983:170; Meron 1985:283) with a few reservations and declarations.[12] During the debates in France the government declared that French law was in conformity with the UN declaration and therefore that new legislation was not necessary.[13] But the rapporteur of the bill in Senate disputed this (Meron 1985:439), noting that the UN Convention called for (1) banning discrimination on grounds of race (Article 2-I-D), and (2) outlawing dissemination of ideas based on racial superiority or hatred, incitement to racial discrimination, or all provocation to such acts, directed against a group of persons, any organization, or association inciting to racial discrimination. The term "racial discrimination" was given a very broad meaning. It included national origin.

None of this was included in French law, which was thus defective and not in accord with the UN Convention.

Less than one year later Parliament passed the statute of 1 July 1972, which along with amendments is the basis of current French law. There was no government bill. Instead, six bills tabled by all political parties (Communists, Socialists, Gaullists, and Centrists) were discussed by Parliament. The reform was adopted unanimously, perhaps a sign of the times.

The contents of the statute can be summarized as follows (Foulon-Piganiol 1972:261):

The statute on the Law of the Press (1881) is amended on three points:

• Incitement to discrimination, hatred, or violence against a person or group of persons because of their origin or of their belonging or not belonging to a given ethnic group, nation, race, or religion are now offenses. The penalties are imprisonment up to one year and/or a fine from 2,000 to 300,000 francs (Article 24 of the 1881 statute, paragraph 5). The innovations are incitement to racial or religious discrimination and to racial hatred or violence. They are very welcome ones as they are directed at incitement per se rather than group libel. "Intent" is not mentioned. The scope of the new offense is extended by the phrases "not belonging to" and "ethnic group," "ethnic," or "nation."

• The definition of group libel is simplified (Article 32, paragraph n.2).

• The procedural reform is no less important. Any association whose legal existence[14] has been recognized for five years from the time that the relevant facts have been brought to public attention and whose aim was to fight racism has *locus standi* to begin proceedings. (If individuals are attacked the association may initiate proceedings only with the individual's permission.) The aim here was to abolish restrictive case law, already mentioned. Besides, there were a number of precedents in French law in which statutes conferred such locus to certain associations in other fields.

The act also amended French law on associations. Under existing law the normal procedure for the government or any individual to seek to dissolve an association was through the civil courts. In addition, a statute of 10 January 1936 empowered the government to ban a number of associations simply by issuing a decree.[15] The 1972 statute added associations inciting violence and hatred on grounds already mentioned, or disseminating ideas or themes tending to condone such acts, to the list of associations that could be banned by decree.

Last, discrimination on the grounds mentioned above becomes an offense, whether committed against a person, an association, or a company, unless there is a "legitimate motive." Penalties are heavier if the author is a civil servant or a person belonging to any public authority (Penal Code, Articles 187-1 and 416).

THE PERIOD 1972–1991

During the past twenty years French law concerning racial incitement and discrimination has been modified several times. The scope of these modifications must be assessed.

First of all, modifications arising from the fact that France has ratified international human rights are instrumental in containing clauses relating directly or indirectly to the issue under discussion. These include (1) the European Human Rights Convention (Article 14) (the right of individual petition was accepted in 1981); (2) Article 14 of the two UN Covenants on civil and political rights and on social and economic rights (see Article 26 of the former); the 1960 UNESCO Convention on discrimination in education (see Articles 1, 2, and 3); and (3) the UN Convention on the elimination of all forms of discrimination against women.

Second, the principle stimulus for modifications from the early 1980s to the present has been the resurgence of a new wave of xenophobia, anti-Semitism, and racial incitement. Depending on the circumstances and the spokesmen, immigrants (especially North Africans and Africans) or Jews (often under the thin disguise of anti-Zionism) have been the targets.

The existing laws on group libel, racial incitement, and unlawful discrimination have been reformed piecemeal, but the general pattern demonstrates the government's and Parliament's resolve to strengthen the legal instruments against racial incitement. Reforms have been introduced in two stages.

From 1975 to 1985 there were five important reforms:

1. The scope of unlawful discrimination: Articles 187-1 and 416 of the Penal Code have been extended to sex discrimination (Statute of 11 July 1975).

2. Legislative clauses prohibiting economic discrimination on ethnic, racial, and religious grounds have been reinforced (Statute of 7 June 1977).

3. A statute of 10 January 1983 has given certain associations (those who have been recognized legally for five years for the purpose of identifying war crimes, crimes against humanity, or to defend the Resistance) a five-year extension to institute criminal proceedings in the following areas: war crimes, crimes against humanity, vindication of war crimes or of collaboration crimes, inscriptions on buildings and tombs, libel or insult (see Articles 2-4 and 2-6 of the Code of Penal Procedure, hereafter CPP).

4. A statute of 13 July 1983 has removed the possibility of invoking "a legitimate motive" in cases of discrimination on grounds of sex, race, or family situation in hiring or dismissal.

5. Another statute of 3 January 1985 extended further the scope of intervention for civil rights associations in cases of homicide, violence, and destruction on ethnic, racial, or religious grounds.

In 1987–1990, the government responded to a series of incidents that pointed to a resurgence of racism by introducing several measures, some through Parliament, related to the following areas:

1. The wearing or public display of Nazi uniforms, badges, or emblems.[16]

Three elements are worth mentioning here: First, the decree prohibits the public wearing or display of uniforms, badges, or emblems recalling those worn or displayed either by members of organizations that have been declared criminal pursuant to Article 9 of the Statute of the International Military Tribunal contained in the 1945 London Agreement, or by a person who has been sentenced by a French or an international court for having committed crimes against humanity within the meaning of the French statute of December 1964. At the Nuremberg trial several groups were declared criminal: the heads of the Nazi Party, the SS, the SD, the Gestapo (not the army). Second, the decree explicitly mentions an international instrument (the London Agreement) and a national statute (that of 1964). The latter declares that the statute of limitations does not apply to crimes against humanity as defined by the UN General Assembly resolution of 13 February 1946. That resolution in turn merely adopted the 1945 definition. In other words, the Nuremburg Law continues to be relevant to French criminal law, as was demonstrated in the Barbie trial. Third, the new prohibition does not apply if the wearing of Nazi emblems or badges as public display takes place in a film, show, or exhibition presenting historical material.

2. Justification (*apologie*) of crimes against humanity (as distinct from that of war crimes, an offense since 1951[17]) was made an offense (Statute of 31 December 1987, amending Article 24, paragraph 5 of the 1881 statute on the press).

3. The statute of 1949 empowers the government to ban the public display of or selling to minors of any publication that endangers young people on any number of grounds (e.g., pornography, promotion of violence). In 1987 the promotion of discrimination or racial hatred was added (Statute of 31 December 1987, Art. 14-II, amending Article 14 of the 1949 statute).

4. The "legitimate motive" clause making discrimination lawful on grounds noted above has been removed (Statute of 30 July 1987, Article 85, amending Article 416-1 of the Penal Code).

5. The same kind of discrimination against legal persons is now prohibited by Article 416-2 of the Penal Code: The text uses the generic word "legal persons" and not as before "association or companies," thus widening its scope (Statute of 30 July 1987, Article 86, amending Article 416-2 of the Penal Code).

6. The legal capacity of associations to introduce criminal proceedings has been extended further. Under a statute passed in 1985 (Statute of 3 January 1985, Article 90, now Article 2-10 of the CPP), an association legally in existence for five years before the event and whose aim is to oppose racism may introduce criminal proceedings in cases of racial discrimination and related offenses—not only in cases of racial incitement. In 1987 the same right was granted to associations whose aim is to *assist* victims of discrimination (Statute of 3 January 1985, Article 67, amending Article 2-10 of the CPP. On these reforms, see Errera 1989:47).

In 1988–1989 several developments in France created pressure for another reform in the legislation related to racial incitement. The development of "revisionist" literature and the vehemence of the xenophobic and anti-Semitic campaigns of the National Front and its leader, Le Pen, stimulated leaders and government circles to consider improvements to the existing legislation. The Socialist Party submitted two bills to Parliament (private member bills—*proposition de loi*—no. 1247, AN, annex to the minutes of the sitting of 2 April 1988, and no. 1004, 15 November 1989) outlawing revisionist literature and making it an offense to negate the Nazi holocaust or minimize its scope. In March 1989, speaking at a meeting organized by the Jewish Students Union, Mr. Fabius, president of the National Assembly and a Socialist, and Mr. Chirac, the former prime minister and a conservative, both agreed that revisionist literature should be banned (*Le Monde*, 26–27 March 1989).

There were further developments in the spring of 1990. Soon after the publication of the yearly report of the National Human Rights Commission (*Le Monde*, 29 March 1990), the then prime minister, Mr. Rocard, invited leaders of all political parties represented in Parliament to a discussion with him on issues related to immigration and racial incitement. Several ideas and suggestions were discussed (*Le Monde*, 30 March and 4 April 1990). Then came the outrage in Carpentras. In this town in Provence, the seat of one of the oldest Jewish communities, several Jewish tombs were desecrated. This led to a mass national protest that included all parties. To date no one has been indicted. In the wake of these events, the Communist Party sent a bill to Parliament containing several reforms designed to strengthen the legal arsenal against racial incitement (private member bill no. 43, AN). This bill, amended by Parliament, became the statute of 13 July 1990. The absence of a government bill and the haste with which the reform was rushed through Parliament are regrettable. The subject deserved a better and more careful treatment, including more consultation with all parties concerned.

The new statute is lacking in unity because it contains several reforms of unequal importance (Statute of 13 July 1990).[18]

These reforms include the four that are discussed as follows:

1. A right of reply of associations: French law provides a right of reply to individuals or legal persons who have been mentioned or clearly alluded to in the press. Under the new law individuals, groups of persons, or associations in existence legally for five years have a right of reply in the press as well as the broadcasting media. If the libel relates to individuals, the association may act only if the individual concerned agrees.

2. Penalties for racial incitement may include suspension of civil rights (e.g., the right to vote or to be elected) for a maximum of five years and publication of the court's decision in the press by a poster.

3. Associations recognized in law as having existed for five years for the purpose of defending the Resistance and concentration camp inmates may initiate criminal proceedings in cases of justification of war crimes, crimes against humanity, crimes of collaboration, and in cases of denial of the Nazi holocaust against Jews.

4. The most important innovation of the statute is the creation of a new offense—the contestation of certain crimes against humanity. This becomes an offense under certain conditions. The crimes in question are those defined as crimes against humanity in Article 6 of the London Agreement. In order to be considered crimes against humanity the offenses must meet one of two conditions: They must have been committed either by members of an organization declared criminal through Article 6 of the statute of the International Military Tribunal (IMT) (here the only crimes against humanity are those committed during World War II), or by a person declared guilty of such crimes by a French or an international court.

THE FUNCTIONING OF THE LAW

The law relating to racial incitement, group libel, and racial injury has been applied extensively since the 1970s. Moreover, the number of private and public prosecutions (the latter by associations now fully empowered to act) is growing, and the sentencing is more severe than it was ten or fifteen years ago. Of great importance is the fact that the cases are decided more rapidly than they had been. The following examples are pertinent illustrations of the working of the law as it operates today.[19]

The first test of the statute of 1 July 1972 became a national and even international cause célèbre. On 22 September 1972 the *Bulletin URSS,* published in Paris by the information service of the Soviet embassy, printed an article entitled "The School of Obscurantism," signed by M. Zanderberg. It began with a reference to the Deir Yassin massacre,[20] claiming that the tragic spirit of the perpetrators continued to guide Israeli policy in the occupied territories and that Israeli schoolboys were taught early to massacre Arabs. The author bolstered his point by referring to the "holy writings" and "moral values" taught in the Israeli schools. The rest of the article, more than half of the text, was an exegesis of the Shulchan Aruch. This exegesis was in fact nothing more than a reiteration of the notorious protocols of the Elders of Zion, a text now known to be a fabrication of the Russian Secret Police at the turn of the century. It claimed that the Jews were conspiring to dominate the world and to despise, exploit, and ultimately kill all other people. This, the author insisted, was the only "morality" of the "Zionist society" the precepts taught to generations of Israelis. The last two sentences of the article state: "These laws of Judaism are written in the bylaws of the Israeli Army and to transgress them is a breach of discipline. They constitute the very essence of the Zionist state policy."

Two associations (the Ligue internationale contre l'antisémitisme, or LICA, and Rencontre) sued the editor for group libel and racial incitement. The hearings, held in March 1973, were very interesting.[21] The editor, a French Communist, confessed that he never read the texts published in his bulletin. The court rejected the argument that the *Bulletin* had the protection of diplomatic immunity, because it emanated from the Soviet embassy. It convicted the editor of group libel and racial incitement. The editor had to pay two fines and the cost of printing the decision in six newspapers and in the *Bulletin* itself.

As in other countries, France had to respond to the publication of extreme statements in which the distinction between anti-Zionism and anti-Semitism was often not clear. This is so in the following two examples.

On 17 June *Le Monde* published a paid advertisement that was identified as such. It was signed by R. Garaudy, a former Communist member of Parliament and philosopher; P. Mathiot, a Protestant pastor; and Father Lelong, a Catholic priest. The text contained a violent denunciation of the power of the "Zionist lobby" in the media—a recurrent and effective theme of anti-Semitism. The article compared the Israeli law on nationality with the Nazi Nuremburg Law of 1935, identifying it as racist legislation, and attacked Zionism as a doctrine.

One civil rights association and a Jewish-Christian association sued the editor for racial incitement and group libel. The lower court rejected the plea on the grounds that the plaintiffs had not mentioned which "group," within the meaning of the statute, was involved (*Le Monde*, 26 March 1983). The Court of Appeal found that the text was a legitimate criticism of the policy of a state and its ideology, which found an echo "in parts of international Jewish opinion" and did not go beyond the limits permissible in free discussion (*Le Monde*, 14 January 1984).

In the same period the left-wing daily *Liberation* published a rabidly anti-Semitic letter from a reader. Under French law the editor is legally responsible for *all* the contents of the newspaper—without exception. The LICA sued the editor for group libel and racial incitement. He was sentenced to pay a fine, damages to the association, and the costs of publishing the decision in three newspapers (*Le Monde*, 7, 8 June and 6 July 1983).

Prosecutions based on racial incitement seem more frequent than those based on group libel. Court decisions sentencing editors or authors can be classified into several categories according to the contents of the publication.

• Racial incitement directed against foreign workers has very often led to conviction.[22]

• This is also the case for plain anti-Semitism.[23]

• Group libel actions have included proceedings against (1) a store selling dolls representing the stereotyped Jew,[24] and (2) the publisher and author of an article attacking young second-generation immigrants (*Le Monde*, 4 May 1990). In a rare occurrence a former Catholic archbishop was suspended *a divinis* by the Pope. Monsignor Lefebvre was sentenced and convicted for group libel and racial incitement against the Muslim community (*Le Monde*, 14 July 1990 and 23 March 1991).

Acquittals, no less interesting to study, are of several sorts:

• Some are based on the very constraints and limits of the law. As mentioned earlier, libel (against a group or individual) is defined by law as the allegation of a fact that besmirches the honor or reputation of a group. In 1989 Le Pen was interviewed by an extreme right-wing newspaper, *Présent*, and he denounced the "big internationals like the Jewish ones that play a conspicuous role in the creation of the anti-national mind." He was prudent enough to add that this did not mean all Jewish organizations or all Jews. The court acquitted him on grounds that he expressed his own political opinions. Opinions in this case were particularly offensive to international Jewish associations.[25]

• Other acquittals seem to be based on a minimalist and strict construction of the statute, a benevolent or detached reading of the text that prompted the proceedings, coupled with a general affirmation of freedom of expression, a constitutional principle in French law. The editor of an extreme right-wing monthly, *Pour un ordre nouveau*, was sued for publishing an article violently attacking the immigrant workers, describing the "black ghettoes," the "idle people looking with hatred at the rare intruders with white skin," "a sordid world," "an army of ultra-poor and underpaid mercenaries," whose only aim in France was to "fill their pockets before returning to their country." This, the association suing the editor contended, was racial incitement. The court disagreed. Its decision makes strange reading. It notes and deplores the fact that discrimination against immigrant workers is a reality. It then describes their living and working conditions. The decision quotes Articles 1 and 2 of the 1965 UN Convention on the elimination of all forms of discrimination but *not* Article 4. Then comes the affirmation of freedom of opinion and of expression in France and the reminder that any statute relating to an offense must be construed restrictively. The decision adds that anyone is free to publish a study on immigration and to make available to the public both personal reflections and conclusions, as long as it is done in good faith and does not violate the law. Opinions may vary on this issue, and it is not appropriate for the courts to act as an arbiter of such controversies. In looking at the article, the courts could not find any appeal to violence against foreign workers or provocations to racial hatred toward them. One may, the judgment went on, regret the lack of restraint in the presentation of the article and, here and there, formulations "that may be thought to be excessive" (such as "there are some districts of big cities that it is impossible to cross at night without risking robbery or rape"). Quoting certain phrases in which the author took some semantic precautions, the court acquitted the defendant.[26] The Court of Appeal quashed the judgment on 17 June 1974 (*Le Monde*, 19 June 1974).[27]

TWO FUNDAMENTAL DEBATES

The existence and contents of laws on racial incitement have been the source of two important public debates that have focused on two questions: Should we have laws against racial incitement and group libel? What should we do with revisionist literature?

Laws against Racial Incitement and Group Libel

In France as well as a number of western countries the debate is over and the issue is moot among scholars, lawyers, and politicians. Such laws have existed for one generation at least, and nobody advocates their repeal. Nevertheless, it is useful to say why they are necessary. This is so, in my opinion, for several reasons:

In some countries an absolutist conception of freedom of speech prevails; here such laws do not exist and would probably be considered unconstitutional. The United States is the outstanding example (Errera 1987:63, 84ff.). A full examination of such laws thus makes sense, if only to contrast legal and social attitudes and policies. In France itself there are indications that it is still necessary to emphasize *why* we need them. Some decisions seem to reflect a lack of understanding of the present state of French society and an incomplete assessment of its recent history.

Fundamentally such laws are necessary if we want to defend the basic civility of our society. We are not to allow an attack against a person or a group of persons and their rights on racial, ethnic, national, or religious grounds. We live in a country and in a century that fully legitimate the use of legal weapons against what is, *and is meant to be*, aggression. Such aggression is directed not only against certain individuals or groups but against the entire body politic and its social and moral fabric. This was expressed more than sixty years ago: The preliminary statement preceding the *décret-loi* of 1939 says explicitly that the creation of group libel as a tort and as an offense is necessary not only to protect the groups under attack but also to protect the interest "of the whole national collectivity."[28] More recently a great American lawyer, Alexander Bickel (1975:72–73), has expressed the same fundamental idea in a telling way:

There is such a thing as verbal violence, a kind of cursing, assaultive speech that amounts to almost physical aggression, bullying that is no less punishing because it is simulated. . . . This sort of speech constitutes an assault. More, and equally important, it may create a climate, an environment in

which conduct and actions that were not possible before become possible. . . . *Where nothing is unspeakable, nothing is undoable.* (emphasis
added)

Skepticism about these laws is based, at times, on a pseudo-utilitarian
argument: According to it, racism and its public expression have underlying psychological, social, or economic "causes." Trying to suppress it by
legal means is an illusion and could make us forget the more fundamental
issues. The only answer is that criminal prosecutions or civil actions will
no more suppress racial incitement than our penal codes have suppressed
murder, theft, or rape. Their aim is to make public, tangible, and known
the position of the polity on this issue, that is, to affirm values. Besides,
there is evidence to show that having such laws and enforcing them has a
restraining and sobering effect.

Revisionism and What To Do with It

In a number of countries (France, the United States, the United Kingdom, Canada) the negation of the Nazi genocide of the Jews has been the
subject of innumerable books, essays, and articles.[29] There is no doubt at
all that such writings are not only a perverse expression of anti-Semitism
but also an aggression against the dead, the survivors, and society at
large, aiming at the desecration or the destruction of the only grave of the
former (i.e., our memory) and the erosion of the very conscience of the
crime. Such an aggression is not to be tolerated. Authors, editors, and
publishers should not escape unpunished. What follows is an analysis of
the legal steps taken in France against revisionist writers and writings.

Administrative Measures. The statute of 17 July 1949 allows the minister of the interior to take the following steps against a publication presenting a danger for young people because of the appearance of racism within
it: prohibition of sales to minors, prohibition of public showing, prohibition of any kind of advertisement. Such decisions, which must be reasoned and taken after due process, have been taken against revisionist
journals (*Annales d'histoire révisionniste*—three prohibitions, *arrêté min-
istériel* of 2 July 1990; *Revue d'histoire révisionniste*—same steps, same
date; *Révision*—decision of 14 June 1990).

Civil Proceedings. These can be of two sorts.
1. Under Article 809 of the civil procedure code, the president of the
civil court is empowered to order, in interlocutory proceedings (*référé*),

any steps that are necessary to prevent imminent harm and to put a stop to a manifestly unlawful trouble (*trouble manifestement illicite*). Such sweeping powers are used by the courts to protect privacy and other rights or feelings (Errera 1990a:67; on *référé* proceedings, see Perrot 1989 and Kayser 1989). In 1987, on the eve of the beginning of the trial in Lyon of Klaus Barbie, a Gestapo official accused of crimes against humanity, a new revisionist journal, *Annales d'histoire révisionniste*, was launched. In an essay on "The myth of the Jews' extermination" one could read the following sentence: "To doubt the historical reality of the extermination of the Jews is not only legitimate, it is a duty, for it is a duty to look for historical truth."

The LICA and four concentration camp inmates' associations asked the court, in interlocutory proceedings, to order the suspension of the distribution of the journal. The next day the president of the Paris civil court first ordered all copies of the journal to be impounded and its distribution to be suspended. Eleven days later, in a second decision, he affirmed that the public exposure and distribution of such a journal, the only aim of which was the negation of the Jews' massacre, amounted, in the circumstances, to a deliberate act directed against the victims of Nazism and all Jews in general. Such an act was, he added, bound to be perceived and resented as a racial incitement and could cause trouble and violent reactions. On these grounds he prohibited temporarily the distribution and the sale of the journal.[30]

2. A number of civil actions for damages have been directed at authors and exponents of revisionist themes. Here are a few examples. R. Faurisson has been, for more than twenty-five years, one of the leading exponents of revisionism in France. In 1978–1979 the LICA and several other associations launched a civil action against him, based on what he had published in two Paris dailies, *Le Matin* and *Le Monde* (in the latter newspaper, by using his right of reply).[31] The Paris civil court, in a closely and very well reasoned decision, distinguished carefully the role of the courts from that of the historian and emphasized that judges are not and should not be historians or rule on disputes between historians. The latter are free to publish their views on any subject, the court said. They do that, however, under their legal responsibility, as does anyone else. Faurisson had said that the Jews' genocide, as well as the existence of gas chambers, were "one and the same historical lie, which made possible a huge political and financial swindle." In doing so, he failed to respect the obligation of prudence, objectivity, circumspection, and intellectual neutrality that were his. The associations suing him, whose aim was to oppose racism and to protect the memory of concentration camp inmates,

had suffered a moral harm. Faurisson was sentenced in order to compensate for it.[32]

Revisionism comes in many guises, and civil actions are more effective in some situations than criminal prosecutions. Here is an example. On 12 September 1987, Le Pen declared in a radio interview that the mass gassing of the Jews by the Nazis was "a point of detail." Deciding on interlocutory proceedings, the Versailles court held that the statement constituted "manifestly unlawful distress" for survivors and their families, and a "fault in the exercise of freedom of expression which, far from being an absolute one, has . . . among its limits . . . the respect of essential values which can be equaled, as is the case here, with the notion of legitimate interest protected by the law."[33] Le Pen was later ordered by the court to pay more than 900,000 francs in damages to the associations suing him.[34] This constituted a valid and appropriate conclusion to four years of litigation.

Criminal Prosecution. Such prosecutions for group libel or racial incitement seem to have been rare. However, two recent cases are notable.[35]

Revisionism in Universities. This topic deserves a separate analysis. What is to be done when exponents of revisionist themes belong to universities?[36] Should specific measures be taken in these cases in addition to the remedies offered by civil and criminal law? The issue is not a purely theoretical one. It relates to the nature and limits of academic freedom. Here are two recent examples.

THE ROQUES CASE.

On 15 June 1985, Roques, an agronomist, presented a doctoral dissertation at the University of Nantes.[37] The subject was: "The Confession of Kurt Gerstein: Comparative Studies of Several Versions." The real subject—Gerstein's manuscript was a mere pretext—was a repetition of revisionist views. It appeared a few months later that all procedural rules and requirements had been knowingly violated by Roques and those academics who helped him, Especially Professor Rivière, the dissertation supervisor and a professor of medieval literature at Nantes University. During the spring of 1986 the Roques case became public in France. On 28 May the secretary of state for higher education, an academic himself, Mr. Devaquet, made a strong statement before the National Assembly. Denouncing the revisionist theses, he announced that he had ordered an inquiry into the procedural aspects of the case, adding that the subject and the contents of a doctoral dissertation were not the business of the minister of education. But he noted that what the panel empowered to decide on the merits of the dissertation (*jury de thèse*) did finally find could not but reflect on all academics.[38] Two kinds of steps were then taken. On 30 July 1986, the minister suspended Professor Rivière for one year, using an old but still valid statute of 1880. This most unusual but, in the circumstances, legitimate decision was upheld by the Conseil d'Etat, France's supreme court for administrative law.[39]

In July 1986 the acting president of Nantes University annulled the presentation of the dissertation on the grounds of grave procedural illegality and fraud. The university did not deliver Roques's doctorate. The Nantes administrative court and the Conseil d'Etat rejected Roques's appeal against the decision.[40] In its report on Nantes University, which was published in 1991, the National Committee in charge of assessing the universities duly mentioned the Roques affair.[41]

THE NOTIN CASE.

In 1989 the journal *Economies et sociétés* published a special issue on "Second Rank France" (*La France vassale*). In one of the articles one could read a reiteration of the revisionist theses on gas chambers, among virulent xenophobic and anti-Semitic ramblings (Notin 1989:117, 121, 123, 128). The author was an assistant professor at the University of Lyon.

The journal was subsidized by the CNRS (*Centre national de la recherche scientifique*), a state body overseeing research in universities and elsewhere. The contents of the article were denounced in the press and in Parliament.[42] The editor of the journal, an academic himself, claimed not to have seen the article before publication and accused one of his collaborators of having inserted it without informing him. That person, he said, had been dismissed. In a circular, the editor asked subscribers (in particular librarians) to tear the article off the journal, as would be done for the copies not yet distributed.[43] The CNRS suppressed its subsidy to the journal.[44]

The University Board (*conseil d'administration*) unanimously condemned the article and the Lyon Law School suspended Notin's course. The minister of education and the mayor of Lyon then asked the university to send Notin before the university's disciplinary board. On 15 May 1990, the University Board asked the minister to take the necessary steps to prohibit Notin from teaching at the university during the next academic year and decided to hold an inquiry on the use of research funds by a "Centre of Linguistic Studies" and an "Institute of Indo-European Studies." It appeared that most revisionists belonged to these institutions.[45] On 18 July, the Disciplinary Board decided to suspend Notin from all teaching and research activities for one year and deprived him of half of his salary.[46] On appeal the National Disciplinary Board decided, on 15 March 1991, to quash the decision on procedural grounds and, instead, deprived Notin of promotion for two years.[47] The university then decided to assign him, from the fall of 1991 on, to a documentary activity.[48] A civil rights association, the Mouvement contre le Racisme, l'Antisémitisme, et pour la Paix (MRAP), also sued Notin for group libel on civil grounds. The Paris court rejected the former and ordered Notin to pay damages to the association.[49]

The lesson of these episodes, which were without precedent in the annals of French universities, is a clear one. It was expressed vigorously by the president of another university in Lyon: Academic freedom is not an absolute, allowing academics to profess, qua professors, any opinion without being answerable before their peers. It is the responsibility of each university or research institution to take the necessary steps, whenever the occasion arises. This is the price of academic autonomy and freedom.[50]

Considering these episodes, one must now answer a last question: What is one to think of the 1990 reform making the negation of the Nazi genocide of the Jews an offense? In my opinion such a move was both unnecessary and unwise. It was unnecessary because French law already contains the relevant civil, criminal, and administrative remedies. It was unwise because denial of the existence of a fact—be it even the worst of crimes—should not be treated as an offense, if only because judges are not historians[51] and because this cannot be the province of criminal law. In addition, a prosecution would offer a supplementary and free public platform to revisionists, who would be immune from prosecution. Do we need that? The acid test came in 1991: Faurisson (again) was sued by several associations for an interview in which he had repeated, in September 1990, his well-known views. Of course he intended, as any defendant would, to argue his views in open court. Counsel for the associations asked the court to forbid him to repeat his views, for reiterating them could, in his opinion, constitute an offense. He also asked the court to exclude the public. Both petitions were rejected. After declaring the statute of 13 July 1990 compatible with Article 10 of the European Human Rights Convention, the court sentenced the editor of the newspaper and Faurisson to pay a fine (which was suspended in the case of Faurisson), to pay the costs of the publication of an extract of the decision in four Paris dailies, and to pay damages to each of the eleven associations.[52]

A FINAL ASSESSMENT

Racist ideologies and conduct, their origin and contents, and what to do about them have been the subject of a number of writings and essays in France during the past twenty years.[53] A few basic elements characterize the present situation.

1. There is, it seems, a marked renewal or increase of xenophobic, racist, and anti-Semitic tendencies, especially as expressed not only in writings and declarations of extremist or maverick elements but by leaders of important political movements. One political party, the National Front, has based its propaganda almost exclusively on such themes (Perrineau and Mayer 1989).

2. Anti-Semitism uses the classic themes, which need not be described here, and is reinforced by two relatively new ingredients: anti-Zionism and revisionism.

3. The main themes of the persistent campaign and agitation against foreign workers and their families can be identified. They relate to demography (France is being "invaded"; immigration is "permanent," although the "real" figures are "hidden"); social rights (foreign workers cost a lot to the country; they use our hospitals and our welfare system); education (the children of foreigners "flood" the schools; their very presence has a negative effect on the quality of education); employment and the economy (in a country where 2.8 million people are unemployed, foreigners "take" the jobs of the French people and are an economic liability for the country); religion (Islam is seen as the enemy of western civilization and of national values; the number of Muslims in France threatens the national identity and is an obstacle to the integration or assimilation of foreigners); crime and insecurity (foreigners are the main cause of crime) (Duraffour and Guittonneau 1991:127ff.).

4. It is clear that the classic themes and arguments of anti-racism as used by civil rights associations and liberal movements in the past do not seem to have had the effectiveness they were supposed to have. P. Taguieff is right to speak of the "crisis of anti-racism"[54] and its rhetoric. The "new" racism focuses less on biology and more on culture and cultural differences. The old Marxist "explanation" (racism as a by-product of economic and social factors) and the UNESCO declarations on racism [55] (science "disproves" racism) are not very convincing nowadays. (Were they ever?) Whatever one thinks of such authors as G. Myrdal or

C. Lévi-Strauss, the societies of the 1980s and 1990s are, for politicians, social workers, social scientists, and not least lawyers, almost a terra incognita in terms of the answers that are needed, and expected, by the public. Hence the general malaise.

5. This being said, the role of the law, of legal instruments and procedures, remains a vital one. Skepticism toward them is untimely and unfounded. It goes without saying that civil or criminal prosecutions will not by themselves suppress racism, group libel, or racial incitement. We do need such instruments in order for society to manifest its values and the limits of what it tolerates, and to enforce the law whenever it is necessary. This is not to say that we automatically need more statutes, more actions before the courts, more international conventions, and the like. The present arsenal has a wide reach; before reforming it or adding to it one should be sure that what we have is being fully and adequately used. If skepticism toward the law has to be resisted, so must some kinds of legal superstitions (making revisionism an offense is an example).

We are entering not only a new century but also a possibly different kind of society. What is at stake here is not only the protection of certain groups or certain people but the protection of the whole social and moral fabric of democracy. The law remains a vital tool of the latter. All lawyers —judges in particular—must be aware of it (Errera 1990b:82).

NOTES

1. On anti-Semitism in France at the end of the nineteenth century and at the beginning of the twentieth century, see Byrnes (1969), Wilson (1989), Marrus (1971), Verdès-Leroux (1969), Wilson (1978), Sorlin (1983). On anti-Semitism and, generally, xenophobia and attitudes toward aliens during the 1930s, see Schor (1985), Bonnet (1976), Milza (1988), Weinberg (1974).

2. "Any public allegation of a fact which is an attack (*une atteinte*) upon the honour or the reputation of a person": Statute of 1881 on the Press.

3. See the case-law of the late nineteenth and early twentieth century: Cour de Cassation, chambre criminelle (hereafter Cass. crim.), 16 February 1893, *Dalloz Périodique* (hereafter *D.P.*), 1894. I.25 (violent attack against Free Masons by a Catholic bishop in Madagascar); Cass. crim., 15 February 1901, *D.P.* 1901 I.62 (attacks against religious orders); Cass. crim., 22 November 1934, *D.P.* 1936 27, note Nast. In 1935 a court in Alexandria, Egypt, decided in the same way (absence of libel against a group unless all its members could be identified and had suffered harm) in an interesting case relating to the May 1933 publication, by the German Club in Cairo, of an anti-Semitic brochure: See the decision in *S*. 1935. 4. 15.

4. This seems to be the first appearance of that word in French legal vocabulary. Another regulation (the *décret-loi* of 29 July 1939) enacting a series of reforms relating

to press and family law, public health, and other matters had, among its subtitles, the following one: "Protection of the race."

5. For example, against Darquier de Pelopoix and another journalist, who were sentenced to a fine and to a prison term. See Marrus and Paxton (1981:283). Darquier de Pellepoix, a rabid anti-Semite, was appointed later by Petain to be general commissar for Jewish affairs. He was sentenced to death in absentia after the war.

6. On Slansky's trial, see Kaplan (1990).

7. Paris Court of Appeal (hereafter C.A.), 9 April 1951; *Gazette du Palais* (hereafter *Gaz. Pal.*) 1951.1.416. This judgment was quashed in 1954 by the Cour de Cassation: Cass. crim. *Bougenot,* 26 June 1954, *Recueil Dalloz* (hereafter *D.*) 1954. 646; *Semaine juridique* (hereafter *J.C.P.*) 1954. 8300; see also Cass. crim. 26 June 1952, *D.* 1952. 641.

8. C.A. Paris, 6 February 1952, *D.* 1952. 693. Other judgments were at the same time less restrictive; however, they related not to group libel actions but to other actions: apology of war crimes (C.A. Paris, 19 March 1952, *D.* 1952. 694) or libel (C.A. Lyon, 2 November 1951, *D.* 1952. 696).

9. C.A. Paris, 26 March 1952, *Roos c. Minisère* public, *D.* 1953. 342. See Foulon-Piganiol (1970a:133).

10. See, for an analysis, Foulon-Piganiol (1970b:163).

11. In November 1969 the editor of *Le Charivari* was prosecuted by the state and sentenced by a Paris court to pay a fine of 10,000 francs for having published in 1967 an outrageously anti-Semitic special issue. See *Le Monde,* 16 October and 6 November 1967. In June 1969 the Paris Court of Appeal sentenced the publisher and the co-author of an anti-Semitic, anti-Zionist, and anti-Israeli tract to pay a fine. See *Le Monde,* 16 November and 7 December 1968 and 27 June 1969.

12. Regarding ratification, see Statute of 28 May 1971. The text of the Convention was published by a decree of 2 November 1971. Reservations relate to Article 4 (freedom of expression) and Article 6 (judicial remedies). Besides, Article 15 of the Convention mentions UN General Assembly Resolution 1514 (XV) on the granting of independence to colonial countries and people, which France did not accept. The government thus declared that the ratification of the Convention could not be interpreted as implying a change in its position toward the Resolution. In addition, France did not then accept the right of individual petition contained in Article 14. It was accepted later in 1982.

13. See the introductory declaration (*exposé des motifs*) of the bill relating to the ratification of the Convention (no. 1617, A.N., 26 January 1971, p. 4); see also the declaration of the secretary of the state for foreign affairs before the Senate. However, he did not exclude new legislative measures if they were necessary (*Journal Officiel* Senate, sitting of 18 May 1971, p. 441).

14. Under French law an association exists legally as soon as its founders have declared it to the local state authorities. Such a declaration includes the name of the association, its object and address, the by-laws, and the names of the president and founders (Statute of 1 July 1901 on association). No restriction may be added (see the Conseil Constitutionnel's decision of 17 July 1971).

15. For example, those inciting to armed demonstrations in the streets, paramilitary associations, or associations directed against the integrity of the national territory or the Republican form of government.

16. Decree of 18 March 1988, now act. R. 40-3 of the Penal Code. See the ministerial circular of 25 March, *Semaine juridique* 1988. III. 614210.

17. For a (rare) example of case-law, see a judgment of the Cour de Cassation (criminal section) relating to Le Pen: Cass. crim. 14 January 1971; *D*. 1971. 101.

18. See the circular of 27 August 1990 on the enforcement of the statute, *Semaine juridique* 1990. III. 64174. For a comment, see Vernon (1990:1).

19. See, for a general study, Bastole, Hanatiou, and Daurmont (1991:319, 435). For an assessment during the mid-1970s, see Costa-Lascoux (1976:181).

20. Deir Yassin was a village of Palestine where the population was massacred by the members of the Irgun and Stern groups.

21. See the minutes of the trial: *Le procès de la LICA contre le Bulletin URSS*, Paris, n.d.

22. See, for example, Grenoble C.A. 9 July 1973, and Grenoble Tribunal de grande instance (TGI), 18 December 1973, *D*. 1975. 489, note Foulon-Piganiol, also reported in *Le Monde*, 20 December 1973. See also Paris TGI, 22 February 1979, *Le Monde*, 24, 25, 26 February and 3 April 1979; Paris TGI; 12 November 1990, *Le Monde*, 16–17 November 1980. In *Le Figaro-Magazine*, M. Courtine, a well-known gastronomic columnist and critic, criticized Chinese cooking but wrote also about the "excessive" number of Chinese people in France and their inconsiderate naturalization, speaking of "invasion" and "bacillar proliferation": *Le Monde*, 16–17 November 1980. See also TGI Paris, 4 July 1988, *Le Monde*, 8 June and 7 July 1988.

23. See Rennes TGI, 12 June 1975, *Le Monde*, 14 June 1975; Paris TGI, 11 December 1979, *Droit et liberté*, January 1980. See also the following decisions: TGI Strasbourg, 11 July 1978, *Le Monde*, 5 and 12 July 1978, upheld in appeal, *Le Monde*, 21 October 1978; same TGI, 19 December 1978, *Le Monde*, 21–22 December 1978 (an early "revisionist," M. Iffrig, denounced in his journal *Elsa* the "myth of 6 million Jews killed by the Germans"); TGI Paris, 28 March 1979, *Le Monde*, 14 January 1978, 2 and 30 March 1979, upheld in appeal, *Le Monde*, 7 June 1980; TGI Paris, 25 May 1982, *Le Monde*, 27 May 1982 (a typical example of an anti-Israeli article using the classical anti-Jewish themes). See also Lyon C.A. 29 June 1989 (anti-Semitic declarations of a maverick Catholic priest; for the story of the case, see *Le Monde*, 21–22 October 1984, 1 April 1989, and 7 July 1989); Paris TGI, 12 February 1985, *Le Monde*, 14 February 1985. For recent convictions relating to anti-Zionist and anti-Semitic articles published during the war against Iraq, see TGI Paris, 1 July 1991, *Le Monde*, 7 July 1991 (denunciation of the "Jewish plot" against the Arabs); Lyon TGI, 16 July 1991: A former spokesman of the Green Party, Mr. Brière, had violently attacked the "beligenous role of Israel and of the Zionist lobby," especially in the media; mentioning Jewish journalists, he added: "It is impossible to make a census of Jews and non-Jews in the media," *Le Monde*, 10 April, 11 June, and 18 July 1991. For an embarrassed and ambiguous exegesis of the article, see Langlois (1991).

Brière was prosecuted. He was declared guilty of incitement to hatred and violence against Jews and sentenced to pay a fine of 20,000 francs and damages to three associations (Lyon TGI, 16 July 1991). The judgment was reversed on appeal on the grounds that Brière's declaration was not uttered in a public place and that he was not responsible for the distribution of its text outside the place where he had been (Lyon C.A. 20 December 1991). The decision has been appealed to the Cour de Cassation.

24. Imported from Germany under another name, the dolls were withdrawn from sale after the LICA decided to sue the store: *Le Monde*, 15 and 31 March 1972; *L'Express*, 13 March 1972. Although the facts were anterior to the 1972 statute, the Cour de Cassation confirmed the *locus standi* of the association, since the reform was a

procedural one: Cass. crim., 15 February 1973, *Semaine juridique* 1973. II. 17480, note Blin.

25. See Paris TGI, 31 May 1991, *Le Monde*, 21–22, 24 April and 9 June 1991.

26. Paris TGI, 23 February 1974, *Gazette du Palais* 6 June 1974, p. 21; also reported in *Le Monde*, 26 February 1974.

27. See also Paris TGI, 6 December 1984, two decisions *Gazette du Palais* 13–15 November 1985, p. 13, note P.B.

28. See text in *D.P.* 1939. 4.351.

29. Vidal-Naquet (1981:193; 1987; 1991). See also "Negationnisme et révisionnisme," *Relations Internationales,* no. 65 (Spring 1991).

30. Paris TGI, 14 and 25 May 1987, *Amicale d'Auschwitz et autres c. NMPP, Gazette du Palais* 1987. I. 369, also reported in *Le Monde*, 12, 14, 16, and 27 May 1987.

31. Professor Noam Chomsky agreed in 1980 to write the preface to the book in which Faurisson published his defense; he defended Faurisson's absolute right to publish his views. See R. Faurisson, *Mémoire en défense contre ceux qui m'accusent de falsifier l'histoire. La question des chambres à gaz,* preface by N. Chomsky (Paris: 1980). On Chomsky's views, see *Le Monde*, 12, 20, 24, and 31 December 1980 and N. Chomsky, "The Faurisson Affair: His Right to Say It," *The Nation,* 28 February 1981.

32. *LICRA et autres c. Faurisson,* Paris TGI, 8 July 1981; *D.*1982.59, note Edelman; also published in *Le Monde*, 18 July 1981; confirmed in appeal: Paris C.A., 23 April 1983; *Le Monde*, 13 September 1988.

33. Versailles C.A., 28 January 1988. *Le Pence Unadis, Gazette du Palais* 129; *Le Monde*, 22 and 30 January 1988.

34. Versailles C.A., 18 March 1991, *Le Monde*, 20, 21, and 27 March 1991, text in *Revue trimetrielle des droits de l'homme,* 1991, 535. For a list of Le Pen's convictions on the grounds of racism and anti-Semitism, see *Face au racisme. I. Les moyens d'agir,* P. A. Taguieff, ed., Paris, Editions de la Découverte, 1991, p. 235.

35. On 14 March 1990 the Versailles C.A. sentenced the editor of a rabidly revisionist and anti-Semitic journal, *Révision,* to a fine and one month of imprisonment for racial incitement: *Le Monde*, 21 March 1990. In 1990 a court in Meaux, near Paris, sentenced the author of a revisionist article for group libel to four months of imprisonment (suspended) and a fine: *Le Monde*, 14 June 1990 and *Le Figaro,* 6 July 1990.

36. With the exception of a few Catholic universities, all French universities are state institutions.

37. Under French law there are two kinds of doctorates: state ones and university ones. The latter are awarded by universities under their own responsibility and have had traditionally less standing.

38. *J.O.A.N.* (Journal Officiel, Assemblée Nationale), 1st sitting, 28 May 1986, p. 1325. On the extent of the Roques scandal, see Tarnero (1986).

39. Conseil d'Etat, *Rivière,* 7 February 1990, p. 27.

40. Nantes administrative court, 18 January 1988, *Roques,* p. 499. Conseil d'Etat, *Roques,* 10 February 1992. *Revue française de droit administratif* 1992, 841.

41. Comité national d'évaluation, *L'Université de Nantes,* Paris, 1991, pp. 40–41.

42. See the debate before the National Assembly, *J.O.A.N.,* 2d sitting, 16 May 1990, p. 1391 and the minister's reply to a written question, no. 30 227, 22 April 1991, in *J.O.A.N. (Questions écrites),* 18 June 1990.

43.   Declaration of Professor Destanne de Bernis, *Le Monde*, 28 January 1990.

44.   *Le Monde*, 18–19 February 1990.

45.   See the declaration of the minister of education, Mr. Jospin, in the National Assembly on 16 May 1990, quoted previously. The minister also asked the Comité national d'évaluation to assess the University of Lyon-III as a whole. See Burgelin (1990:7). The Notin case is analyzed in the report of the Comité: *L'Université Jean Moulin Lyon III*, Paris, 1992, pp. 36–38.

46.   *Le Monde*, 20 July 1990.

47.   *Le Monde*, 20 March 1991.

48.   *Le Monde*, 21 March and 10 April 1991.

49.   Paris TGI, 11 July 1990; reported in *Le Monde*, 13 July 1990.

50.   M. Cusin, "Révisionnisme et libertés académiques," *Le Monde*, 17 May 1990.

51.   See Réberioux (1990:92). See also, generally, Bredin (1984) and Kiejman (1984).

52.   Paris TGI, 18 April 1991.

53.   See, inter alia, Guillaumin (1972), Varet (1973), de Comarmond and Duchet (1960). The most recent essay is that of Taguieff (1987).

54.   In *Face au racisme* (no date), vol. 2, p. 13, in an essay entitled *Les métamorphoses idéologiques du racisme et la crise de l'antiracisme*.

55.   See *Quatre déclarations sur la question raciale*, Paris: UNESCO, 1969.

3

Incitement to Racial Hatred in England

Avrom Sherr

INTRODUCTION

This chapter considers the law of incitement to racial hatred in England and Wales covering the period from major proto-fascist agitation in the 1930s prior to World War II and outlines the judicial and legislative responses to these problems.

The chapter then proceeds to consider the major changes in the law with the adoption of more specific racial incitement legislation in 1965, moving onward to the most recent legislation in the Public Order Act 1986. The level of prosecution under each of the various common law and legislative offenses is noted. The chapter also considers the effect of both the existence of offense and the level of prosecution on racial propaganda, freedom of speech, and some social perceptions of these laws.

Although a comprehensive exposition of existing law is not attempted, the discussion is intended to provide an overview of the origins, content, controversy surrounding, and administration of such laws.

In particular, legal regulation of racial incitement and racial discrimination generally causes quite different problems in relation to freedom of speech and democracy in a jurisdiction without a written constitution such as that of England and Wales. In the absence of any carpet "freedoms" or "rights," the limitations such laws might have on freedom of speech are greater. The "chilling effect" mentioned in much of the American constitutional literature could occur in such cases.

It is proposed that prosecution policy in England and Wales has tended to overplay this factor in limiting the number of prosecutions. Thus, the balance of democracy is maintained (or not maintained) through unmonitored prosecutorial discretion, which is not easily susceptible to either political or judicial check. This position is compared with so-called constitutional jurisdictions in which the balance between freedom of speech and the racial incitement itself can be considered openly by a trial or appellate court. In England and Wales the court may only consider whether the crime, or crimes, in question have been committed.

ORIGINS OF RACIAL INCITEMENT LAWS

In December 1985, the European Parliament issued a report entitled *Enquiry into the Rise of Fascism and Racism in Europe.*[1] The report charted the beginnings of the extreme right in Britain from 1902, with the formation of the British Brothers League at the time of large-scale immigration from Eastern Europe, on throughout the 1930s and the formation of Sir Oswald Mosley's British Union of Fascists. The report followed the growth of the Mosleyite Union Movement, the National Labour Party of John Bean and Andrew Fountains, the White Defence League, the Racial Preservation Society, the British National Party, the Greater Britain Movement (under John Tyndall), the National Socialist Movement (which became the British Movement), and the emergence of the National Front in 1967. The report also remarked on the "entryism" of extreme right-wing groups such as Tory Action, Wise, The Swinton Circle, and David Irving's Focus Policy Group.

International links were shown to exist between certain Arab embassies, Palestinian groups, and right-wing extremist groups, as well as international collusion between the National Front, the British Democratic Party, and Column 88 with other neo-Nazi groups in Germany, Belgium, and Italy.

Right-wing groups caused problems for public order, including racial incitement, throughout this period. The 1920s and 1930s in England had been a period of great social change. The Great Depression of the inter-war years had begun to bite, the National Unemployed Workers Movement was formed, and there were many marches of the unemployed down to London to protest their condition. The General Strike of 1926 brought matters to a head, and there were numerous confrontations between groups of the "impoverished unemployed" and the forces of law and order (Bowes 1966).

As the 1930s progressed, the circumstances of the Great Depression turned the minds of the unemployed toward possible scapegoats for their plight. At this time the rise of the fascist movement under Sir Oswald Mosley provided a major focus for anti-Semitic activity. Sometimes the fascist image of militarism and authority appeared to be more acceptable to the police force than the less organized groups of Socialists, Communists, and Jews who attended the fascist meetings in order to demonstrate against them (Kidd 1940). It became clear that legislative action was needed first to distinguish a set of offenses which would bring the problems of public disorder into focus and eliminate some of the discretion which had allowed the police to favor one side or the other (Kidd 1940).

The Public Order Act 1936 was the result. Section 5 made the use of threatening, abusive, or insulting words or behavior an offense.

Prior to section 5 of the Public Order Act, incitement to racial hatred could have fallen under two other headings: sedition (or seditious libel) and public mischief.

It has also been suggested that it might have fallen under the rather vague and general heading of treason, but this seems to have been academic supposition rather than practical sense and there were certainly no prosecutions of that nature.

RACIAL INCITEMENT AS SEDITION

In Article 93 of the 1883 edition of the *Digest of the Criminal Law*, Stephen described sedition as "an intention to bring into hatred or contempt or to incite disaffection . . . or to promote feelings of ill-will and feelings of hostility between different classes of subjects."

The latest reported case of sedition was *R. v. Caunt* in 1947 over an article appearing in *The Times* on 18 November 1947 concerning the responsibility of British Jews in the Hagana's "execution" of two British soldiers. In the period before the emergence of the state of Israel, the British Mandate was threatened by the efforts of the Israeli Hagana and other groups to secure independence there. Two British soldiers were killed. Caunt's article, which suggested that British Jewry was responsible for the action of the Hagana, had been published in the *Morecambe and Heysham Visitor*, with a limited circulation. Although there had been protests in many parts of the country, including violence at a synagogue in Coventry, it was not possible to prove that this was a direct effect of Caunt's article. Caunt denied that he had intended violence to result even though he had intended his article to be offensive to Jews. The judge directed the jury to consider that intention, and Caunt was acquitted.[2] This case clearly showed the unreliability of the crime of sedition as a means of controlling racial incitement.

RACIAL INCITEMENT AS PUBLIC MISCHIEF

Public mischief was a common law offense used against a wide range of behavior. For example, it was used against the producers of the Prostitute's Directory in *Shaw v. The DPP* (Director of Public Prosecutions), and against private investigators who pretended to be banking officials in *R. v. Withers*. The vagueness of this offense did not lend itself to clarity of purpose that would assist effective prosecution. Nor was a tort of group defamation possible, as a result of *Knuppffer v. London Express Newspapers Ltd.* (1944 AC 116), which decided that members of a racial or religious group would have no defamatory redress unless the defamation was referable to particular members of the group. This is an interesting illustration of the legal preference for individual rights rather than group rights. This makes recognition of racial incitement more difficult (Lustgarten 1986:11) unless the incitement is more specifically prohibited.

RACIAL INCITEMENT AND THE 1936 ACT

Section 5 of the Public Order Act 1936 was the result of Parliament's concern over the public disorder generated by the clashes between fascist groups, unemployed groups, and the police. It became an offense "in any public place or at any public meeting to use threatening, abusive or insulting words or behaviour . . . with intent to provoke a breach of the peace or whereby a breach of the peace was likely to be occasioned." Early attempts to enforce the Act against the fascists ran into the partiality of the British police, some of whom (until World War II) saw Moseley and his supporters as much less of a threat to public order than those who opposed them.

The most effective and well-known use of this provision in a racial incitement case was that of *Jordan v. Burgoyne* (1963 2 A11 ER 225) in 1963. Colin Jordan and John Tyndall were active members of right-wing nationalist groups including the National Front, and many of the legal cases concern their activities. *Jordan v. Burgoyne* concerned a public meeting in Trafalgar Square organized by far-right-wing organizations, at which Jordan and Tyndall addressed the public. It was found that there was a crowd of some 2,000 people of which about 200 or 300 young people were positioned together immediately in front of the speaker's platform. This mixed group contained "many Jews, supporters of the Campaign for Nuclear Disarmament [CND], and Communists." Colin Jordan in his opening words said:

As for the Red rabble here present with us in Trafalgar Square, it is not a very good afternoon at all. Some of them are looking far from wholesome, more than usual I mean. We shall of course excuse them if they have to resort to smelling salts or first aid. Meanwhile, let them howl, these multiracial warriors of the Left. It is a sound that comes natural to them, it saves them from the strain of thinking for themselves.

A bit later, at about 5:15 P.M., when the crowd had grown to about 5,000 people, Colin Jordan said,

More and more people everyday are opening their eyes and coming to say with us "Hitler was right." They are coming to say that our real enemies, the people we should have fought, were not Hitler and the National Socialists of Germany, but world Jewry and its associates in this country.

At this point there was disorder, an outcry, and a general surge forward by the crowd toward the speaker's platform, although a large police cordon surrounded the platform. Jordan was arrested and charged with "using insulting words whereby a breach of the peace was likely to be occasioned" under section 5 of the Public Order Act 1936.

Lord Chief Justice Parker, giving judgment in 1963 in the appeal court with some curious wording, suggested two tests for the necessary intention required by the section for an offense to be committed. The first test was a more objective one. The situation was assessed from the view of the reasonable citizen,

I cannot myself, having read the speech, imagine any reasonable citizen, certainly one who was a Jew, not being provoked beyond endurance and not only a Jew but a coloured man, and quite a number of people in this country, who were told that they were merely tools of the Jews and that they had fought in the war on the wrong side, and matters of that sort. (*Jordan v. Burgoyne* 1963 2 QB 744 at 748)

He then stated, seemingly in complete contradiction to the previous assertion, that the test was not what would provoke a reasonable citizen; rather, it was necessary to take one's particular audience as one found it, a more subjective formulation concentrating on the specific facts of each case and who happened to be in the audience. Although Jordan was "first in the field" in having obtained the platform in Trafalgar Square by organizing a public meeting there, since the views he expressed were unpopular both to his audience of Jews and CND supporters and the Divisional Court, he was criminally liable.

The more subjective formulation, if it is in fact different from the first, went as follows:

If in fact it is apparent that a body of persons are present—and let me assume in the defendant's favour that they are body of hooligans—yet if words are used which threaten, abuse or insult—all very strong words—then that person must take his audience as he finds them, and if those words to that audience or that part of the audience are likely to provoke a breach of the peace, then the speaker is guilty of an offence. (*Jordan v. Burgoyne* 1963 2 QB 744)

The effect of this case was to suggest two possible formulations for understanding the guilty intent necessary for the section. In one, any racial incitement would be judged on whether it would provoke a "reasonable citizen" to a breach of the peace. In the second, it did not appear to matter how reasonable the audience members were, provided that they *were* actually provoked.

Although it was not targeted specifically at racial incitement, section 5 of the Public Order Act 1936 was therefore a fairly effective means of dealing with racially incitable behavior provided it fell within the wording of this section. The Public Order Act 1963 increased maximum penalties for this offense and provided that offense could be tried on indictment before a jury. All of this appeared to strengthen the possibilities for dealing with racialist and anti-religious utterances. However, those who tried to incite racial or religious hatred but did not cause a breach of the peace did not come under section 5, and it was this gap that section 6(1) of the Race Relation Act 1965 was intended to fill.

CONTENT OF THE LEGISLATION

The Race Relations Act 1965:
Specific Offense of Racial Incitement

Section 6(1) of the Race Relations Act 1965, the first so-called incitement to racial hatred provision, read as follows:

A person shall be guilty of an offence under this section if, with intent to stir up hatred against any section of the public in Great Britain distinguished by colour, race, or ethnic or national origins—

(a) he publishes or distributes written matter which is threatening, abusive or insulting; or

(b) he uses in any public place or at any public meeting words which are threatening, abusive or insulting, being matter or words likely to stir up hatred against that section on grounds of colour, race, or ethnic or national origins.

In its 1964 election manifesto, the Labour Party had pledged itself to introduce legislation dealing with incitement to racial hatred. Section 6(1) was the result. This was part of a wider approach toward race relations generally, which had become problematic in the 1950s and 1960s. A large number of Afro-Carribeans had been attracted to the United Kingdom during this period, especially to take up jobs in nursing and on the bus system. Events in East Africa were beginning to provide an influx of Asians as well. Difficulties between the insular indigenous communities and the new immigrants had begun to occur, and the new Labour government wished to address them. Of special note is the necessary criminal intent (mens rea), "with intent to stir up hatred." This meant that a court would have to prove that an offender intended to stir up hatred, rather than simply discuss the racial issue concerned, and that the written matter or words were *likely* to stir up hatred.

Prosecution could be instituted only with the consent of the attorney general. The attorney general gave consent to the prosecution of at least twenty-one people for alleged offense under the section, and up until 30 June 1969 he had received approximately 106 complaints to consider for such prosecution. The majority of those prosecutions occurred in 1966 and 1967, and it seems that the failure to convict defendants in the *Southern News* case in 1967 (see subsequent discussion) dissuaded prosecution thereafter.

The first case, *R. v. Britton* (1967 1 A11 ER 486), was of a seventeen-year-old laborer who smashed the glass door of Sidney Bidwell, member of Parliament (MP) for Southall and long campaigner against racism, and left a racialist pamphlet at the door. Lord Chief Justice Parker held that there was no "distribution" and that the MP and his family did not come within the definition of a "section of the public." Britton was therefore acquitted.

The next prosecution was against Colin Jordan, by then leader of the National Socialist Movement, and his accomplice Mr. Pollard (see *The Times*, 26 January 1967), who had published and distributed a racist pamphlet and anti-Semitic stickers. Jordan claimed his intention was only to inform and encourage a patriotic desire by lawful means. The trial judge, Mr. Justice Phillimore, instructed the jury to look for Jordan's real intention and the policy and purposes of the National Socialist Movement. Both were convicted.

The first prosecution regarding racist *speech* rather than publication or distribution concerned Michael Abdul Malik (Michael X) for a speech made at a "black power" meeting in Reading (*The Times*, 9 November 1967; see also [1968] 1 A11 ER 582). Malik was found guilty and sentenced to twelve months' imprisonment. In November 1967 four members of the Universal Coloured People's Association were prosecuted for a series of speeches at Speaker's Corner, Hyde Park, where the defendants were said to have called on black nurses to give white patients the wrong injections. The defendants were found guilty and fined a total of £270.00 (*The Times*, 29, 30 November 1967).

The Malik case and the latter case brought tremendous press coverage for the black power movement—much more than their ordinary meetings would have been able to give them. This publicity, which was much greater than the trials of the white racialists, led to the erroneous impression that there had been more prosecutions against blacks under the Act than against white racialists.

Four members of the Racial Preservation Society were prosecuted in 1967 for distribution of the *Southern News* in East Grinstead, seeking a "humane solution to the problem of coloured immigration" (*The Times*, 28, 29 March, 1 May 1968). The prosecution was not able to prove the necessary intent or that the publication was insulting matter which was likely to stir up racial hatred. The trial judge stated the issue as being a choice between whether the material was "intentionally inflammatory" or "innocently informative." The jury found the defendants not guilty, and the defendants published a souvenir edition of "the paper the government tried to suppress." Finally, on 15 June 1984, the National Front clashed violently with an anti-fascist group called "Liberation" in the center of

London in Red Lion Square. A student was killed in the disorder which followed, and a major public inquiry was ordered by the home secretary to be presided over by a senior Court of Appeal judge. Lord Justice Scarman's report on the Inquiry into the Red Lion Square disorders (Cmnd. 5919, para. 125) included some paragraphs on section 6. He described it as "an embarrassment to the police" and called for a "radical amendment" to make it effective, so that police action could properly be taken against offenders.

Back to the 1936 Act

The stage was set for new legislation. Section 70 of the Race Relations Act 1976 repealed the previous racial incitement section and inserted, instead, section 5A into the Public Order Act 1936, thus placing the offense within the category of public order offense rather than within the category of race relations and discrimination generally. This pattern has since been followed in the 1986 Public Order Act, which includes a range of legislation dealing with "racial hatred" (see subsequent discussion).

Section 5A(1) set up an offense that did not involve proving that there had been an "intention to stir up hatred." A person would commit an offense if

(a) he publishes or distributes written matter which is threatening, abusive or insulting; or

(b) he uses in any public place or at any public meeting words which are threatening, abusive or insulting in a case where, having regard to all the circumstances hatred is likely to be stirred up against any racial group in Great Britain by the matters or words in question.

"Racial groups" meant "a group of persons defined by reference to colour, race, nationality or ethnic or national origins"; although religion is not mentioned, it is thought that Parliament intended the legislation to include Jews (Williams 1967:320).

The meaning of the words "threatening, abusive or insulting" is quite well defined by cases under the similar wording of the public order legislation. They are fairly strong words, and it is up to the jury to decide in each case whether the behavior in question matches those words. However, they may not be very useful in terms of racial incitement as opposed to problems of public order. Racist propaganda can be insidious and can occur at a lower, continuous level. A defendant who fixed stickers to a factory door that read "Keep Britain White" and "Niggers Go Back to

Africa" was convicted under the section (*The Times*, 26 July 1978). However, a jury in *R. v. Jones and Cole* cleared two defendants of charges brought under section 5A regarding insulting references made to shoppers in Warwick marketplace about black people.[3] This view was very well expressed by Lord Justice Lawton in the *Relf* case (1979 1 Criminal Appeal Reports 111):

In this class of cases, constant repetition of lies might in the end lead some people into thinking that the lies are true. It is a matter of recent history that the constant repetition of lies in Central Europe led to the tragedy which came about in the years 1939 to 1945.

Prosecutions were still only to be brought with the consent of the attorney general, according to section 5A(5). Some doubt was expressed about whether the political nature of the attorney general's appointment made this offense appropriate for consent to be given by him. The attorney general is an office of the Crown and an appointee of the government. It was feared that a particular party complexion might influence a decision in a particular case.

Prior to the passing of the Act, Enoch Powell, a right-wing intellectual member of Parliament who made an infamous "rivers of blood" speech about the problems of different races and different cultures in 1968, made a similar speech suggesting that when the new section 5A was brought in, he would thereafter be gagged and prevented from making similar comments (*The Times*, 22 January 1977). Powell was an otherwise respected, if eccentric, member of the House of Commons who claimed no popular grouping of followers but felt the need to state sincerely held racist views in an emotive manner. The issue of his right to speak became bound up in media discussion of the new legislation, giving his words undue prominence.

It was not clear whether it was the intent element of the old section that had been the problem. In *R. v. Read* (*The Times*, 7 January 1978), subsequent to the 1976 act a jury found that a man who used the words "niggers, wogs and coons" in a speech and also said about the murder of an Asian youth, "one down, a million to go" was *not guilty* of the offense. Judge McKinnon QC (not known for his liberal views) had directed the jury that the section was for dealing with an agitator who tried to stir up racial hatred, but that it was not intended to cover arguments aimed at stemming immigration or advocating repatriation. The line between the two grew ever thinner. Even with the intent element gone, it was difficult for a jury to find the most obvious racial inciter guilty if other elements in the legal system put barriers of this nature in its way.

The *Read* case was an excellent example of the deficiencies in forcing social change only through legal modification. Law and lawyers are unhappy to be ahead of mores, and their natural position is to reflect changed attitudes subsequent to their evolution. Laws attempting to prevent or control racial incitement must be accompanied by input of other educational and social resources in order to have a value greater than that of the paper on which they are written. A law cannot police itself. Where there are competing demands on the police, prosecutorial authorities, and the courts, it is necessary for all these to have the goodwill and understanding that come from a full comprehension of the social dangers of the prohibited behavior.

In essence it may come down to the distinction between the different political views and understanding of a judge such as Lord Justice Lawton (not always a liberal) in *Relf* and Judge McKinnon (always right-wing) in *Read*. Effective appellate controls do help, but time and effort is necessary to change widely accepted but unspoken prejudices which affect even judges, prosecutors, and juries.

Section 70(6) allowed a defense for those publishing or distributing to a section of the public "consisting exclusively of members of an association of which the person publishing or distributing is a member." This gave a "private club" exemption for racist literature to be published or distributed among other racists belonging to an association. It was thought to be a good way of letting off some of the steam which had built up among racist groups without giving them a wider, public audience for those views. This was an interesting idea in practical terms, but it suffered from philosophical difficulties. Racist publications were likened to pornographic literature and films which could be shared by club members but not sold to the public. The theory seemed to be that the behavior was victimless. However, racial incitement even within a closed group could have massive repercussions on other racial groups outside, and therefore it presented a strong social danger.

Between 1 January 1979 and 19 March 1986 some fifty-nine people were prosecuted for the offense.[4] Many of the problems of the legislation were definitively set out in an article by Geoffrey Bindman (1982). He pointed out that material published to members of an association or to a group in private was excluded from the legislation, but that the effect of such propagation of views seemed to be equally morally wrong. He noted also that the offense was not arrestable, unlike its neighbor in section 5 of the Public Order Act 1936. A policeman could therefore only stand by helplessly if he witnessed the offense being committed. Subsequently the policeman would have to obtain a summons of the attorney general. The decision in *Thorne v. BBC* (1967 2 A11 ER 1225) had already shown that no individual could bring a civil claim based on section 6.

When in January 1981 (Cmnd. 8092-1) the attorney general published his criteria for prosecution, he stated that he considered not only the prospects of conviction but also his view of whether a successful prosecution does more harm than good to the cause of racial equality. Clearly, the chances of failure as in prosecutions such as *Read* would hold heavy sway in an uncertain case. The political burden of media attention given to a racist who was found not guilty could be enough to push the attorney general further toward caution than the circumstances of a particular case merited. To this political climate of uncertainty of prosecution were added the results of two inquiries which reported the use of racist literature. There had been complaints at the Inquiry into Red Lion Square (Cmnd. 5919) that racialist leaflets were being distributed in schools and at school gates. In May 1981, the Centre for Contemporary Studies also published an inquiry showing the methods employed and campaigns initiated by extreme right-wing groups in Britain to attract and recruit schoolchildren ("Nazis in the Playground," cited in Bindman 1982).

The removal of the need to prove intention and the insertion of the phrase, "in a case where having regard to all the circumstances hatred is likely to be stirred up" did not prove as successful as was hoped. In some cases—such as *Jones* and *Cole*, and *Read* in 1978—the court considered the spoken words or publication to have been so contrary to decent human sentiment that they were likely to provoke sympathy to the intended victims rather than revulsion. This was hardly the view of the legislators. Cotterrell (1982) notes the strong arguments that committed fascists have no respect for judge or law and can hardly be reasoned with. Another social suggestion that is often made is that the problem of racial incitement forces us to "distinguish determined political action from mere delinquency," and the danger of overreaction (using a "hammer to break an eggshell," as it was put in one case) has been stressed in opposition to extension of the law or even to its more vigorous enforcement.[5]

At the same time, studies in police operations at different levels have shown how policy from above can be mediated and filtered down to the lower ranks where views on combating racial harassment, incitement, and violence may be seriously inadequate (Cotterrell 1982:380).[6] Both Bindman and Cotterrell advocated a move toward a crime of group defamation, exposing a group to hatred, ridicule, or contempt, rather than the need to include "threatening, abusive or insulting" behavior (7 August 1980 HC 756-1 and HC 756-2).

The review of the Public Order Act 1936 and related legislation placed before Parliament in April 1980 (Cmnd. 7891) made clear that changes were likely to be made when public order was reviewed more generally.

The 1986 Act

A new Public Order Act was passed in 1986 containing an entire Part III dealing with the offense of "Racial Hatred." Sections 18 and 19 are singled out here since they cover the behavior which had previously been dealt with by the amended section 5A of the Public Order Act 1936. The other sections deal with public performances of plays; distributing, showing, or playing a recording; broadcasting or including programs in cable program services; possessing racially inflammatory material; powers of entry, search, and forfeiture in relation to such material; and other supplementary provisions.

Section 18 follows the line of the previous Public Order legislation in using "threatening, abusive or insulting words or behaviour," but it includes both a specific intention (or mens rea) and the "having regard to all these circumstances" formulation seen previously. However, there is a defense for somebody falling under the "having regard to all the circumstances" test if they can prove no intention for their words, behavior, or written material to be, and were not aware that it might be, threatening, abusive, or insulting. The strange sub-sections 2 and 4 conform with other parts of the new Public Order Act 1986 but seem not to have relevance or significance for this particular area. Indeed, such behavior inside mixed racial council estates had been discussed in the parliamentary debates prior to the passage of the Act as being a major reason for changing the law.

Section 18 reads as follows:

(1) A person who uses threatening, abusive or insulting words or behaviour, or displays any written material which is threatening, abusive or insulting, is guilty of an offence if (a) he intends thereby to stir up racial hatred, or (b) having regard to all the circumstances racial hatred is likely to be stirred up thereby.

(2) An offence under this section many be committed in a public or a private place, except that no offence is committed where the words or behaviour used, or the written material is displayed, by a person inside a dwelling and are not heard or seen except by other persons in that or another dwelling.

(3) A constable may arrest without warrant anyone he reasonably suspects is committing an offence under this section.

(4) In proceedings for an offence under this section it is a defence for the accused to prove that he was inside a dwelling and had no reason to believe that the words or behaviour used, or the written material displayed, would be heard or seen by a person outside that or any other dwelling.

(5) A person who is not shown to have intended to stir up racial hatred is not guilty of an offence under this section if he did not intend his words or behaviour, or the written material, to be, and was not aware that it might be, threatening, abusive or insulting.

(6) This section does not apply to words or behaviour used, or written material displayed, solely for the purpose of being included in a programme broadcast or included in a cable programme service.

From (3) it will be seen that for the first time this offense has been made an arrestable offense, thus dealing with one of the major criticisms previously expressed. However, under section 27(1) proceedings for an offense under part 3 of the Act cannot be instituted except by or with the consent of the attorney general. The previous "private club" exemption seems to have disappeared as a result of the formulation of 18(1) and (2). Apart from the "dwelling" exclusion, the offense may be committed either in public or private. Similarly, section 19 also removes the "private club" exemption and now criminalizes all racist literature even among members with like views. Section 23 makes it an offense for such literature or other racially inflammatory material to be possessed.

19(1) A person who publishes or distributes written material which is threatening, abusive or insulting is guilty of an offence if (a) he intends thereby to stir up racial hatred, or (b) having regard to all circumstances racial hatred is likely to be stirred up thereby.

(2) In proceedings for an offence under this section it is a defence for an accused who is not shown to have intended to stir up racial hatred to prove that he was not aware of the content of the material and did not suspect, and had no reason to suspect, that it was threatening, abusive or insulting.

(3) References in this Part to the publication or distribution of written material are to its publication or distribution to the public or section of the public.

It seems somewhat surprising, since the old "private association" defense has now been removed, that section 19(3) refers to publication or distribution to the public or section of the public. It is not clear why this was left in the new legislation. It is possible that it was intended to deal with the *Britton* type case in which publication was only to one person or one family.

The definition of "racial hatred" for all sections is to be found in section 17 as "hatred against a group of persons in Great Britain defined by reference to colour, race, nationality (including citizenship) or ethnic or national origins." There is still some question about what is covered by these groups, and specifically whether Jews are included. Apparently a New Zealand case, *King-Ansell v. The Police* (1979 2 NZ LR 531) has held that Jewish persons are protected by the phrase "ethnic origins," and the better view seems to be that this is also the case in Great Britain (Smith 1987:151).

To summarize, the main changes in the new act allow for intention to be proved or circumstantial evidence to be shown that hatred was likely to be stirred up. The legislation also now allows for a police constable to arrest anybody suspected of committing the offense. Behavior in a private place or at a private club exemption has been removed.

It is not yet clear what effects these changes in the law will have. It is clear, however, that racial incitement legislation is likely to be a definite, if still somewhat controversial, inclusion in the Statute Books of England and Wales.

CONTROVERSY

Comments have already been made on some of the controversy surrounding early cases, as well as the reactions of people such as Enoch Powell to changes in the law.

Much of the lightweight discussion in the media has surrounded the issue of whether it is right to legislate against people's likes, dislikes, or preferences. With due English eccentricity, the often-expressed view is that "an Englishman's home is his castle, wherein he may think and feel and say whatever he likes. An Englishman's mind is also his castle, and he can take his thoughts outside of his home and express them in the local public house and elsewhere socially." Little distinction was made between such private or social intercourse and a more public face with real external effect. A major television soap opera, "Till Death Do Us Part," portrayed the Alf Garnet character as a typical working-class Englishman for whom racial thought and speech was endemic and expected. If such soap operas are indicative of social values, it is interesting to see a black member of the cast in more recent episodes. This person is an articulate, intelligent young man who is working as Alf Garnet's cleaner. Although he still receives a fair amount of abuse, he probably wins the day. This particular barometer of social values would seem to suggest that changes at this level of discussion appear to have occurred. The Englishman's right to sound off at whomever he pleases has not changed, but there is also a recognition of the rights of others.

At the more substantial level of comment, criticism in the academic world has centered around the question of efficacy of law in general in changing the mores, attitudes, and behavior of people. It is quite clear that law by itself is not effective. Educational, social, and political changes are necessary, and law is a useful backstop. In this sense law cannot forge ahead, but it is helpful for it to be there. Even if laws are not used by an overwary prosecutorial system, it is useful to have those laws firmly in the statute book for symbolic reasons alone.

Elsewhere the enactment of such legislation might well fall foul of more general concepts of freedom of speech entrenched within a constitution or a bill of rights. England does not have a written constitution or, as yet, a bill of rights, so the rhetoric of discussion is centered somewhat differently. This means that there is no balancing act carried out by appellate courts between the prohibited conduct on the one hand and individuals' rights of free speech on the other. In England the only question is whether a crime has been committed.

Many have suggested that creating a bill of rights would be a panacea for the difficult problems that exist in the area of demonstrations (Lester 1984:46). A number of attempts have been made to import the European Convention on Human Rights into English law itself. It is argued elsewhere that Lester is not clear that this will make the difference that is claimed for it (Sherr 1989:181–204). The usefulness of a constitutional-type guarantee of freedom of protest may be good in theory, but it may not be particularly effective in practice.

The arguments are rehearsed only in outline here. England, New Zealand, and Israel are the only countries that do not have a classic "written" constitution. Israel has been evolving a set of laws judicially formed by the Israeli Supreme Court which define the human rights of the individual vis-à-vis the state including freedom of expression, religion, and movement. This leaves only England and New Zealand. Although England may have been the cradle of democracy and the mother of parliaments, it effectively exported the European Convention to many of the countries of the old Commonwealth when they were granted independence.

England is also beginning to be more and more affected both by the European Convention and by the constitutional approach. Cases decided by many countries in the old Commonwealth come to the English Privy

Council for final decision. The Privy Council is made up of the same judges as sit on the Judicial Committee of the House of Lords. They are asked to consider such issues and will often turn, as the courts in those countries have already, to decisions of the U.S. Supreme Court for guidance. It becomes even more difficult to say therefore that English judges would be incapable of handling such issues. They must do so in relation to the European Convention, since our own citizens can go to the European Court of Human Rights and we must therefore take into account what they might say.

It is suggested, however, not so much that the constitutional model would be dangerous but that it would not necessarily provide as much control of the police as is necessary and would not necessarily guarantee the rights it purports to uphold.

In a human rights system there is a floor of rights, a line at which it is possible for a court to state, "above this you may go, below this you may not." The English system has instead a circle or goldfish bowl of human behavior. Inside the goldfish bowl exist all sorts of sponge-like and amoeba-like creatures called laws, including ones that deal with crimes and civil obligations. People can swim around in this behavioral sphere wherever it is possible to do so without coming up against these areas of "no-right."

In the goldfish bowl, the edges of the crimes are not always clear and they have the tendency of expanding at the whim of prosecutors, magistrates, and judges. The effect is that it is not always possible to tell exactly where one can swim although some areas are clearer than others. Over on the floor of rights, although everyone knows that at some point they will hit that floor, it may take a long time before a particular issue gets to the Supreme Court in order to determine exactly where that floor is.

The English case of *Jordan v. Burgoyne* (1963 2 Q.B. 744) and the American case of *Feiner v. New York* (1951 340 U.S. 315) can now be compared.[7] These two cases both consider whether freedom of speech should be given only to those who speak with the agreement of their audience. Both cases concern speeches involving possible racial incitement of different forms.

Feiner was inviting listeners to attend a meeting whose venue had been changed at the last moment because the local authorities canceled a permit to use a particular building. The trial court found that his speech gave the impression he was trying to "arouse the negro people against the whites, urging that they rise up in arms and fight for equal rights." The reaction of the crowd was such that Feiner was charged with the offense of disorderly conduct, and the U.S. Supreme Court found that he was properly convicted (there was also a strong dissenting judgment).

The "inciting" words of Colin Jordan, when he was addressing a public meeting in Trafalgar Square, have been presented earlier in this chapter. Jordan was arrested and charged with an offense under section 5 of the Public Order Act 1936, similar to section 5 of the new 1986 act. The Lord Chief Justice Parker said that although "a man is entitled to express his own views as he likes," the words spoken "were words which were intended to be and were deliberately insulting to that body of persons" who were present. In other words, in both cases a "heckler's veto" applied.

The constitutional principle of freedom of speech did not allow Feiner to speak in the same way as the crime of section 5 of the English act did not allow Jordan to speak. It matters not whether one agrees with what they were saying, the freedom was not there.

Such comparisons are extraordinarily difficult to make, and it is possible that one is not comparing like with like. However, the comparison can be taken further if we look at the events of the "Skokie-Nazi" cases in the United States in 1977 and compare them with similar happenings regarding the English National Front and the Irish Republican Army in the United Kingdom.[8] The Skokie cases were well litigated and found many freedoms of protest, but it is interesting to note that the Nazis never marched in Skokie. Although English law prohibits a large number of the behaviors that the courts finally allowed in the Skokie cases, many of those behaviors were occurring on marches in England at the time— marches that *did* take place.

It is not clear from this evidence whether constitutional guarantees would make an enormous amount of difference to behavior in general and specifically in relation to racial incitement. They would allow courts to consider the balancing act more openly. However, this might mean that judicial decisions are made for other reasons than those expressed on paper.

ADMINISTRATION

One of the major problems in relation to the legislation has been the necessity for decisions regarding prosecution to be made at the highest level. Although this may mean that decisions are highly refined, it may also mean that decisions are taken for more political reasons than would otherwise be the case. The political dangers from failed prosecutions seem to have played a much larger part than they should have.

An important sociological study would monitor the effect of numbers of prosecution and the types of defendants prosecuted against growth of public and private misbehavior. The latter is, however, difficult to monitor and assess. It is clear that the high-level prosecuting authorities do consider the entire context of offense, what society will bear, and the results of educational change. They may also be carefully considering issues of freedom of speech, such as they exist in England, without articulating them.

It is difficult to second-guess discretionary decisions made out of the public eye, but it is clear from the changes in numbers of cases prosecuted at different periods that policy is being made and followed. It is also often clear that pressure groups can have an effect on policy if they use their power constructively and constantly. The political sphere reacts to background policy, usually formed by civil servants, but it also reacts to the immediacy of politically charged events. A good pressure group can manipulate this well. There is some evidence that the Board of Deputies of British Jews, for example, has been able to do so.

CONCLUSION

It is too early to gauge whether the 1986 legislation will change the way prosecutors, judges, or even the public behave. The objective test of section 18(1)(b) is substantially watered down by the possible defense of section 18(5). The movement back toward intention with such swings of the pendulum from objectivity on one side to specific intent on the other do not seem to bode terribly well for the way in which the legislation will be used, and intention has now come full circle.

The dwelling exemption seems totally inapplicable to racial incitement. Either such an exemption covers domestic disputes within a family, in which case stirring up racial hatred is unlikely, or the exemption or defense covers neighbor disputes in which stirring up racial hatred in (say) public housing estates might actually be a real problem.

It would, in any event, be wrong to expect that law by itself can change the thoughts, attitudes, or behavior of individuals. Law can assist in doing so; it has a symbolic effect and can also be used as a stick if enough policing and prosecution successfully occur. However, there can never be saturation policing, and laws are obeyed largely by the consent of the public rather than because they exist. People who disagree with low speed limits on a motorway amply demonstrate this.

It is difficult to assess the effect of racial incitement laws without looking more closely at the social context in which they operate. It is clear that social views have changed since the early 1960s, when the first legislation to deal specifically with this issue was enacted. It is not clear whether views have changed simply because of the law, or whether the law followed those changes.

Charting the more extreme movements is also different from charting the views of the average citizen. Although they do not obtain an enormous amount of media coverage all of the time, the National Front and other right-wing organizations are powerful in England and Wales, as they are in Europe (European Parliament 1985); and history has shown that times of high unemployment can cause further outbreaks of racialism. At best the racial incitement laws are not terribly relevant for most people. At worst the previous inability of the police to step in and make immediate arrests, and the need for attorney general permission, have brought such law into disrepute on both sides of the political spectrum.

NOTES

1. Draughtsman: Mr. Dimitrios Evrignis; it is also known as the European Parliament Report (Brussels, 1985). See also the resolution of the European Parliament adopted on 16 January 1986 as a result of the findings of the Committee of Inquiry.

2. Note that this direction, which has not been taken up by an appellate court in the United Kingdom, has been followed by the Canadian Supreme Court in *R. v. Boucher* (1951) 2 DLR 369.

3. Cole said they brought diseases into Britain and were taking hospital beds. Jones was convicted of an offense under section 5 of the Public Order Act. See *The Times*, 26 July 1978, Warwick Crown Court.

4. House of Commons, March 1986, vol. 94 c. 188.

5. See Cotterrell (1982) and *House of Commons Home Affairs Committee Report, The Law Relating to Public Order*, vol. 1. Report HC 756-1 (1980), paragraphs 96 *et seq*.

6. For the background to these criticisms, see the fifth report of the Home Affairs Committee, 1979–1980.

7. See also A. H. Sherr, *Freedom of Protest, Public Order and the Law* (Oxford: Blackwell, 1989).

8. Ibid., pp. 193ff.

4

The Judicial Treatment of Incitement against Ethnic Groups and of the Denial of National Socialist Mass Murder in the Federal Republic of Germany

Juliane Wetzel

INTRODUCTION

The Allies believed that by trying war criminals and through de-Nazification they could rid Germany of "nationalism and militarism"—these are the actual words of the Law of Liberation passed by the Council of Provinces in the American Zone and approved by the military government in March 1946. The majority of the German population also considered the matter of their co-responsibility a closed book after those proceedings were over. But it was soon evident that all such efforts by the occupying forces were rather ineffective. In areas such as the administration of justice there were no criminal convictions because of a person's National Socialist past, and the same personnel continued to work in these areas after 1945. Those in other areas who had been convicted were soon released and quickly employed in their old positions or in even better

This article was translated from the German by Professor Gerald Chapple, Department of Modern Languages, McMaster University, Hamilton, Ontario.

ones. The political focus had shifted, and the Cold War relegated the crimes of National Socialist Germany to the background. Prime offenders were soon considered to be merely tainted; those who had helped sustain the Nazi regime were changed into mere fellow-travelers who were then "exonerated," if not actually turned into Resistance fighters. Similarly, "re-education" in the spheres of education and journalism proved to be only marginally successful. Not the least reason for all this was the German people's failure to come to grips with the Nazi past on its own; it did so only when effective measures were dictated to them by the Allies. This could only make the ultimate goal of sincere German atonement more difficult, as it had the opposite effect of pushing them into a defensive attitude and fostered a mechanism of repression that has persisted up to the present day. Even though the Law of Liberation was absorbed as Article 139[1] into the provisional constitution of the soon-to-be-established Federal Republic of Germany, which became the Basic Law of May 1949—this was done simply to ensure that the Law would not be superseded by the provisions of the Basic Law—the substance of the Law contained in Article 139 was relegated to a position of merely symbolic value.

This did not mean that there was no reflection on the past. But to this day the majority of Germans are devoid of sensitivity when it comes to anything relating to the fate of the Jews under the National Socialist regime. This lack of empathy runs through the entire spectrum of political parties in the Federal Republic, from the Greens to the extreme right. From the Occupation on, extreme right-wing ideas were circulating here and there because right-wing groups in particular can still hark back to a long tradition that was in no way broken or destroyed after the Allies marched into Germany. But the extremists did not dare go public again after the collapse of the Nazi regime.

THE BANNING OF THE SOCIALIST REICH PARTY

The failure of this so-called cleansing process became most obvious when, on 2 October 1949, the Socialist Reich Party (SRP) was founded. The SRP should be seen as the successor of the Nazi Party, the *National-sozialistische Deutsche Arbeiterpartei* (NSDAP) because it carried on old National Socialist traditions. Because of the SRP the federal German constitutional organs were involved for the first time in defending against Nazism. In November 1952 the federal government filed an application with the Federal Constitutional Court to determine whether the SRP was unconstitutional. The government described the SRP as a party based upon the "Führer principle" and one that should be considered as the successor to the NSDAP. Evidence was adduced in the form of documents and tape recordings of speeches by leading party functionaries. The Federal Constitutional Court heard the case in July 1952. That same month the SRP announced that it was voluntarily dissolving the party throughout the Federal Republic. The Federal Constitutional Court's decision was finally handed down on 23 October 1952. The party, which in spite of everything had garnered about 11 percent of the total votes cast (and sixteen seats) in the May 1952 provincial elections in Lower Saxony, was declared unconstitutional and dissolved; furthermore, it was no longer permitted to create similar organizations.[2] The federal government had already determined in May that the SRP, to judge by its stated goals and the behavior of its members in pursuing them, was intent on doing harm to free democratic constitutional order, as defined in Article 21 of the Basic Law (concerning political parties); moreover, the government placed a ban on the Reichsfront, a subsidiary organization of the SRP, because they had violated the constitutional order (according to Article 9, paragraph 2 of the Basic Law[3]).

In its written opinion the Federal Constitutional Court had made it clear that at issue was not merely the substance of the SRP platform and the party's aims—since these could very easily be disguised—but rather the behavior of the party's "followers," for that is what reflected the party's intentions most accurately. The Federal Constitutional Court was not fooled by the SRP's argument that those who wrote the incriminating speeches or letters either were not party members or had ceased to belong to the party; the court was of the opinion that anyone was an SRP supporter who was active on the party's behalf even if that person was not a confirmed party member.[4] The court went on to say that there was a strong suspicion that the SRP represented an attempt at resurrecting radical rightist ideas that "had last been manifest in National Socialism," and that the evidence presented confirmed this impression by demonstrating that the SRP leadership was largely made up of "former 'veteran fighters' and active National Socialists."[5] In addition, a questionnaire given to functionaries and campaign workers of the SRP provincial executive in Lower Saxony had specifically asked about any previous activity in the NSDAP[6]—which meant that having a Nazi record was enough to enable anyone to obtain a party post even before joining the SRP. The Federal Constitutional Court did not accuse the SRP of going to inordinate lengths to attract former Nazis, but rather of bringing together the unreconstructed Nazis in particular, those who had "remained loyal" to the old doctrine. The court stated too that the party platform's distinct similarity to that of the Nazi Party with regard to "loyalty to the Reich" and the superiority of the "German race" showed that the SRP had made no attempts to integrate former Nazis into a democratic system but had tried instead to perpetuate and spread National Socialist ideology.[7] The court added that the party's aim of destroying the free democratic constitutional order was clearly evident in that "the same circles which had made it possible for Hitler to lead Germany to its ruin" would soon be voicing "their claims to political leadership," and this would all be achieved by following the same route Hitler did in the 1930s. Now the Federal Constitutional Court did mention the fact that to avoid possible legal action, the party literature and speeches had disguised the party's true goal of creating a dictatorship. In its written opinion the court cited as proof excerpts from a letter written by the provincial leader of Baden-Württemberg, Dr. Krüger, in which he disclosed that it was in the party's interests "not to be branded as a neo-fascist organization" and that to speak out against dictatorship to a limited extent was "necessary, given the mere fact of the Federal Constitutional Court's existence."[8] In the end it became clear that in spite of all these camouflaging maneuvers by the SRP, the constitutional bodies of the Federal Republic were not about to tolerate the SRP's activities; on the contrary, they took steps to counter them.

Another major reason for this was the resuscitation of anti-Semitism, which the Federal Constitutional Court called a particularly serious matter, adding that by using Stürmer slogans and songs, such as *O Arier hoch in Ehren* (Great honor to the Aryans), the SRP had violated human rights and the principle of equality before the law.[9] This was reason enough for classifying the SRP as anti-constitutional, for stripping SRP officials of their seats in legislative assemblies, and for seizing party property and turning it to public use.

THE LAWS USED TO COUNTER EXTREME RIGHTIST AGITATION

The case of the SRP has served to illustrate how the Basic Law provides the legal system with means for taking action against extreme rightist political thinking and agitation. These means are limited mainly to the suppression of parties and associations insofar as these organizations contravene constitutional order. Moreover, the legal system has recourse to Article 18 of the Basic Law, which provides that fundamental rights of freedom of speech, of the press, and of assembly, among others, may be suspended if, under Article 18, a violation of the free democratic constitutional order is involved.

Just as the historical purpose of the Basic Law is to oppose National Socialist and racist activities, the Criminal Code deals with these offenses by including articles aimed at protecting the democratic state of law and public order. These articles describe criminal offenses such as disseminating propaganda for anti-constitutional organizations (Criminal Code, Article 86)[10] or using propaganda to continue the work of a former National Socialist organization, that is, spreading, producing, or introducing extreme rightist political agitation. The propaganda must of course exhibit—to quote the article itself—an "active, militant, aggressive stance" against free democratic constitutional order; furthermore, it must be evident that National Socialist endeavors are being continued—soliciting for the Nazi regime is not, in and of itself, sufficient to warrant a conviction. The article excludes publications that appeared before the Federal Republic was founded, e.g., Hitler's *Mein Kampf*, a common item in the antiquarian book trade. Among other criminal acts listed in the same article (Article 86a)[11] are the use or circulation of the symbols of former Nazi organizations, including flags, SS runes, swastikas, and certain salutations, for example, "Heil Hitler!" (Kalinowsky 1985:153ff).

Article 130 of the Criminal Code[12] addresses the crime of public incitement against groups of people. In the aftermath of anti-Semitic and neo-Nazi incidents at the end of the 1950s, an amendment to this law was passed on 30 June 1960 that was intended primarily to keep the public peace. According to the amendment, whoever incites hatred toward any group of people, promotes violence or arbitrary measures against those people, insults them or maliciously causes them to be vilified or defamed is to be imprisoned for a period of three months to five years. This law covers those Jews residing in the Federal Republic of Germany as well because they belong to a group of people whose fate has given them an extremely high profile and toward whom a particular sense of responsibility exists. The claim of the Jewish people for recognition of Jewish persecution under National Socialism has to be understood in this context. But the legal language of Article 130 is phrased in such a way that the mere denial that the Jews were persecuted is still not treated as an attack on the legal substance of human dignity. A criminal act is deemed to exist only if the denial of genocide is combined with the assertion that the so-called lie of Auschwitz has resulted in fraudulently obtaining claims for reparations. And, of course, the mere denial of the annihilation of the Jews by itself constitutes evidence of libel (Criminal Code, Article 185) (Kalinowsky 1985:158ff).

The final point to mention is Article 131[13] of the Criminal Code, which makes it an offense to display publicly, put up a poster, publicize, or otherwise make accessible the glamorizing or minimizing of violence or inciting to racial hatred. The article primarily affects written material resulting in any of these offenses; the reporting of historical or contemporary events is of course exempted. This restriction is perfectly justifiable, for how else could historians accurately report on events in the Third Reich? But the same legal exception often permits right-wing extremists and those who tamper with history to distort, deny, or question the facts under the guise of depicting history accurately; their techniques are so cleverly hidden that owing to the restriction in the paragraph, these people escape prosecution although in actual fact they engage in criminal activity. Similar difficulties are met with time and again regarding the interpretation of the same restriction in Article 86a, which makes it a crime to similarly circulate identifying symbols with National Socialist features. Practical experience has shown how differently this problem has been resolved. For example, the Provincial Court in Karlsruhe ruled that model airplanes with swastika markings be confiscated; yet the prosecuting attorney's office in Frankfurt did not view the placing of National Socialist emblems on toys as a criminal act because it was not done for propaganda purposes, whereas a Munich auction house was able to offer Nazi memorabilia for sale—among them a yellow Star of David and a Jewish identity card—although charges had been repeatedly laid, all because the Bavarian Ministry of Justice delivered itself of the opinion that the sale of such objects was "only for scholarly and historical purposes" and therefore came under the legal exemption (Ratz 1979:159f). Much can come onto the market like this if it is palmed off as contemporary history.

THE LAW IN PRACTICE

If we inquire into the relationship between the Weimar Republic and the Federal Republic with regard to legal decisions against radical rightists, we must first raise the question as to whether today, as in the Weimar of yesterday, conditions favorable to strengthening rightist circles are being created by leniency on the part of the judicial system toward acts of violence by the radical right and toward their incitement against ethnic groups and their racial hatred. To answer this properly it is necessary to describe some judicial experiences as they relate to the political intentions of the extreme right.

Just before the SRP was suppressed, two Party members were arrested and sentenced: Major-General (ret.) Otto Ernst Remer, the SRP vice-chairman and former Hitler Youth leader who, as commanding officer of the Berlin Guards, had played a part in crushing the coup attempt of 20 July 1944 and who often turned up in trials of right-wing extremists either as witness or defendant; and Dr. Franz Richter (alias Fritz Rößler), another founding member of the SRP who, as a member of Parliament for the "German Law Party–Conservative Party," had given an anti-Semitic speech in November 1951 for which he was arrested in February 1952 (Arndt and Schardt 1989:275). In March of that year Remer received the minimum sentence of three months' imprisonment for slander for denigrating the memory of deceased persons.

In the 1950s there were more convictions for insulting German Jewish citizens and for disseminating anti-Semitic literature, along with bans on extreme right-wing associations and groups (Arndt and Schardt 1989:275ff). Then, in January 1958, the provincial court in Offenburg initiated criminal proceedings against Ludwig Zind, an Offenburg teacher, who was charged with approving of the mass crimes of National Socialism. Zind was sentenced to one year in prison for denigrating the memory of deceased persons. Later, in the first half of the 1960s, about six hundred people were convicted of criminal acts stemming from radical right or anti-Semitic motives. After the founding of the National Democratic Party (NPD) in 1964, the Office for the Protection of the Constitution detected a precipitous rise in Nazi and anti-Semitic incidents during 1965. Then, in 1967, the state prosecutor's office in Munich laid charges against Dr. Gerhard Frey because of continued incitement against social groups, agitation threatening to the state, and libel. Frey was the publisher of the *Deutsche National-Zeitung* (German National Newspaper) who then founded the Deutsche Volksunion (DVU), which subsequently joined forces with the NPD in the federal elections, hoping to beat the 5 percent clause in order to be able to sit in Parliament. But the so-called headlines trial of Frey's provocative newspaper headlines was suspended in September 1974 (Arndt and Schardt 1989:289). In light of the fact that the *Deutsche National-Zeitung* has today the second-largest circulation of any weekly newspaper other than the liberal *Die Zeit* in Hamburg, this was indeed a decision fraught with serious consequences.

But in a different case with a different outcome, the Federal Constitutional Court refused to judge a suit against an organ of the state brought by the NPD and even permitted the federal minister of the interior to continue describing the NPD as a party having anti-constitutional goals and activities, as being radical rightist, extreme rightist, an enemy of freedom, and a threat to free and democratic order.

Similarly, the annual report of the Office for the Protection of the Constitution, issued by the federal minister of the interior, lists the parties, groups, associations, and publishing houses that, in the ministry's view, are to be classified as being either extreme left or extreme right. To appear in the Office's report is to have the label of being "anti-constitutional" hanging over one's head like a sword of Damocles. The question is frequently asked as to why one party or another does not appear on the list. To this day the Republicans, for instance, have not been put on it even though they advertise newsreel videos of Hitler's speeches in their magazine, *Credo*; not only that, but their party chairman, Franz Schönhuber, who boasts about having been in the Waffen-SS, has been constantly building up his party into a "Führer" party with a highly suspect ideology. He maintains relations with other extreme right-wing groups and parties, although he always publicly distances himself from them. Members of the National Democratic Party of Germany crossed over to the Republicans, mainly during its formative phase at the beginning of the 1980s, and some could in fact be numbered among its founding members. In July 1978 Schönhuber prohibited co-operation with members of extreme right-wing parties, but he continued to maintain contacts with the likes of the leader of the French extreme right-wing Front National, Jean-Marie Le Pen. Schönhuber's public distancing of himself from extremist positions was not done merely to prevent losing possible votes from the democratic far right; it was also an expression of fear because of the threat of being included in the report of the Office for the Protection of the Constitution, and that would certainly have negative consequences in an election. Several provinces are debating the issue of including the Party in that report, but until this actually happens the Party can operate within the law of the Federal Republic.

Even passing stiffer laws would not prevent parties like the Republicans from shifting back and forth between legality and illegality. They would also keep trying to appear to the public as if they were operating within the free democratic constitutional order, but they would nevertheless attempt to accomplish their real goals by circuitous routes. Stricter measures would therefore not eliminate the problem of right-wing extremism; it would have the opposite effect of helping to promote those found guilty into heroes in the eyes of the radical right.

Another dangerous result of new, tougher legal measures might be the reduction of the basic rights of assembly and freedom of speech, which must be defended and preserved at all costs. Efforts along this line would, in doubtful cases, make it impossible for other democratic groups and organizations to express criticism openly. In summary, the problem lies in the way existing laws are presently interpreted, laws that are still applied more leniently against agitation from the extreme right than against agitation from the extreme left.

From the mid-1972s on, the extreme right was thoroughly transformed into militant and terrorist neo-Nazism, which has had further effects on trials in criminal courts. There has been a rise in the number of convictions for possessing a weapon, murder, planting bombs, and forming terrorist groups. Then, too, acts of defamation of deceased persons and incitement against ethnic groups persisted, often as part of terrorist crimes. This new situation intensified discussions about the necessity of the criminal law providing protection against these extreme rightist actions (Kalinowsky 1985:279ff). After some appropriate changes in the criminal law were made during the 1960s and mid-1970s, later discussions (at the end of the 1970s and the beginning of the 1980s) concentrated on creating a special, so-called lie of Auschwitz article that was ultimately written into the German Criminal Code as its Twenty-First Amendment.

THE FEDERAL COURT'S DECISION
OF 18 SEPTEMBER 1979

The direct cause of this action on the part of the lawmakers was the trial of a gardener from Mainz, Karl-Franz (Curt) Müller, in the Federal Court in Karlsruhe. A complaint had been filed by a twenty-nine-year-old student whose Jewish grandfather had lost his life in the concentration camp at Auschwitz. The young man felt that his own and his late grandfather's honor were offended by the posters on a wall in Müller's garden that routinely displayed radical right literature claiming that the murder of millions of Jews in the Third Reich was a "Zionist hoax" and that "the lie of the six million gassed Jews" was intolerable.[14] The Provincial Court had already found for the plaintiff, but the decision was overturned when the defendant brought an appeal before the Superior Provincial Court in Koblenz. In the end, the student was upheld in the Federal Court when it ruled that the Superior Court's decision was legally in error. In its decision the court first affirmed that "no one can plead for protection by claiming freedom of speech if that person makes statements denying the historical fact that Jews were murdered in the 'Third Reich.'" The court found further that the evidence for the destruction of millions of Jews is overwhelming and that, contrary to the claim of the accused, the point was not to cast the slightest shadow of a doubt on the estimated figure of six million murdered Jews. If the statements on the posters had only kept to the charge that historians were writing untruths, then the plaintiff would not have been offended by them. According to the court, however, what was at issue here was the additional phrase that it was all a "Zionist hoax," a fabrication calling into question the barbarous fate to which the Jews had been subjected solely on the basis of their "racial" origin. The court said it was basing its decision on the fact that the accused had disputed the fact of the genocide as such, not just the numbers; in the wording of the decision:

"Whoever attempts to deny these events, denies to each and every one of them [the Jews] their value as human beings which they may rightfully claim as their own." This means that such a person would be denying a guarantee to this group of persons, who had been singled out by fate, that discrimination will not occur again, a guarantee that represents a fundamental precondition for living in the Federal Republic.

The decision stated further that numerous verdicts from the 1950s and 1960s prove that the criminal division courts of the Federal Court have long been treating cases involving libelous statements against "the Jews" as cases of individual libel. The Federal Court said it recognized, in so doing, the particular fate of those people as a group, in contrast to the narrow definition it otherwise adopts toward group libel, because this group forms a distinct segment in the community. The view of the appellate court in Koblenz that the plaintiff was not a Jew himself, and therefore not a member of this especially prominent group, was ruled by the Federal Court as being too narrow. It reasoned that the plaintiff at least had a Jewish grandfather and would have been classified as the grandson of a "full Jew," or at the very least as a "second-degree mongrel," in the terminology of the Nazi racial laws; consequently, he too would have been discriminated against and categorized as belonging to a group considered to be "inferior" (*minderwertig*). The criminal division court did not sustain the objection that the plaintiff was not born until 1950 and therefore was not vulnerable to persecution of this kind, arguing that the decisive point was not the fate of an individual but rather the historical event, which has done harm to the image of every Jew as a person. The court concluded by saying that it follows that the insult to the plaintiff's honor must be recognized, and the stipulation that as a rule, only a widow or children can lay charges of denigrating the memory of deceased persons, does not apply in this case (Decision of Sixth Civil Chamber, 18 September 1979).

After the Federal Court handed down its decision upholding the plaintiff's charge, the radical rightist *Deutsche Wochen-Zeitung* (The German Weekly) (which was acquired by Dr. Gerhard Frey in 1985) published an article on 9 November 1979—the forty-first anniversary of the "Reichskristallnacht"—on the Karslruhe trial with the headline, "Federal Court Blocking Historical Research? Jews in Germany Get Special Civil Rights." The article labeled the court's recognition that every single Jew living in the Federal Republic is now afforded a special position under the criminal law as being tantamount to giving them a "privilege in law." This supposed privilege prompted the question "whether a veteran or his grandchild born after him now had the right to sue to protect their personal honor if they had been slanderously defamed as 'murderers in uniform'." The court had of course unequivocally determined that group libel is to be recognized only in the special case where Jewish citizens of the Federal Republic are affected; thus, if it can be put this way, a special legal practice will be applied. The *Deutsche Wochen-Zeitung* article clearly draws a parallel between the murdered Jews and soldiers killed in World War II, a comparison typical of the radical right. So it demonstrated once again how right-wing extremists try to minimize the special fate of the Jews—except, of course, when they choose to deny it altogether.

There are no special laws pertaining to Jews in the Federal Republic. This is proper because, in keeping with democratic principles, no one group of people in the country should receive special treatment; the laws must be drawn up in such a way that all citizens of the Republic are provided equal protection. The "lie of Auschwitz" law makes only the trivializing or denial of Nazi crimes punishable under the law. It does not protect Jewish citizens from anti-Semitic attacks in general; in fact, it provides protection for all categories of Nazi victims, including gypsies (i.e., Sinti and Roma), against slander, usually in libel cases denying or trivializing their fate. The law is naturally concerned with Jewish citizens first and foremost because they suffered so drastically from persecution, but it is meant for others as well. Only extreme rightists take this piece of legislation as being a "special law of privilege" for Jews. The largely violent acts of aggression against foreigners, especially against Turks, are prosecuted under the existing criminal law that applies to all citizens living in the Federal Republic. On this point it is worth mentioning that there is a very marked distinction between the attacks on Jews and on Turks. The Turks or other foreigners seeking asylum in Germany are slandered and mistreated aggressively because they are living in the Republic, because of a popular belief that they take away jobs and housing, and because they are said to place a strain on social services paid for by the community as a whole. This reveals a fundamental fear for their livelihood and standard of living on the part of the general population. On the other hand, Jews see themselves as open to anti-Semitic prejudice that is absolutely without any basis in fact; it ultimately harks back to the phenomenon of an "anti-Semitism without Jews," to the old, ever-recurring prejudice that has nothing to do with fears that one's own existence is threatened.

Another statement in the *Deutsche Wochen-Zeitung* article supports this last point: "But it is even more dubious when federal judges pass judgments on history ex cathedra, as it were, which they are neither professionally qualified nor trained to do. There is a danger here that scholarly and critical research—given the possible interpretations that even the mere choice of words creates as a basis for decision making—might some day be stifled by the law." A little farther on, the author has the temerity to claim that "(t)here can be no talk whatsoever of having inviolable, ironclad 'material,' as convinced as the Federal Court is of this; we should instead speak of allegations that, however, are still waiting to be proved, especially as far as the method of killing and above all the total figures are concerned." In referring to "Gardener" Müller's wall posters, the newspaper article merely questioned whether the manner of proceeding was particularly tactful—what is meant, of course, is whether the threat of criminal prosecution was appropriate in this case—because, the article concluded, these subjects are too serious and far-reaching "for our people" to be dealt with "on the street by means of political agitation."

In the face of statements like these we have to ask ourselves how effective court decisions against radical rightist and demagogic ideas actually are. As in the case of political parties, one easily gets the impression that the criminal law is used only against explicitly stated Nazi ideas or obvious and open imitations of the NSDAP—witness the SRP. But how do we deal with parties and statements that do not make their ideology or ultimate objectives known, and that always wear a public disguise, or at least—as they say themselves—proceed with caution in order not to wind up in the machinery of the law? Where can we draw the line between tolerable, legally acceptable extremism and the kind of rightist extremism that can be prosecuted under criminal law? There is a strong impression that in the first few years of the Federal Republic's existence rather firm measures were taken against these political trends, but then there was a lull, in spite of increasing right-wing extremism. Not until the end of the 1970s and the beginning of the 1980s did the authorities show renewed interest, but they did not then—nor do they today—move as energetically against the right as they did, and still do, against the left.[15] This does not equate the behavior of the current authorities with that of the Weimar Republic, when leftists were mercilessly persecuted while rightists were treated with kid gloves, because nowadays the violent crimes of the extreme right are prosecuted with all available means, and the courses of action available through the law and to the police for moving against those crimes appear to be adequate. With regard to criminal activity and agitation, however, there was a need for more action, which still exists, by and large, today.

The trial of "Gardener" Müller in Karlsruhe demonstrates that anti-Semitic baiting and the provocative denial of historical facts need to be tried in the Supreme Court in order to generate a decision that will lay the legal basis for the future as well. The trial also made it crystal clear how shaky the legal basis has been, until recently, for prosecuting someone who denied the holocaust: That person could be charged only if one of the thirty thousand Jewish citizens of the Federal Republic brought a suit for libel. That this would be difficult for all those persecuted by the Germans in the Third Reich, to say nothing of their descendants, needs no further explanation.[16] This was a feeling shared by Heinz Galinski, the president of the Jewish Community and chairman of the Central Council of Jews in Germany, when he pointed out that it was unreasonable to require those affected to lay a personal complaint in court against those whose outrages should be brought to a halt by the state itself. His point was, therefore, not only to spare Jewish citizens from being put into this situation but to remind ourselves that it is necessary for a committed democracy to prevent the apologists for the Brown (i.e., Nazi) plague from having any room whatsoever to operate within the law.[17]

THE LAW AGAINST THE "LIE OF AUSCHWITZ"

In November 1979 the then minister of justice of the Socialist-Liberal coalition, Dr. Hans Jochen Vogel (SPD), announced that in the light of increasing neo-Nazi activity, the federal government was declaring itself in favor of further measures to fight this form of extremism. Vogel referred to several loopholes in the criminal law that were to be plugged; for instance, it was illegal to use and circulate objects bearing Nazi insignia but not to manufacture or import them. He explained further that there was a need to take action regarding published material. The Federal Court's decision of 25 July 1979 on the distribution of Hitler's *Mein Kampf* showed, he said, that the distribution of this kind of propaganda material is liable to prosecution only if it was published after the Federal Republic was founded. Moreover, he continued, legal means should be created to have the *Deutsche-Nationalzeitung* taken to court. He concluded by saying that from now on, anyone offended by the paper's "disgusting headlines" should not be expected to have to bring criminal charges (*Frankfurter Rundschau*, 7 November 1979). Even during the Socialist-Liberal coalition there were conflicting views as to whether the matters Vogel addressed required a new basis in law, and if they did, as to what form it should take.

In 1980 Justice Minister Vogel introduced a bill dealing with these matters, but for the Free Democratic Party (FDP) members in the coalition it went too far with regard to the circulation of National Socialist propaganda publications. A second bill, brought in by Vogel's successor in Helmut Schmidt's Social Democrat (SPD) minority government, Jürgen Schmude, took the FDP's objection into account, but then the matter was dropped. In 1982, just before the New Year and two days before the dissolution of the Bundestag, Schmidt's cabinet adopted the bill and sent it on to the Bundesrat (Upper House) for its approval, but it was rejected by the Christian Democratic Union/Christian Social Union (CDU/CSU) majority that controlled the Bundesrat. After the change of government, Hans A. Engelhard (FDP), the justice minister in Federal Chancellor Helmut Kohl's (CDU) new government, introduced a bill closely resembling the SPD/FDP coalition's bill; it had a provision making "the lie of Auschwitz" a special criminal offense. However, the CSU in particular blocked the project; a fierce argument ensued—with increasing public involvement—over whether a new law was at all necessary and whether the act of trivializing or denying the genocide of the Jews should be prosecuted by the state. If such a law were to be passed, the CSU insisted on having the denial of "crimes against the Germans" included along with it. As things turned out, the CSU's demand *was* incorporated, although it was formulated more broadly than before (Böhme 1985:10–12). By now it had become obvious how interconnected, even in democratic right-wing circles, the mass murder of the Jews and the fate of German exiles during the expulsion actually were. There is still no sensitivity to the fact that Auschwitz was unique. To link the persecution of the Jews and the suffering of the Germans in this manner is to equate two historical events that occurred under completely different circumstances. The Jews were persecuted simply because they were Jews; the Germans, on the other hand, were driven out of Eastern Europe as a consequence of war because the Nazis had committed great wrongs against the Czechs, Poles, Hungarians, and others. Moreover, one wonders why denying crimes against the Germans has to be made a crime at all. The historical fact is not disputed by either side.

The Bundestag, after receiving the report requested from the Committee on Laws in March 1985, again debated the bill, now formally called the Twenty-First Amendment to the Criminal Code. It was almost identical to its two predecessors but went further by providing for the seizure of extreme right-wing publications, even after the expiry of any statute of limitations on prosecution—a reference to the law governing the press, under which prosecution must take place within six months. If prosecution has not begun within that time, the author can no longer be prosecuted, although his publications can be withdrawn from circulation if the Federal Court so decides. This actually happened following a decision of the Federal Court in February 1983 against Wilhelm Stäglich's book, *The Myth of Auschwitz—Legend or Reality?* The author was charged with incitement against ethnic groups and inciting to racial hatred. Stäglich, a civil servant, had already been subjected to a disciplinary hearing in 1974 resulting from an article published in October 1973 by the extreme rightist monthly magazine, *Nation Europa*. On that occasion his "eye-witness report from Auschwitz" earned him a 20 percent cut in salary for five years (Arndt and Schardt 1989:288). Another book to be prosecuted was *The Lie of Auschwitz* by the neo-Nazi Thies Christophersen, the leader of the radical right Farmers' and Citizens' Initiative who had received several sentences and later fled to Denmark. Christophersen, who continued to disseminate his propaganda piece, *Die Bauernschaft* (The Peasantry), from Denmark, is one of those for whom the new bill would make it impossible to export propaganda material into the Federal Republic. But the main reason why a new regulation appears necessary is because of the importing of material from the United States, more specifically, from Gary Rex Lauck's NSDAP Foreign Organization in Lincoln, Nebraska. Lauck exports his *NS-Kampfruf* (Nazi War Cry)—the worst sort of hate propaganda preaching incitement against ethnic groups—and Nazi insignia; he supports neo-Nazi convicts in German jails, is a defense witness in trials of those who share his opinions, and maintained very close contact with the most militant neo-Nazi in Germany, Michael Kühnen, who died of AIDS in 1991. It was precisely because of Lauck's activities that the Conference of Provincial Justice Ministers had made an earlier appeal to the Federal Ministry of Justice protesting the importing of this kind of propaganda (Ratz 1979:163).

The chief concern of the SPD regarding the bill, besides the ban on importing extreme rightist propaganda material, was to make a new law whereby an accusation of denying National Socialist atrocities—an explicit reference to the persecution of the Jews—would not be dependent on an aggrieved person's laying of a charge, as the bill of January 1984 stated, that "to deny National Socialist atrocities" is to disturb "the public peace and thus a public right," the violation of which "must be criminally liable independent of a decision taken by an individual on his own volition" (Publication 10/891 of the German Bundestag, 18 January 1984). Furthermore, the SPD insisted that the Bundestag had to pass the bill by 8 May 1985, the fortieth anniversary of the end of World War II. Since the FDP too was fully convinced that conditions favorable to getting the State Prosecutor's Office into action must be created as quickly as possible, a compromise was struck (after frantic negotiations), which was brought before the Bundestag on 14 March 1985, directly before the debate.

In the debate itself, a spokesman for the SPD pointed out at the start that his party had repeatedly requested decisions on the Twenty-First Amendment to the Criminal Code, but as of that day no vote had been taken in the Committee on Laws. The member went on to say that it appeared at first that a broad consensus on the proposed amendment would prevail in the Bundestag particularly since the bill introduced by then Justice Minister Engelhard was almost identical to the SPD's. Of course, there wasn't much to be seen of that consensus now. The spokesman for the CDU/CSU, on the other hand, raised the old question as to whether there was any need at all for the law, considering that recent decisions of the criminal courts were already deeming the denial of the destruction of the Jews in the Third Reich to be slandering or denigrating the memory of the deceased. He also wondered whether the proposed new version of the law could prevent or even restrict extremist propaganda, which could be effected by a law only in a limited way; other means were necessary if it were to be possible at all. However, as had been said many times before, what was at issue was to review the problematic legal situation: that any criminal charges could only be laid by members of a particular group—the Jewish citizens of the Federal Republic.

When the Bundesrat stated its position on the bill it had further concerns that trials initiated on the basis of the law as then written might provide extremists with an opportunity for turning the courtroom into a propaganda forum (Publication 10/1286 of the German Bundestag, 11 April 1984). But this objection is not convincing because in recent years right-wing extremists had been able to use court trials as a platform for political agitation time after time. There are numerous examples of this happening. Take, for instance, the neo-Nazi leader, Michael Kühnen, the founder of the Aktionsfront Nationaler Sozialisten (Front for National Socialist Action), who, along with like-minded supporters in the so-called Bückeburg Terrorist Trial, was allowed to stage a propaganda show and deliver this parting shot: "They [i.e., his followers] don't want to gas Jews and don't want to kill Communists—for the time being" (Klein 1984:99). In the same way, Erwin Schönborn, an old-time Nazi and vicious anti-Semite, was allowed to speak in court with impunity—Erwin Schönborn, who had been the leader of the Reich's Labor Service and who, after 1945, founded the Aktionsgemeinschaft Nationales Europa (National Europe Group for Action), the Kampfbund Deutscher Soldaten (Fighting Alliance of German Soldiers), and the Arbeitsgemeinschaft Nationalsozialistische Demokratische Arbeiterpartei (Working Alliance of the National Socialist Democratic Workers' Party). Schönborn always came out of the courtroom pretty well unscathed, although when he stated publicly, "anybody who still claims today that even a single Jew was gassed is either a completely stupid idiot or an agent of that state filled with war criminals, Israel," he received an eighteen-month sentence for slander, calumny, and duress. The charge of incitement against an ethnic group was dropped (Klein 1984:103). But what are those statements if not incitement against an ethnic group? Schönborn was acquitted in another trial for making similar statements on the grounds that he had a right to express his opinions freely. Wrong-headed decisions like these are no longer possible after the precedent-setting Federal Supreme Court decision of 18 September 1979 that found against "Gardener" Müller.

What is needed is a basis in law allowing for a unified approach to sentencing when dealing with right-wing extremists, one that does not ultimately require a Supreme Court decision to overturn obviously wrong decisions made on the basis of elastic clauses. Hopes that a new law would be passed were dashed by the Twenty-First Amendment, which came into effect in August 1985. The revised version of Article 140 that the SPD had planned, in which the denial or trivializing of National Socialist genocide were to get their own proper basis in law, was ineffectual. Nor could they push through the "lie of Auschwitz" as a separate criminal offense at that time. This offense will continue to come under Article 194 on *Beleidigung* (Libel and Slander) as in the past; it was slightly changed, so that besides the trivializing and denial of Nazi crimes, the crimes of "other violent and arbitrary regimes" were also made subject to punishment and even "to criminal charges laid by state justice officials as well."[18] A welcome feature of this new version of the law is that a criminal prosecution is no longer to originate solely with charges made by a survivor or a member of a murdered person's family; now, the state prosecutor can act himself. Thus, a criminal offense that used to be prosecuted only at the request of a private party has become an offense to be prosecuted by the state. However, to include the slandering of victims of crimes of other "violent and arbitrary regimes," which unequivocally refers only to German refugees in 1945, is still a dubious action. And this happened in spite of the words Justice Minister Engelhard had written in April 1984 in the *Frankfurter Allgemeine Zeitung*: "You cannot treat unlike things as equals—there is no direct connection between war crimes and the systematic, even bureaucratically organized elimination of millions of people" (cited in Böhme 1985:12).

The Twenty-First Amendment to the Criminal Code that was passed on 13 June 1985 also made slight changes to Article 86a, with the result that from then on the manufacture, storing, or importing of objects displaying the symbols (flags, insignia, etc.) of unconstitutional organizations became criminal offenses (*Bundesgesetzblatt* Nr. 29, 15 June 1985). Article 131 had already been modified in February of that same year in connection with the law creating new regulations to protect young people in public. According to the new regulations, a fine or up to a year's imprisonment face anyone (as the revised version of the law of 2 January 1975 already stated) whose writing incites to racial hatred, or who in any way portrays cruel or otherwise inhuman acts of violence toward people, or who expressly glorifies or trivializes those acts of violence. Any person who depicts the cruelty or inhumanity of such acts in a way that violates human dignity may suffer the same punishment (*Bundesgesetzblatt*, Nr. 12, 5 March 1985).

It remains to be seen whether these minimal corrections to the legal situation will really assist the courts in proceeding against those trends on the extreme right that are growing stronger and stronger. And we are not even talking about the vengeance expressed in the insolent opinions of beer-hall regulars (*Stammgäste*), for in those cases hardly any court could successfully prosecute an accused able to talk his way out of the charge because he was legally incompetent (e.g., by being under the strong influence of alcohol). We are also not talking about the fact here that hardly anybody would want to report these opinions to the police or take a person to court because of them. There is also some doubt as to whether the debate on the amendment itself will have any influence on judges in the Federal Republic.

Had there really been no legal basis before 1985? Or was it the way the judicial system dealt with Nazi crimes and the neo-Nazis that contributed to the radical right's venturing so boldly and brazenly into the public sphere again? Although the initiative for the Twenty-First Amendment originated with the Social Democrats and the Socialist-Liberal coalition, the SPD admitted in its bill of January 1984 that the existing laws actually would be sufficient, except in very few cases, to permit criminal prosecution for denying and trivializing Nazi crimes. The resurgence of right-wing extremism cannot be attributed to legal loopholes, but the state believed itself to be under pressure, not the least reason for this being the mockery of the "spineless state" by the radical right (Braunbehrens 1984:16). Public discussion and debates in the Bundestag on the wording of the Twenty-First Amendment and, too, the enormous delay make it clear how difficult it still is for the Germans to deal with their past and demonstrate that legal measures tend not to help solve this problem.

More important is how all this sheds light on events during the Nazi dictatorship, mainly for the educational sector and youth groups. It has been shown that through personal appeals and encouraging the process of identification with the victims these historical facts can be communicated most effectively. This has been proven by reactions to school and public lectures given by survivors, as well as to films like *Holocaust*. Related to this is the exemplary decision of a juvenile court in Frankfurt that found against two youths who hung up posters with National Socialist slogans like "Death and extermination to all foreigners and Jews" or others calling for a "Reichskristallnacht" with the words "Now let the people [Volk] rise up and the storm break out!" They were let off with a warning—which, however, was tied to the judge's order for them to read the report on Auschwitz, *Anus mundi*, by Wieslaw Kielar, a Warsaw Resistance fighter, and to submit an essay about it in three months to prove they had read it (*Frankfurter Rundschau*, 3 October 1979). In spite of this imaginative punishment, it must be noted that the reason for the court's warning that what was involved in this case were adolescent aberrations and not political motives is not without its problems. The police and the courts tend to dismiss all too readily the desecration of Jewish cemeteries or graffiti with Nazi slogans as "the stupid pranks of kids," but they are making it too easy for themselves. Extreme right-wing groups and parties are putting more and more effort into recruiting their followers from among young people. They are succeeding more easily of late because of unemployment among young people and because their future holds no prospects.

Surely the most pernicious devices for gaining converts are the Nazi computer games, which at the moment are usually distributed in schoolyards for free or at low cost. Games such as "Hitler the Dictator," "Stalag I," "Anti-Turk Test," or "Aryan Test" are already making the rounds in the age group from six to eight and offer the children the chance "to gas someone" on screen, or to check out their "Aryan ancestry" by playing question-and-answer games; if, of course, they have dark hair and eyes, they are "ready for the gas chamber." Here the law is faced with what is virtually an insoluble problem: No manufacturers and distributors can be discovered, and the blacklisting by the "Federal agency for investigating literature harmful to children," which has already happened with the games traced up to now, only increases their attraction for young people, who want to get hold of the banned games in spite of the fact that their design is usually unfamiliar to them and that they conceivably get no fun out of playing them. Many of these games are already on the index, but the number of undetected copies is still very high, because pirating and purchasing them via post office boxes pose no problems for computer freaks.

In the meantime, new areas for extreme right-wing propaganda work have opened up in the former German Democratic Republic (GDR), as have new, untapped markets for the manufacturers of those computer games and other material designed to promote incitement against ethnic groups.

Even before reunification, at the beginning of the 1980s, an extreme right subculture was growing larger in the GDR, so that before the merger of the two countries the potential was there among young skinheads and the fascist-prone (Faschos) for extreme right-wing behavior. Anti-Semitic feelings were evident and, all during the first weeks and months after the GDR was opened up, neo-Nazi acts of violence—primarily against foreigners, but against Jewish cemeteries as well—were on the increase, thanks in part to the support of neo-Nazis from the Federal Republic. During the more or less lawless period between the dissolution of the GDR and the adoption by the five new provinces of the Basic Law of the Federal Republic of Germany, these violent attacks were carried out with relative impunity, particularly those against Africans and Asians living in the GDR. The ineffectualness of the GDR security forces was also evident when they tried to put a stop to some extreme rightist events staged by Michael Kühnen and his followers from both the East and the West. They were obviously afraid to lay a hand on them, and those arrested were soon released.

The burgeoning number of violent neo-Nazi acts in the former GDR must, in the final analysis, be regarded as a temporary phenomenon, as the result of the breakdown of taboos giving vent to thoughts and feelings denied or repressed until then on the part of misguided youths; dealing with them in the courts under the existing laws of the Federal Republic should present no difficulties. The potential threat from organized right-wing extremists will be rapidly reduced to the same level that we in the Federal Republic have been living with for years—unlike in other countries in Europe—during which time it has not played a significant role in the political life of Germany, just a limited and ineffectual one. But what the lawmakers and the courts cannot do, of course, is to combat xenophobia and the mentality that thinks "the boat is full," that is, to battle the open racism and hatred of foreigners that took on the surprising forms they did in the GDR. Hatred of those who do not look like you, of those seeking asylum, of immigrants and migrants, together with the fear of being "swamped by foreigners"—these are products of the high standard of living enjoyed in the Federal Republic, to which can now be added the fear of former citizens of the GDR for their very existence. All of this gives every reason for serious concern. To eliminate these trends is not the task of the lawmakers but of society, which means the politicians and educators, the family, and last but not least, every individual citizen.

The conflict in North America between civil libertarians and those who argue for legal restrictions on freedom of the press, of speech, and of expression is reflected in similar debates in the Federal Republic, particularly in those that sprang up over the performance in 1985 of Rainer Werner Fassbinder's play, *The City, Garbage and Death*, in the Frankfurt Kammerspiele. A character simply called "the Rich Jew" plays the lead, and this touched off a fight between those advocating artistic freedom and those who considered the work anti-Semitic and therefore not to be performed. (The affair was reminiscent of a similar scandal in the mid-1960s, at the premiere of Rolf Hochhuth's play, *The Deputy*.) The supporters of Fassbinder's play espoused the view that artistic freedom means that societal norms may be violated and that this freedom is subject to no restrictions whatever. Nevertheless, those who saw a danger in the play's controversial anti-Semitic features were successful in their demand that the play be canceled.

This is precisely the point at which we can most clearly perceive the difference between the two political cultures of North America and the Federal Republic of Germany. In the latter case, the notion is that it is quite proper for a democracy to impose limits on itself for its self-defense, especially when there is a threat of racism or incitement against ethnic groups. Where the line separating "harmless" anti-Semitism from the more virulent form actually lies is still an open question. And the reaction of the general public, as with Fassbinder's play, will vary from case to case and is very much dependent on the political situation at a given time.

All in all, there is still much to be done to combat extreme right-wing agitation and other criminal activity; but there is some doubt as to whether it would be reasonable and efficacious to rectify the situation by passing new laws. It strikes one as questionable that until the German people themselves have seriously come to grips with their own past, the legislative bodies in the Federal Republic—whose members are drawn from their ranks—are attempting to regulate certain criminal offenses whose historical bases they themselves have still not grasped in their full extent, or cannot even approach with the requisite sensitivity. As to the Jewish population in the Federal Republic, it would seem to have been imperative, on moral grounds alone, to make "the lie of Auschwitz" a separate statutory offense without linking it to the fate of the refugees. This would have been the best possible way of protecting the Jewish populace from further slander and of demonstrating to them that they have not been left on their own, that their fate is taken seriously.

NOTES

1. Article 139 of the Basic Law reads, "The legal regulations issued to 'free the German people from National Socialism and militarism' are not affected by the provisions of this Basic Law."

2. Compare the Federal Constitutional Court's decision of 23 October 1952 on determining the anti-constitutionality of the Socialist Reich Party, published by members of the Federal Constitutional Court, Tübingen, 1952.

3. Article 9(2) reads, "All associations are prohibited whose purposes or whose activity run counter to the criminal laws or are directed against the constitutional order or opposed to the principle of understanding among peoples."

4. Federal Constitutional Court's decision, 23 October 1952, p. 25f.

5. Ibid., p. 27.

6.   Ibid., p. 30.
7.   Ibid., pp. 43, 52f.
8.   Ibid., p. 63f.
9.   Ibid.
10.   Article 86 of the Criminal Code reads:

(1) Whosoever disseminates or produces for purposes of dissemination within the territory in which this law applies, maintains a supply or imports into this territory, propaganda

1. of a political party declared unconstitutional by the Federal Constitutional Court, or of a political party about which it has been incontestably determined that it is a substitute organization for such a political party,

2. of an association which has been incontestably prohibited because it is ranged against the constitutional order or against the principle of understanding among peoples, or about which it has been incontestably determined that it is a substitute organization for such a political party,

3. of a government, association or institution outside the territory in which this law applies, which is active on behalf of the purposes of the parties or associations designated under 1. and 2., or

4. propaganda whose content are directed at continuing the efforts of a former National Socialist organization

shall be punished by a term of imprisonment of up to three years or a fine.

(2) Propaganda in the sense of Paragraph 1 are only those writings (§11 para. 3) whose content is directed against the free democratic constitutional order or the principle of understanding among peoples.

(3) Paragraph (1) does not apply if the propaganda or the action serves to advance political or civil education, to protect against unconstitutional actions, to promote art or science, to advance research or teaching, to report events of contemporary or historical interest or other such purposes.

(4) The court may refrain from imposing penalties according to these regulations in cases when the guilt is modest.

11.   Article 86a reads:

(1) Whosoever

1. within the territory in which this law applies disseminates symbols of one of the political parties or associations designated in §86 para. 1 no. 1, 2 and 4 or, publicly uses them in a meeting or in writings disseminated by him, or

2. produces, maintains a supply or imports into the territory in which this law applies objects which represent or contain these kinds of symbols for dissemination or use in ways specified in number 1

shall be punished with a term of imprisonment of up to three years or a fine.

(2) Symbols in the meaning of para. 1 are particularly flags, insignia, parts of uniforms, slogans and forms of greeting.

(3) §86(3) and (4) shall correspondingly apply.

12. Article 130 states:

Whosoever attacks the human dignity of others, in a manner capable of disturbing public peace, by

1. inciting hatred against sections of the population,

2. calling for violent or arbitrary measures against them, or

3. insulting them, maliciously exposing them to contempt or slandering them

shall be punished by a term of imprisonment of not less than three months and not exceeding five years.

13. Article 131 states:

(1) Whosoever

1. disseminates,

2. publicly exhibits, posts, presents, or otherwise makes accessible,

3. offers, leaves or makes available or accessible to a person below the age of eighteen, or

4. produces, procures, supplies, keeps in stock, offers, advertises, recommends, undertakes to import into, or export out of, the territory in which this law applies, in order to use them, or parts of them, in the manner indicated in number 1 to 3 above, or to enable others to do so, writings (§11, para. 3) which incite to race hatred or which describe cruel or otherwise inhuman acts of violence against human beings in a manner which glorifies such acts of violence, or makes them appear harmless, or represents the cruel and inhuman aspects of such acts in a manner offending human dignity, shall be punished by a term of imprisonment of up to one year or a fine.

(2) Likewise shall be punished whosoever disseminates by radio broadcasts, such representations as indicated in para. 1.

(3) Paragraphs 1 and 2 do not apply when the act serves to report on current events or history.

(4) Paragraph 1 number 3 is not to be applied if the action is done by the legal guardian of the person.

14. From the judgment of the Sixth Civil Chamber of the Federal Supreme Court on 18 September 1979.

15. Interest in the trial of "Gardener" Müller was not very great. There were few editorials on it, and the *Süddeutsche Zeitung* (in Munich), for example, buried a small report about it on page six. The limited interest so apparent in this case is typical of media coverage of other people on the extreme right, with the exception of Franz Schönhuber's Republicans. On the whole, the general public rates information about the extreme left more highly, which is also reflected in courtroom proceedings. For example, lawyers in trials of members of the "Red Army Faction" have been searched and those accused were not permitted to speak with one another. Things were very different in 1977 during the trial in Bückeburg of the neo-Nazi Michael Kühnen and some of his followers, where the lawyers were *not* searched, the accused *were* allowed to talk with one another, and both the lawyers and the accused were permitted, in court and with no restrictions, to deliver themselves of Nazi slogans and statements promoting incitement against ethnic groups. Even today, a double standard is operative in trials of terrorists. This is true not only of how trials are conducted but of the general population as well.

16. Compare *Süddeutsche Zeitung*, 25, 26 August 1984.

17. *Blick nach rechts* (Look to the Right), 11 March 1985.

18. Gesetzgebungsdienst (Legislation Service) *Juristen Zeitung*, Nr. 12, 9 August 1985. The first two paragraphs of Article 194 read as follows:

(1) Prosecution for insult shall be instituted only upon petition. When the act is committed by disseminating or making publicly accessible a writing (§11, para. 3), or in an assembly or by means of broadcasting, a petition is not required, if the insulted person was persecuted as a member of a group under the National Socialist or another violent and arbitrary dominance, if the group is a part of the population and if the insult is connected with such persecution. However, there shall be no prosecution ex officio if the injured person opposes it. The opposition may not be withdrawn. If the injured person dies, the right of petition and of opposition passes to the next of kin as specified in §77, para. 2.

(2) If the memory of a deceased person is denigrated, the next of kin as specified in §77, para. 2 have the right to lodge a petition. If the act is committed by disseminating or by making publicly accessible a writing (§11, para. 3), or in an assembly or by means of broadcasting, a petition is not required, if the insulted person was persecuted as a member of a group under National Socialist or another violent and arbitrary dominance and the denigration is connected with it. However, there shall be no prosecution ex officio if the person entitled to launch a petition opposes it. The opposition may not be withdrawn.

5

Racial Incitement Law and Policy in the United States: Drawing the Line between Free Speech and Protection against Racism

Donald A. Downs

HATE CRIMES IN THE UNITED STATES AND THE FIRST AMENDMENT

This chapter will address the legal status of hate-inspired crime and racist speech in the United States. I will begin by discussing the nature of hate crimes in the United States and the special limits that the First Amendment of the U.S. Constitution places on laws that prohibit hate-oriented expression. I will then discuss the nature of relevant laws and their implementation.

The U.S. historical experience with racism and ethnic conflict has been profound and unique. On the one hand, the legacies of slavery, officially sanctioned segregation, and prejudice against new immigrants have left deep wounds. The recent riots in Los Angeles over police brutality against blacks reveals the seemingly ineradicable tensions. On the other hand, the United States has absorbed more ethnic groups than virtually any other country, leading to unusual ethnic diversity and pluralism; and many minorities have made political and legal gains in recent decades. The American experience is a combination of hope and conflict (Horowitz 1985).

The nation no longer witnesses the widespread racial lynchings that plagued the land in the heyday of the Ku Klux Klan (1870–1930). Nonetheless, various types of "hate crimes" directed at minorities in neighborhoods and campuses have apparently surged in recent years. The most extreme incidents involve hate-inspired killings or beatings. In Portland, Oregon, in 1988 a white hate group, acting with the encouragement of a Klan leader in Los Angeles, attacked and killed an Ethiopian resident alien. In 1989 someone sent bombs through the mails to selected targets in the South. In both cases, the culprits were eventually apprehended and charged (Southern Poverty Law Center 1991:3).

Unfortunately, although there are numerous state and local laws against hate-inspired violence and acts against persons and property, government agencies have not compiled the data needed to authoritatively assess trends in this area and the effectiveness of law. The federal government's Uniform Crime Reports have never monitored crimes generated by racial animus per se, nor (until very recently) have the crime reporting systems of the states. In April 1990, however, President Bush signed the Hate Crimes Statistics Act, which requires police departments to keep statistics of all bias-motivated crimes (crimes related to race, religion, sexual orientation, and ethnicity), and report them to the Federal Bureau of Investigation. The deputy attorney general for civil rights must then establish criteria that determine which crimes are hate- or bias-animated (*New York Times,* 28 April 1990). As of the late 1980s, eight states had enacted similar statutes. Because these laws are also of recent vintage, states have not yet generated meaningful data (Anti-Defamation League 1988:3–4).

Nevertheless, private organizations dedicated to combating racism have compiled some suggestive data. According to them, the number of violent and lesser assaults and intimidations has risen in recent years after having fallen off in previous years. These acts often involve various forms of verbal intimidation or harassment and racist-inspired damage to property. The *New York Times* (28 April 1990) has recently reported that "most incidents . . . [involve] vandalism like the scrawling of 'K.K.K.' on doors and walls or harassing phone calls and letters. While most cases did not result in physical harm to the minority families . . . they had a serious emotional impact" (see also Mason and Thomson 1985:85). Yet violent racist-inspired acts have also increased. The Southern Poverty Law Center reported twenty murders in 1990 "linked to white supremacists or motivated by violence." This was almost triple the number in 1989, and the most the Center has reported since it began recording such acts ten years ago (Southern Poverty Law Center 1991:4). The Center reported a "dramatic rise in hate crimes" in recent years, especially housing-related incidents, which constituted 75 percent of federally prosecuted cases in 1988 and 1989 (up from about 50 percent in previous years) (Southern Poverty Law Center 1991:2). For 1990, the Center reported a 50 percent increase in cross burnings, a 33 percent increase in religious vandalism, and a 22 percent increase in violent assaults (Southern Poverty Law Center 1991:4). Furthermore, these reports probably understate the problem, as many incidents are never reported. The Center's Pat Clark states that "since there is no national data collection on hate crime, our figures are necessarily incomplete, so we are probably looking at only a fraction of the violence that actually occurred" (Southern Poverty Law Center 1991:2).

Another source supports the Center's conclusions. The Anti-Defamation League (ADL) has tracked anti-Semitic violence since 1979. From 1979 to 1981, such incidents rose dramatically from 120 to 974. From 1982 to 1987, however, a downtrend occurred. The ADL attributed this reversal to "a more effective response from law enforcement agencies, heightened public awareness of the problem, a greater willingness of victims to report these crimes, and, most importantly, the enforcement of laws aimed at punishing this type of crime more severely" (Anti-Defamation League 1988:1). I will discuss some of these new laws later. In 1987 the number of incidents began climbing, and it continues to grow. The number of vandalistic attacks in California alone rose over 100 percent in 1987 (from 62 to 137). The ADL also reported 324 incidents of the separate crimes of assaults, threats, and harassments in 1987.

Finally, nonsystematic evidence from college campuses supports the conclusion that hate-inspired acts and communications have increased. Almost two hundred university and college campuses have recently witnessed well-publicized incidents of verbal harassment and related expressions of racial hate. At my own institution, the University of Wisconsin, Madison, the dean of students investigated over 170 complaints of racial and sexual harassment in 1989 alone (Statement by Mary Rouse, U.W. Madison, Dean of Students).

In response to racist incidents, states, national government, and campuses have passed laws or regulations that deal with the specific hate elements of the crimes just discussed, including threatening, intimidating, or harassing racist speech. These laws supplement pre-existing laws that originated mainly in the post–Civil War period (when the national government began to protect, with varying degrees of success, the basic rights of the newly freed ex-slaves) and the period of black immigration to the North during the mid-twentieth century (when racial tensions grew).

Before we look at the major laws, one crucial issue must be addressed: the constitutionality of laws restricting racist expression. All laws restricting racist expression in any form must meet the stringent constitutional standards of the First Amendment to the U.S. Constitution, which prohibits all laws "abridging freedom of speech, or of the press." The United States is, perhaps, unique in the amount of protection it provides racist speech. Thus, one must grasp basic First Amendment doctrine in order to evaluate laws against incitement to racial hatred in the United States.

The First Amendment and the Law

For the most part, laws in the United States providing criminal or civil sanctions against racism at both the state and federal levels have dealt with discriminatory *action* or speech closely tied to illegal *conduct*. This narrow approach stems from basic constitutional doctrine that has developed over the years. Laws against general racist rhetoric (or "group defamation" or "group libel") are constitutionally problematic, even if such rhetoric encourages violence. Only four states have group libel laws (Connecticut, Indiana, Massachusetts, and West Virginia), and they seldom enforce them. No such national law exists.[1] In 1952 the U.S. Supreme Court upheld a group libel law, but changes in other areas of First Amendment law since then cast serious doubt on the validity of such laws.

Under the Supreme Court's interpretation of the First Amendment, the right of free speech normally outweighs the social interest in protecting society from the *offense* and *potential danger* of such expression. Governments may restrict racist speech only when the harm or danger of the speech is clear, imminent and substantial; otherwise, according to the Supreme Court, the best remedy for racist rhetoric in a pluralistic environment like the United States is the maintenance of an open marketplace of ideas in which counterviews are given the opportunity to reply. First Amendment doctrine is premised on democratic theory: The law deems it inappropriately paternalistic for the state to abridge politically relevant speech because of disapproval of its content or undifferentiated concern about its potential to influence the acts of others.[2]

In addition to protecting general racist rhetoric, this approach also protects the right to organize parties on the basis of racist doctrine, for the freedom of expression entails freedom of association as well.[3] As a result, hate groups like the Klan, Nazis, and skinheads are active in at least forty-three states (Southern Poverty Law Center 1991:4–5).

The precepts of many other western countries and international law differ. For example, the International Covenant on Civil and Political

Rights of 1966 endorses freedom of expression but states that "advocacy of national, racial, or religious hatred that constitutes incitement to discrimination, hostility, or violence shall be prohibited by law." Article 4 of the International Convention on the Elimination of All Forms of Racial Discrimination requires member states to criminalize the dissemination of hate propaganda.[4]

Dozens of countries have ratified the Convention or promulgated laws consistent with its logic. England passed the 1965 Race Relations Act in response to the rise of neo-Nazism in the 1960s. A 1976 amendment to this act (put into the Public Order Act 1936) makes it an offense if one "publishes or distributes written matter which is threatening, abusive, or insulting" or "uses in any public place or at any public meeting words which are threatening, abusive, or insulting" (Public Order Act 1936, section 5A (5) (b)). France and Denmark prohibit racial defamation, racial degradation, racial insults, and incitement to discrimination, hatred, and violence (French Penal Code, Art. 1, 3 Act 72-546, 1 July 1972).

Germany has many laws against racist speech and the organization of racist political parties. A variety of laws proscribe Nazi organizing, slogans, signs, and uniforms (including the "Heil Hitler" greeting); and it is illegal "to write, print, or distribute writings that glorify acts of violence against human beings and incite hatred" (Bollinger 1986:256).

Most of the laws just mentioned would be unconstitutional in the United States. To be sure, the United States finally signed the International Covenant on Civil and Political Rights in early June 1992. Yet the government attached a set of exceptions including the assertion that the signing in no way compromises the status of First Amendment rights in the United States.[5] Indeed, this very concern was a major reason why the United States had refused to sign the Covenant for so long. Although the inclusion of exceptions has met criticism, it is consistent with the long-standing constitutional principle that the treaty power of the national government is subject to the same constitutional limitations as any other exercise of governmental power (Henkin 1975:137). The First Amendment limits restrictions of speech, compelling the state to use other means to effectuate ethnic harmony and justice. The different historical circumstances that surrounded the development of free speech doctrine in the post–World War II era may partially explain the difference between U.S. and European policies. European policy is partly a reaction to the atrocities of Hitler. The development of modern free speech doctrine in the United States is an offshoot of the civil rights movement itself. The Supreme Court decided in the 1960s that a policy of strict neutrality concerning the content of politically oriented speech constituted the best guarantee of free speech for unpopular groups. In a quid pro quo fashion, the speech rights of civil rights and other dissenting groups were secured at the price of granting similar protection to hate groups ("freedom for the thought we hate").[6] Most prominent Jewish and black groups in the United States still favor this mutual pact because they believe it is the best security for their own rights.

Constitutional Law and Free Speech

The constitutional law governing free speech commenced in 1919 with Supreme Court decisions concerning federal prosecutions of individuals whose speech threatened to disrupt the draft during World War I. For a number of decades the Court allowed restrictions of speech on two primary grounds: (1) if it posed a "clear and present danger" to society. Under the Court's interpretation of this test, however, speech constituted a clear and present danger if it simply had a "dangerous tendency" to lead to unlawful action; (2) if the speech did not possess sufficient "social value" to merit protection, regardless of any specific danger presented. In 1942, the Court stated in *Chaplinsky v. New Hampshire* that such forms of expression as obscenity, lewd and offensive speech, libel, and "fighting words" (words likely to injure emotionally or to provoke a violent hostile reaction) were not protected because "such utterances are no essential part of any exposition of ideas, and are of such slight social value as a step to truth" (315 U.S. 568 (1942), at 571–572).

These approaches provided ample leeway for governments to restrict racial incitement and other expression of questionable moral value. Though states did not always enforce such laws conscientiously in the area of race relations, doctrine did permit states to punish racial rhetoric when they so desired. A representative case involved the conviction in Illinois of a leader of the Chicago "White Circle" Party who circulated racially inflammatory leaflets on a streetcorner. In *Beauharnais v. Illinois* (1952), the Supreme Court upheld this conviction for "group libel" on the grounds articulated in *Chaplinsky*. The Illinois law resembled the international laws already mentioned; it made it a crime to manufacture or exhibit any material that "portrays depravity, criminality, unchastity, or lack of virtue of a class of citizens, of any race, color, or creed or religion which said publication or exhibition exposes the citizens of any race, color, creed, or religion to contempt, derision, or obloquy or which is productive of breach of peace or riots" (Ill. Rev. Stat. Ch. 38, Sec. 471 (1949), repealed in 1962). Beauharnais's leaflets beseeched the city government to "halt" the movement of blacks to Chicago and exhorted "one million self respecting white people to unite. . . . If persuasion and the need to prevent the white race from becoming mongrelized by the negro will not unite us, then the aggressions . . . rapes, robberies, knives, guns, and marijuana of the negro, surely will" (*Beauharnais v. Illinois,* 343 U.S. 250 (1952), at 252).

The Supreme Court associated Beauharnais's speech with libel and fighting words, which *Chaplinsky* had excluded from First Amendment protection. Quoting from another case involving incitement to religious animosity, the Court remarked that "[R]esort to epithets or personal abuse is not in any proper sense communication of information or opinion safeguarded by the Constitution, and its punishment as a criminal act would raise no question under that instrument." (*Beauharnais,* citing from *Cantwell v. Connecticut,* 310 U.S. 296 (1940)).

Thus, as of 1952, racist speech in a public context was punishable whether or not it was targeted at a particular individual. Yet social and legal change loomed on the horizon. The civil rights movement, the anti-Vietnam War demonstrations, and more general changes in social mores (cultural and value pluralism) led the Court to be more distrustful of the exceptions to free speech established in *Chaplinsky* and to be more suspicious of government claims that potentially dangerous speech needed to be suppressed. During the 1960s and 1970s the Court made it harder to limit speech based on clear and present danger, and it restricted the exceptions to speech established in *Chaplinsky.* The Court narrowed the scope of the "obscenity" exception to very sexually explicit "hard core" pornography and gave significant constitutional protection to fighting words and libel in the context of public debate.

The Court made it very difficult to punish offensive speech and fighting words by holding in *Cohen v. California* (403 U.S. 15 (1971), at 35) that laws against offensive speech are inherently unconstitutionally vague, and that offense is often too subjective a matter to justify legal restriction except in special contexts in which the right to privacy is paramount (offensive expression should be tolerated in other contexts because "one man's vulgarity is another's lyric"). This decision was rendered against the backdrop of the "heckler's veto" cases, in which the Court had protected the rights of civil rights protesters to demonstrate despite authorities' claims that angry hecklers or hostile audiences threatened disorder. Police must attempt to control disruptive audiences, if possible, before asking speakers to forsake their speeches.[7] Furthermore, in ruling that the First Amendment protected Cohen's wearing a jacket that had "Fuck the Draft" emblazoned on its back, the *Cohen* Court limited the doctrine of fighting words to face-to-face encounters in which violence is imminent. *Cohen* and subsequent fighting words cases established the standard that racist and other offensive speech can be prohibited only if it is extremely personally abusive and directed at a specific target.[8]

Finally, the Court narrowed the clear and present danger test in a series of cases culminating in *Brandenburg v. Ohio* (1969), a case that involved a Klan group's advocacy of racial violence from a farm field (reported on the television news). Brandenburg was convicted under an Ohio criminal syndicalism statute for "advocat[ing] the duty, necessity, or propriety of crime, sabotage, violence, or unlawful methods of terrorism as a means of accomplishing industrial or political reform" and for "voluntarily assembl[ing] with any society, group, or assemblage of persons formed to teach or advocate the doctrines of criminal syndicalism." The Supreme Court reversed the conviction, holding that the First Amendment protects the advocacy of unlawful action or violence "except where such advocacy of the use of force or of law violation is directed to inciting or producing imminent lawless action and is likely to incite or produce such action." (395 U.S. 444 at 447(1969)). The mere possibility of future harm ("dangerous tendency") is an insufficient basis.

Although the Supreme Court and other courts have not defined "incitement" with great precision, *Brandenburg* essentially protects advocacy and incitement of racial violence unless they constitute "triggers" to imminent illegal action. Government may not prohibit rhetorical pleas for illegal action, or even sincere pleas that fall short of triggering imminent lawlessness. Accordingly, the Supreme Court reversed the conviction of a man who told an audience before the White House that "if they ever make me carry a rifle the first man I want to get in my sights is [President] L.B.J." (*Watts v. U.S.*, 394 U.S. 705 (1969), at 706). On the other hand, the Supreme Court of Florida upheld a conviction of a protester for "extortion" because his expression fit the *Brandenburg* test. The defendant led an angry crowd in chants that urged assassination of a sheriff in order to compel dismissal of a deputy for shooting and killing a young black man. "Two, Four, Six, Eight! Who shall we assassinate? Deputy, sheriff, and the whole bunch of you!" he beseeched the crowd (*Matthews v. State,* 363 So. 2d 1066 (1978)). The court ruled that this was a "true" threat, not merely rhetorical.

A famous case in the later 1970s epitomizes the extraordinary protection the First Amendment now extends to racialist rhetoric in the United States. In 1977 a small Nazi party in Chicago announced its intention to hold a public demonstration in Skokie, a northern suburb where about a thousand survivors of Nazi death camps resided. The party planned to wear its uniforms, replete with swastikas, in front of the village hall (a classic public forum, where speech rights are most extensive) and carry signs that asserted "White Power." The party's threatened appearance in

Skokie opened severe psychological wounds. Resisters threatened substantial violence in the event the Nazis came to town. Skokie officials used two legal means to keep the Nazis out. They obtained an injunction in state court and passed three permit ordinances modeled on the Illinois statute in *Beauharnais* that prohibited the issuance of a permit to demonstrate if the applicant planned to engage in "racial slurs" and wear a military uniform. The Nazis challenged the ordinances in federal court. Under *Beauharnais v. Illinois* and the European laws already discussed, the ordinances and injunction would have been valid exercises of governmental power.

But after a year of legal and political jockeying, both state and federal courts ruled that Skokie's respective measures violated the First Amendment. The Illinois Supreme Court decision in the injunction case relied strongly on *Cohen v. California* and later fighting words cases in concluding that the context of the proposed demonstration (a classic public forum, with no targeting of private domains) made the fighting words rationale inapplicable (*Village of Skokie v. National Socialist Party of America*, 373 N.E. 2d 21 (1978)). The federal court decisions concerning the ordinances utilized *Brandenburg, Cohen,* and related cases in ruling against Skokie.[9] The Supreme Court tacitly approved the lower courts' rulings by refusing to hear Skokie's appeal.

Skokie stands as a landmark of the U.S. commitment to freedom of speech, including calculated racist rhetoric. Nevertheless, the Supreme Court did not review the *Skokie* decisions, so the constitutional status of fighting words in the context of hate speech was left dangling. But this constitutional limbo changed suddenly in the summer of 1992 when the Court declared St. Paul's Bias Motivated Criminal Ordinance unconstitutional in *R.A.V. v. City of St. Paul, Minnesota* (1992 Lexis 3863, No. 90-7675). Although the *R.A.V.* decision left room for governments to act against hate speech, Justice Antonin Scalia's inexorable logic staked out new grounds for limiting the basis of governmental action in this domain. St. Paul's ordinance stated:

Whoever places on public or private property a symbol, object, appellation, characterization or graffiti, including, but not limited to, a burning cross or Nazi swastika, which one knows or has reasonable grounds to know arouses anger, alarm, or resentment in others on the basis of race, color, creed, religion or gender commits disorderly conduct and shall be guilty of a misdemeanor. (St. Paul, Minn., Legis. Code, section 292.02 (1990)).

St. Paul applied this ordinance against a teenager who, along with others, burned a cross in a black family's yard; cross burning is a universally recognized symbol of hate historically directed against blacks by the Ku Klux Klan.

The Minnesota Supreme Court upheld the St. Paul ordinance by construing it to prohibit fighting words. However, a majority of the U.S. Supreme Court ruled that the ordinance transgressed the First Amendment because it singled out certain types of fighting words for proscription while ignoring others. By prohibiting only fighting words dealing with race, color, creed, religion, and gender, St. Paul premised its ordinance upon a viewpoint discrimination that disadvantaged some forms of fighting words over others. Such viewpoint discrimination stemming from "underinclusive" statutes (i.e., those that do not cover all forms of fighting words, but only certain categories) suggests that the government is playing favorites in speech policy based on ideological or moral agendas or preferences. This type of underinclusion violates the cardinal First Amendment principle that the law must treat all viewpoints equally when it comes to free speech policy. I quote Scalia at length because of the importance of this recent decision:

[E]ven as narrowly construed by the Minnesota Supreme Court, the ordinance is facially unconstitutional. . . . [T]he ordinance applies only to "fighting words" that insult, or provoke violence, "on the basis of race, color, creed, religion or gender." Displays containing abusive invective, no matter how vicious or severe, are permissible unless they are addressed to one of the specific disfavored topics. Those who wish to use "fighting words" in connection with other ideas—to express hostility, for example, on the basis of political affirmation, union membership, or homosexuality—are not covered. The First Amendment does not permit St. Paul to impose special prohibitions on those speakers who express views on disfavored subjects. . . . St. Paul has no such authority to license one side of the debate to fight freestyle, while requiring the other to follow Marquis of Queensbury Rules. . . . Selectivity of this sort creates the possibility that the city is seeking to handicap the expression of particular ideas. . . . St. Paul's comments and concessions in this case elevate the possibility to a certainty. (1992 U.S. Lexis 3863, pp. 10–12)

R.A.V. casts serious doubt over the constitutional validity of many state laws on hate speech. The majority's theory concerning underinclusive classifications of fighting words is sure to meet controversy. Indeed, four of the nine Justices in *R.A.V.* dissented from Scalia's logic, pointing to the fact that underinclusive laws preserve more freedom of expression than more generic laws directed against all fighting words; these Justices concurred with the result in the specific case, however. But if Scalia and the majority's logic prevails, laws directed against hate speech will have to be crafted in generic, neutral terms that emphasize disturbance of the peace and protection against significant verbal harassment without singling out expression that vilifies on grounds of race, gender, religion, and related categories. In addition, *R. A.V.*'s doctrine could sound the death knell for group libel laws that prohibit racist rhetoric, a fortiori, for these laws single out racist group libel and are less narrowly crafted than fighting words laws. *Beauharnais* is now an endangered species.

On 23 June 1992, one day after *R.A.V.* came down in Washington, the Wisconsin Supreme Court revealed *R.A.V.*'s potential effect when that court decided *State of Wisconsin v. Todd Mitchell* (State of Wisconsin Supreme Court, No. 90-2472-CR). The Wisconsin court struck down Wisconsin's "hate crime" statute, which provided for enhanced criminal penalties for specified crimes in which the victims were selected on the grounds of animus due to race, religion, color, disability, sexual orientation, national origin, or ancestry (Wisconsin Code, section 939.645, Stats. (1989–90)). *Mitchell* dealt with an enhanced criminal penalty given to a black man who directed the brutal group beating of a white man who happened to walk by the group after they had watched the movie *Mississippi Burning*, a film about racial violence and justice in Mississippi in the 1960s. Drawing on *R.A.V.* and other sources, the Wisconsin Supreme Court ruled that the penalty enhancements were based on the thought process behind the act (as the acts were already prohibited under separate laws), thereby running afoul of the First Amendment and criminal law principle that government may not punish thoughts as distinguished from actions.

Mitchell indicates that the many other state penalty enhancement laws are in jeopardy, although states need not follow *Mitchell's* lead (they are bound only by the U.S. Supreme Court). It should be noted that *Mitchell* goes farther than *R.A.V.*, for its principle governs enhancement laws whether they apply only to specific categories of animus or not. *Mitchell's* ruling reaches a principle of thought control that transcends *R.A.V.'s* concern for viewpoint discrimination in the context of underinclusive coverage.

Despite the developments just discussed, the Supreme Court has never ruled that freedom of speech is absolute. Racist and other disturbing speech may be limited in certain contexts, though courts will carefully construe such limitations. After *R.A.V.*, of course, all such limits must be crafted in a viewpoint-neutral fashion that does not single out certain types of hate speech for restriction. Three limiting conditions are most important. (1) Fighting words, obscenity, and libel are still unprotected, though the Supreme Court has narrowed their scope. In terms of fighting words and assaultive expression, the speech must be extremely personally abusive and targeted directly at vulnerable individuals. (2) More generally, if the speech is sufficiently integrated with illegal action, it is not protected. As Franklyn Haiman has stated, there is a difference between "speech which incites to illegal conduct" and "speech that is an integral part *of* illegal conduct" (Haiman 1981:245; emphasis in original). The latter is "performative" in nature, linking it to action in a substantial way. Solicitations, conspiracy, direct incitements of imminent lawlessness (as in the Florida case), and substantial threats are of this nature and will be examined more closely in the subsequent discussion. (3) Potentially harmful or upsetting speech that merits protection in most contexts (especially in print or in public forums) may be less protected in other contexts in which it interferes with competing interests or values. For example, racist speech in the context of employment may be restricted as illegitimate "harassment" or as interference with the right to make contracts. And managers may restrict speech if it fosters the wrong public image and thereby harms the mission of a company or government agency (e.g., racist comments by a police officer, even in a public forum, jeopardize the integrity of the police force).[10] A related standard is the "captive audience" doctrine. Because freedom of speech entails the right not to be an unwilling auditor, speech may be restricted if it *substantially* interferes with the right of privacy and the right not to listen, and if the targets cannot reasonably avoid exposure to it.

Judgment in First Amendment cases is often difficult. Courts must balance the implications for free speech doctrine with the right of privacy and the right to be free of undue verbal abuse and intimidation. The Supreme Court has not fashioned definitive doctrine in many of these areas, but the standards enunciated in *Cohen* and *R.A.V.* provide a basic framework for analysis. Let us now apply these standards and examine the constitutional status of the most important laws that limit racist expression and race-motivated crime.

LAWS AGAINST RACIST EXPRESSION

In this section I will treat speech-related laws in two distinct categories: speech that involves encouragement to crime, and speech that inflicts direct harm on vulnerable targets. I will also mention enforcement successes and problems where relevant.

Encouragement to Crime:
Conspiracy, Solicitation, and Advertising

The first type of "performative" speech that often falls outside of First Amendment protection is speech that induces others to commit crime. In addition to the type of incitement treated by *Brandenburg,* typical laws prohibit criminal solicitation, conspiracy to commit crime, criminal agreements and attempts, and advertising for illegal services or products. These types of "inchoate" crimes are often lumped together. Section 2 of the U.S. Criminal Code, for example, states, "Whoever commits an offense against the United States or aids, abets, counsels, commands, induces, or procures its commission, is punishable as a principal." Illinois law designates such actions "solicitation."[11]

Conspiracy entails verbal agreement between or among two or more persons to commit a specific crime, and some concrete action taken toward that end. In general, the Supreme Court has held that agreements to engage in unlawful action are not protected by the First Amendment. The fact that such agreement "necessarily takes the form of words does not confer upon it, or upon the underlying conduct, the constitutional immunities that the First Amendment extends to speech" (*Brown v. Hartlage,* 456 U.S. 45 (1982), at 55). Some important federal laws in the area of race relations deal with conspiracy, especially in association with threats and intimidations. These laws have reduced the number of serious violations of rights, as the number of cases of severe violence are lower than in the earlier twentieth century. As is always the case, the incentive to enforce the law is at least as important as actual passage of the law. Unfortunately, authorities have encountered more difficulty in identifying the perpetrators of more clandestine illegal acts in neighborhoods, and the number of violent incidents has risen relative to more recent times.

Congress passed the Civil Rights Act of 1870, now section 241 of Title 18 of the U.S. Criminal Code, "originally to cope with the intimidation and violence practiced by hooded groups of the Ku Klux Klan" (Haiman 1981:218). Today it is the basis of federal prosecution of violations of rights that state authorities refuse to prosecute. It imposes significant fines and imprisonment

if two or more persons conspire to injure, oppress, threaten, or intimidate any citizen in the free exercise or enjoyment of any right or privilege . . . or if two or more persons go in disguise on the highway, or on the premises of another, with intent to prevent, harm, or hinder his free exercise or enjoyment of any right or privilege.

Section 241 has companion legislation, section 242 (based on the Civil Rights Act of 1866), which provides lesser penalties for the "willful" deprivation of rights "under color of any law, statute, ordinance, or custom."

Sections 241 and 242 are the criminal counterparts of several federal laws that furnish civil remedies for violations of rights made "under color of state law" or in a private capacity. The most important in terms of conspiracy is section 2 of the Civil Rights Act of 1871 (the Ku Klux Klan Act), which became section 1985 (3) of Title 42. Section 1985 (3) sanctions civil damages "if two or more persons in any state or Territory conspire or go in disguise on the highway or on the premises of another, for the purpose of depriving, either directly or indirectly, any person or class of persons of the equal protection of the laws, or of equal privileges and immunities under the laws."

Although these civil and criminal laws have been on the books since right after the Civil War, enforcement has mushroomed in recent decades in the aftermath of the civil rights movement and concomitant Supreme Court expansion of the statutes' respective scopes. Section 1985 (3) actions became much more prevalent after a key Supreme Court ruling in a 1971 case concerning the beatings and intimidations of blacks mistaken for civil rights activists. The Court ruled that the law applied to private conspiracies to deprive individuals of their rights as well as conspiracies "under color of the laws," thereby significantly increasing the statute's reach.[12]

Likewise, the Court gave greater breadth to criminal actions brought under section 241 in a famous 1966 case involving the murder of three civil rights activists in Mississippi (the politics of this case was the centerpiece of the movie *Mississippi Burning*). Again, federal action was necessary to bring the culprits to justice. Local police arranged the scenario that led to the murders, though they had not committed the actual killing themselves. The federal indictment stated that the defendants "conspired together . . . to injure, oppress, threaten, and intimidate" the three victims "in the free exercise and enjoyment of the rights and privileges secured to them by the Fourteenth Amendment." The lower federal court had dismissed the indictment because it maintained that the law did not cover the types of rights (Fourteenth Amendment) at issue in the case. The Supreme Court disagreed, thereby expanding the statute's coverage (*U.S. v. Price,* 383 U.S. 787 (1966)). Combined with the national government's rekindled incentive to apply the law, this ruling has had a substantial impact. Federal prosecution of the Los Angeles police officers in the now infamous Rodney King beating case is based on Section 242.

Although the Supreme Court has ruled that the First Amendment does not protect conspiracy, one part of section 241 does pose another First Amendment issue that has recently arisen: the provision making it unlawful to "go in disguise on the highway or on the premises of another with intent to prevent or hinder" the free exercise of civil rights. This provision has furnished the basis for at least twenty-one state and fifty local laws against wearing hoods or masks (Klan symbols) in any public demonstration. The Klan claims that the statute and its local derivatives violate its right of free association. In May 1990 a Georgia state court judge ruled that a Georgia law outlawing the wearing of masks violated the Klan's free speech rights. According to the *New York Times,* the judge "ruled that widespread hostility to the Klan meant that members might need the anonymity provided by a mask to exercise their First Amendment rights without fear of reprisal. He also said the law impeded the Klan's ability to attract new members." A Georgia appeals court reversed this decision ("Georgia Judge Rules Klan Is Persecuted," *New York Times,* 26 May 1990:6). Because the statute is written in a neutral fashion (it does not apply to certain types of masks), it does not appear to run afoul of *R.A.V.*

Another type of encouragement to crime includes specific inducements such as solicitation and advertising. The First Amendment declines protection of solicitation and related inducements because "they *do* something rather than *say* something" (Greenawalt 1989:245). Offers of rewards and similar inducements are prime examples of such speech acts.

A major federal law that addresses illegal inducement in the context of race relations is the Fair Housing Act of 1968 (Title 42 U.S. Code, Section 3604 (e)), which makes it illegal "for profit to induce or attempt to induce any person to sell or rent any dwelling by representations regarding the entry or prospective entry into a neighborhood of a person or persons of a particular race, color, religion, or national origin." Realtors have challenged this law as an impermissible infringement on their free speech, but the courts have consistently disagreed. The speech's link to illegal action and its "commercial" nature render it less entitled to First Amendment status (Haiman 1981:252).[13] This law has certainly opened up the housing market in comparison to previous practices. Yet informed commentators allege that the law has not been a total success. Realtors often "steer" minorities to particular neighborhoods without manifestly violating the letter of the law (Bell 1973:640–643 and, generally, Chs. 11, 12).

Individuals who offer monetary inducements or "bounties" to kill or harm are likewise denied First Amendment protection; such speech obviously possesses negligible First Amendment value. Two cases in which courts issued restraining orders stand out. In 1977 a court stopped a Nazi Party's taped telephone message that promised two hundred dollars "to the first white man or woman who will exercise his right to protect his life and property and blow one of these black criminals away."[14] In addition, in a criminal case related to the Skokie affair, a national director of the Jewish Defense League was prosecuted in 1979 for soliciting murder in a press conference. Irving Rubin told the press:

We are offering five hundred dollars, that I have in my hand, to any member of the community, be he Gentile or Jewish, who kills, maims, or seriously injures a member of the American Nazi Party. . . . The fact of the matter is that we're deadly serious. This is not said in jest, we are deadly serious.

The appellate court concluded that the speech was an invitation to political assassination and a criminal solicitation based on the imminence of the possible result.[15] Because such expression is clearly performative in nature, the First Amendment provides ample grounds for government action. Consequently, few instances of such expression have occurred in recent years.

In a related vein, the First Amendment does not protect advertising for illegal goods or activity. The Supreme Court has consistently allowed governments to ban such expression because of the lower constitutional status of commercial speech and because it is an integral part of illegal conduct. Thus, the Supreme Court has upheld the Fair Housing Act and has ruled that governments may prohibit the use of gender-specific advertising columns because this is part and parcel of illegal gender discrimination.[16]

Finally, group libel laws may be considered encouragements to commit crime. As mentioned, group libel laws are constitutionally suspect today, especially after *R.A.V.* Indeed, Illinois rescinded the group libel statute upheld in *Beauharnais* in 1962. Consequently, following the Skokie cases' lead, lower federal courts have consistently struck down group libel–related civil or criminal actions in recent years. One court has held that a group libel action may succeed only if specific intentional harm to an individual can be demonstrated.[17] This makes group libel operative in only fighting words contexts.

Specific Directed Harms

In this section I will discuss the most important laws dealing with the direct infliction of emotional harm, mainly through threats, harassment, or intimidation. Unlike speech that encourages crime or advocates illegal action, this type of speech *is harmful in itself*. Authorities may not restrict speech just because others happen to find it offensive—especially if such individuals are not "captive" auditors. But some offensive speech is threatening and intimidating enough to justify suppression. The fighting words exception to free speech constitutes the major constitutional support for laws prohibiting threatening or intimidating speech, especially in captive or related special settings.

Though limited after *Cohen,* the fighting words doctrine is not a dead letter. According to Kent Greenawalt, the courts will uphold legislation directed against fighting words and racial slurs if certain criteria are satisfied. "The common direction concerning fighting words and racial and ethnic slurs has been to demand very narrowly drawn statutory language focusing on imminent violence. This direction fits comfortably both with the general distaste for content-based restrictions and with the modern treatment of the hostile audience [heckler's veto] problem." The state concern for protecting individuals from *substantial* intimidation (whether or not a violent retaliation is likely) may also provide a rationale for punishing fighting words. (Greenawalt 1989:295; Downs 1985:122–153). Of course, after *R.A.V.* such laws must be drafted in content-neutral fashion. An important yet underappreciated case in Texas reveals that the fighting words doctrine may accommodate the latter concern as well, at least in certain contexts.

In the early 1980s the Knights of the Ku Klux Klan began intimidating Vietnamese fishermen in the Galveston Bay area of Texas. On one occasion, the Klan and its associates took a boatride near Vietnamese fishermen in the bay. They wore full military regalia and hoods on their faces, brandished weapons, hung an effigy of a Vietnamese fisherman, and circled within eyesight of the fishermen. The Vietnamese sued for injunctive relief on grounds of intimidation and distress, contractual interferences, and the violation of property and personal rights. The federal district court sided with the Vietnamese, ruling that the Klan's symbolic expression was a mere pretext for intimidation. The Court noted the intent and purpose of the demonstration and the probable and natural impact on the targets. The "provocative statements" amounted to "conduct" and "fighting words."[18]

It is important, however, to note how the facts of *Vietnamese Fishermen's* differ from *Beauharnais*. The Klan in Galveston Bay directed its symbolic wrath at a discrete, vulnerable target who could not avoid the intimidating message, whereas Beauharnais simply distributed his leaflets on a busy streetcorner. The *Vietnamese Fishermen's* case establishes two standards that will prove useful in the ensuing analysis: (1) Racist speech merits less protection in "captive" or "targeted" contexts involving vulnerable targets of hate; (2) If expression is a "pretext" for substantial intimidation or harassment, it is less worthy of constitutional protection.

Hence, the fighting words exception applies only in fairly extreme cases of harassment or intimidation, so applying the fighting words exception to other anti-racial harassment and intimidation laws and rules is more problematic. If such expression accompanies concrete actions like desecration and vandalism, it is clearly punishable. Many states already have laws against such obviously unprotected conduct. As of 1988, thirty-three states had laws against institutional vandalism of some sort; most of these provide additional punishment if the vandalism was committed by reason of one or more of the following: the victims' race, color, religion, sexual orientation, or national origin (Anti-Defamation League 1988:1). *R.A.V.* and *Mitchell* cast doubt upon these laws, though their status at the moment is unclear. Statutes that punish speech alone raise more constitutional questions. Until the U.S. Supreme Court makes a ruling in this regard that is more definitive than *R.A.V.*, state courts and lower federal courts are likely to generate inconsistent rulings.

Several important state and federal laws deal with various aspects of threatening or harassing speech. More traditional laws include federal laws against "extortions and threats," including threatening the president. To qualify, such threats must be "unequivocal, unconditional, and specific as to the person threatened."[19]

State courts have tended to restrict laws concerning threats, intimidations, and harassment in similar fashion. As of 1989, thirty-one states had laws against intimidation and harassment in some form, many of which were passed in the preceding fifteen years (Anti-Defamation League 1988:1). Oregon's 1981 harassment statute, for example, prohibited the commission of any of four underlying crimes—third degree criminal mischief, harassment, fourth degree assault, and menacing—"by reason of the race, color, religion or national origin of another person." In upholding the law, an Oregon court narrowly construed the statute to make it consistent with the Oregon constitution. The harassment must be "likely to be followed by unlawful acts" (705 P. 2d 740 (1985), at 749). This statute is very vulnerable in the wake of *R.A.V.*, as it singles out harassment based on race, religion, and national origin. Indeed, in a previous case, *State v. Robertson*, the Oregon Supreme Court ruled Oregon's criminal coercion law unconstitutional because it covered threats that were entitled to First Amendment protection. In addition to stressing that the law failed to distinguish coercive or extortionate speech made in public as opposed to private contexts, the court mentioned eight other factors that bear on such laws' constitutionality. Kent Greenawalt summarizes:

The Oregon court at one point suggested a variety of possible relevant elements for determinations about constitutional protection: (1) the lawfulness of the demanded conduct, (2) the nature of the threatened conduct, (3) the aim and the motive of the person making the threat, (4) the relationship of the parties to the demand or the threatened consequences, (5) the relationship between the demand and the threatened consequences, (6) the means of expression employed in the demand or threat, (7) the likelihood and imminence of the threatened acts, and (8) other distinctions in the social setting or function of the demand. (Greenawalt 1989:221)

Greenawalt concludes that *Robertson* (written by a nationally respected First Amendment scholar) "casts doubt on the validity of provisions in many other states" (Greenawalt 1989:221).[20]

In 1984 the Oregon appeals court used *Robertson* to strike down Oregon's intimidation statute (ORS 166.065(1)(b)), which enhanced the penalty for harassment when crimes are motivated by the race, color, religion, or national origin of the victim. The complainant in *State v. Harrington* charged that "The defendant [by] reason of race and color and with intent to harass, annoy and alarm John Thomas Ritchey, [did] unlawfully publicly insult John Thomas Ritchey by abusive words in a manner likely to provoke a violent and disorderly response, by repeatedly calling John Thomas Ritchey a 'fucking nigger.' " The court said that such expression did not fit the fighting words exception to free speech in light of *Cohen* and post-*Cohen* U.S. Supreme Court cases (680 P. 2d 666 (1984)). *R.A.V.* provides a coup de grace to this logic. The Oregon cases reveal the constitutional hurdles that laws against racist intimidation, threat, and harassment face. Such hurdles are not insurmountable, however, as long as legislatures are willing to be careful and precise, following the guidelines suggested in *Robertson, Cohen,* and *R.A.V.*

The courts are more tolerant of laws against racist expression that intrudes into private domains or other special contexts in which the free speech right is subordinated to other interests. Courts have upheld state and federal laws against intimidation or harassment in the workplace, courtroom, voting process, housing market, and related areas. Government enforcement and private litigation have fortified rights in these domains in recent decades. Section 594 of Title 18 makes intimidation and threats in the context of voting illegal, punishing "Whoever intimidates, threatens, coerces, or attempts to intimidate, threaten, or coerce, any person for the purpose of interfering with the right of such person to vote or not to vote as he may choose, or of causing such other person to vote for or not to vote for, any candidate for the office of President, Vice-President, presidential elector." In the 1950s, southern authorities systematically denied blacks the right to vote by law or by intimidation at the polls.

Today blacks have made dramatic electoral gains, as federal authorities have enforced voting law strongly. Note that this law is neutral in terms of the grounds for intimidation, thereby conforming to *R.A.V.*'s mandate.

"Harassment" (a verbal act akin to threats) is also punishable in certain contexts. I will discuss the most important. First, federal and state laws prohibit harassment over the telephone, including threats. Kent Greenawalt (1989:291) remarks, "Since a telephone call intrudes on a private domain of the listener, the government may well have authority to prohibit communications that would be protected in a face-to-face encounter; if so, disturbing telephone threats may be punishable even if the ordinarily stringent constitutional standard is not met."[21]

Racial slurs in the highly regulated context of labor bargaining and elections are also subject to civil sanctions on harassment or related grounds. For example, in *National Labor Relations Board v. Katz,* the Seventh Circuit Court of Appeals ruled that a company's allegation that racial and religious slurs were made by a priest at a union organization meeting in conjunction with other threats of violence and loss of jobs established a prima facie case for overturning a union election.[22] In a similar vein, both section 1981 of Title 42 and Title 7 of the 1964 Civil Rights Act provide civil relief for racial, ethnic, and sexual harassment (including racist expression) in employment and contractual contexts.[23] Racist or unnecessarily race-related comments made by a prosecutor in a criminal trial constitute automatic grounds for a mistrial in most jurisdictions.[24] Because these rulings are based on more general norms of fair procedure, they do not violate *R.A.V.*'s neutrality principle.

These cases reveal that racist rhetoric, while protected in public-oriented contexts (public forums, newspapers, books, etc.), may be subjected to various restraints (criminal or civil) in other contexts where privacy, procedural integrity, or security need protection. The authority to restrict threatening or harassing racist speech is less extensive, however, in general face-to-face encounters.

Falling between open public forums and speech in protected contexts, threatening or intimidating speech in general (non-context specific) face-to-face encounters constitutes an intermediate realm in terms of First Amendment protection. An interesting area in this regard is the university or college campus. On the one hand, the university is the crucible of free thought.[25] On the other hand, the university possesses many special contexts in which civility and decency are required (e.g., the classroom, the dormitory, the library, etc.). Racial incidents have erupted on many campuses in recent years. In reaction, many have passed or considered measures restricting racist expression. Three of the most prominent measures were passed or considered by the University of Wisconsin, Stanford University, and the University of Michigan. Stanford has debated passing a new rule that would prohibit words that intentionally harm or harass when "directly addressed" to specific individuals and the use of "words, pictures, or symbols that are commonly understood to convey, in a direct and visceral way, hatred or contempt for human beings of the sex, race, color, handicap, religion, sexual orientation or national and ethnic origin in question" ("Free Speech and Insults on Campus," *New York Times,* 25 April 1989:1, 11).

In April 1988 the University of Michigan adopted a Policy on Discrimination and Discriminatory Harassment in response to what the Board of Regents considered a "rising tide of racial intolerance and indifference on campus." Among other things, the policy disciplined "Any behavior, verbal or physical that stigmatizes or victimizes an individual on the basis of race, ethnicity, religion, sex, sexual orientation, creed, national origin, ancestry, age, marital status, handicap or Vietnam-era status" and that implies a threat to the individual's performance or academic environment. A federal district court declared the policy unconstitutional in 1989 because it covered expression that the First Amendment protects.[26]

After undergoing several revisions, the University of Wisconsin's rule is presently narrower than the University of Michigan's. In *UWM Post, Inc. v. Board of Regents,* however, a federal court ruled that the first version did not conform to the fighting words exception (774 F. Supp. 1163 (E.D. Wis. 1991)). After intense debate, the university responded by reissuing the rule in tighter form limited to fighting words. However, the rule explicitly punishes only fighting words based on race, gender, sexual preference, religion, and disability, so it directly conflicts with the principles articulated in *R.A.V.*, which became law right after the university adopted the new policy. If Justice Scalia holds his majority, this new rule will also fall. For unfathomable reasons, University of Wisconsin officials have refused to reconsider the new rule as of this writing.

Campus racist speech restrictions must meet the same standards that the Oregon courts have applied to Oregon's harassment and intimidation statutes, as well as the conditions of *Cohen* and *R.A.V.* Rules that apply to special contexts like dormitory rooms and classrooms will fare better than broader ones; and rules that are viewpoint-neutral and limited to serious threats or intimidation in face-to-face encounters will prove to be more acceptable than less constrained rules.

CONCLUSION

Compared to other countries, the United States has chosen to grant exceptional protection to racist rhetoric. The Supreme Court has made a fundamental value choice under the aegis of the First Amendment: Outside of specific contexts in which nonspeech values predominate, freedom of expression will prevail over the interest in protecting society from the offense racist speech inflicts and the fears associated with its potential to encourage violence and discrimination. Speech in public forums and print media receives the most constitutional protection. As a result, the First Amendment allows hate groups to organize and proselytize their views.

However, the First Amendment permits restriction of racist speech in three major contexts: (1) when such speech is an integral part of illegal action, as in conspiracy, solicitation, or direct incitement to imminent illegal action; (2) when such speech occurs in nonpublic domains and jeopardizes privacy or other interests, such as voting, employment relations, or trials; (3) when racist speech is targeted at discrete individuals outside of the contexts just mentioned and is sufficiently threatening, harassing, or intimidating. In each of these situations, racist speech either constitutes the perpetration of a substantial direct harm or is part and parcel of illegal action ("performative"). As long as governments conscientiously tailor laws to these conditions, and do so in a viewpoint-neutral fashion (*R.A.V.*), the laws will pass constitutional muster.

In deciding whether present First Amendment doctrine is wise legal policy, several points must be borne in mind. First, the policy protects anti–hate group speech as well as hate group speech. The overwhelming majority of public discourse in the United States favors racial and ethnic equality (though there is often heated contention over the nature or content of equality). As the Supreme Court has held, good counterspeech is one remedy for bad speech. Second, police possess ample alternative means to control hate groups. The Constitution permits appropriate surveillance and infiltration of such groups, and national and local police agencies have taken advantage of these methods of control. Third, we have seen that the United States enforces many laws that prohibit racial discrimination and expression closely linked to discriminatory action, such as racist comment in employment or bargaining contexts. The extraordinary protection given racist rhetoric in the public forum does not extend to other racist speech acts.[27] Laws against such discrimination have made a substantial difference in the workplace and elsewhere.

Finally, it is not evident that laws restricting racist rhetoric in the public forum would achieve their ends. Drawbacks[28] of group libel laws include the following three points. (1) A lack of consistent enforcement may lead to charges of discrimination when they are applied. (2) Targets of the laws may appear to be victims, as in the Klan mask case in Georgia. Given the prevalence of the content neutrality doctrine in recent First Amendment law, carving a new exception to free speech for racist expression could be interpreted as favoring some groups over others, thereby exacerbating racial tensions rather than assuaging them. Restrictions of racist speech on campus have spawned precisely these claims. The potentially monumental *R.A.V.* case addresses these concerns. (3) Application of the rule may be made against the very minorities the law was designed to protect. The Race Relations Act in England has been enforced against blacks quite often, and the claimant in the University of Michigan case discussed previously was a black student. In addition, it is possible that granting these groups free speech rights constitutes a measure of cooptation. Would they commit more serious clandestine acts if they lost their speech rights?

Thus, as long as government vigilantly enforces anti-discrimination and speech-related laws in proper contexts and keeps a watchful eye on hate group activity, the present constitutional protection of racist rhetoric appears to be justified in light of the special legal and social environment of the United States.

NOTES

1. See Haiman (1981:90). Illinois once had one, as we will see, but it was rescinded in 1961.
2. See, for example, Tribe (1988: Ch. 12, secs. 1, 2).
3. See, for example, *NAACP v. Alabama,* 357 U.S. 449 (1958).
4. See, for example, Sohn and Burgenthal (1973).
5. Nexis, States News Service, 3 June 1992, eighteenth story, pp. 2–4.
6. These are the words of Justice Holmes and Aryeh Neier. On the relation between minority rights and the content neutrality doctrine, see Kalven (1965). See also Neier (1979).
7. See, for example, *Edwards v. South Carolina,* 372 U.S. 229 (1963).
8. See, for example, *Gooding v. Wilson,* 405 U.S. 518 (1972).
9. See, for example, *Collin v. Smith,* 578 F. 2d 1197 (7th Cir. 1978), cert. denied, 439 U.S. 916 (1978). For a treatment of the Skokie case, see Downs (1985).
10. See the discussion in *Rankin v. McPherson,* 483 U.S. 378 (1987). Though the Supreme Court said in this case that an employee of a sheriff's office could not be fired for rhetorically telling a friend over the phone that she wished President Reagan had been killed by John Hinkley in 1981, the Court developed a test that is less protective of free speech in such contexts.
11. 18 U.S.C., sec. 2; Ill. Revised Stats., Ch. 38, sec. 211-i. See Haiman (1981:245).

12. *Griffin v. Breckenridge*, 403 U.S. 88 (1971). On the sharp increase in federal litigation in these areas after an important Supreme Court case in 1961, see Low and Jeffries, Jr. (1988), esp. Chapters 1 and 2. The key 1961 case is *Monroe v. Pape*, 365 U.S. 167 (1961), which expanded the reach of section 1983 of Title 42, U.S. Code. Section 1983 grants civil relief for violation of rights made "under color of" state law or custom. Section 1983 actions have skyrocketed since 1961 and have been an integral part of the civil rights movement and struggle.

13. See, for example, *U.S. v. Bob Lawrence Realty*, 474 F. 2d 115 (5th Cir. 1973), cert. denied 414 U.S. 826 (1973).

14. See Haiman (1981:264). A similar case arose in Houston in 1979.

15. See *People v. Rubin*, 96 Cal. App. 3d 968, 158 Cal. Rptr. 488 (1979), cert. denied 449 U.S. 821 (1980). See also Greenawalt (1989:250).

16. See *Hoffman Estates v. Flipside, Hoffman Estates, Inc.*, 455 U.S. 489 (1982); *Pittsburgh Press Co. v. Pittsburgh Commission on Human Relations*, 413 U.S. 376 (1973).

17. *Michigan United Clubs v. CBS News, Inc.*, 485 F. Supp. 893 (W.D. Mich. 1980). See also, for example, *Sambo's Restaurant, Inc. v. City of Ann Arbor*, 663 F. 2d 686 (6th Cir. 1981).

18. *Vietnamese Fishermen's Ass'n v. Knights of the Ku Klux Klan*, 543 F. Supp. 198 (S.D. Tex. 1982), esp. at 207–208. See also 518 F. Supp. 943 (S.D. Tex. 1981). The court did not indicate that the absence of weapons would have made any difference in its ruling.

19. 18 U.S.C. Sec. 871 *U.S. v. Kelner*, 534 F. 2d 1020 (2d Cir. 1976), at 1027, cert. denied 429 U.S. 1022 (1976). See Greenawalt (1989:291).

20. *State v. Robertson*, 6 2P. 2d 56 (1982). The justice was Hans Linde. See Greenawalt (1989:221). See also 649 P. 2d, at 581.

21. See, for example, *Gormley v. Director Connecticut State Department of Probation*, 632 F. 2d 938 (2d Cir. 1989), cert. denied 449 U.S. 1023 (1980).

22. 701 F. 2d 703 (7th Cir. 1983). See also *National Labor Relations Board v. Silmermann's Men's Wear, Inc.*, 656 F. 2d 53 (3rd Cir. 1981).

23. See, for example, *Patterson v. McClean Credit Union*, 109 S. Ct. 2363 (1989).

24. See, for example, *State v. Wilson*, 404 So. 2d 68 (1981); *State v. Noel*, 693 S.W. 2d 312 (1985); *Commonwealth v. Alican*, 381 N.E. 2d 144 (1978).

25. See *Davis v. White*, 533 P. 2d 222 (1972).

26. See *Doe v. University of Michigan*, 721 F. Supp. 852 (E.D. Mich. 1989).

27. See Bollinger (1986) on how free speech doctrine protects a special realm of freedom that is distinguishable from other realms in society.

28. I discuss these and other drawbacks in Downs (1985:145–150). Interview with Robert Sedler, the counsel in *Doe v. Michigan*, March 1990.

6

The Prevention of Racial Incitement in Israel

Gerald Cromer

Ever since its establishment in 1948, the State of Israel has had laws that can be used in the fight against racial incitement. However, they were never invoked. Before Meir Kahane's election to the Knesset (Israel's parliament) in 1984, the problem was not regarded as serious enough to warrant attention; after his electoral success, it was widely considered to be too urgent to be dealt with by means of the existing laws. Only a few of his opponents suggested using them. Emphasis was placed instead on the need to introduce new ones. Only in this way, it was argued, would the urgency of the situation be made clear to all.

It is the reforms that were, in fact, introduced in the wake of Kahane's entry into the Knesset that constitute the subject matter of the discussion that follows. I will describe the various measures taken and the debate they engendered. However, before analyzing the legal response, it is necessary to look, albeit briefly, at the ideas that prompted it in the first place—at Kahane's policies toward the Arab minority in Israel.

CLERICAL FASCISM

Ever since he established the Jewish Defense League (JDL) in 1968, Meir Kahane was engaged in a continuous "clash with the gentile" (Ravitsky 1986:96). In the United States he fought against different forms of anti-Semitism, especially amongst New York blacks and in the Soviet Union. On arriving in Israel in 1971, Kahane turned his attention to the Christian missionaries and the Black Hebrews in Dimona. However, they soon conceded pride of place to the local Arab population. In August 1972, less than a year after arriving in the country, Kahane arranged a show trial of Muhamad Ali Jaabari, the mayor of Hebron, for his part in the 1929 massacre. From then on, he was always at pains to point out the ways in which the Arabs constitute a threat to the Jewish state. It is, of course, beyond the confines of this chapter to present a detailed analysis of all his allegations in this regard. Attention will be focused instead on just two of them—the twin threats posed by assimilation and demography. It is Kahane's policies vis-à-vis these issues in particular that prompted the various preventive measures that I will describe.

In his early writings, Kahane (1981:55) portrayed the State of Israel as the only viable solution to the problem of intermarriage. Only there, he argued, can Jews "preserve and create their own specific tradition and way of life, free of the spiritual and social assimilation of a foreign and abrasive culture." However, Kahane later took a much less sanguine view of the situation. Israel, he felt, was as devoid of Jewish content as the diaspora. It is like any other western liberal state—or, what he regards in less flattering terms, a "Hebrew-speaking Portugal." It is not surprising, therefore, that assimilation and intermarriage are rampant.

The plague has not spared the Jewish state. . . . A generation has grown up that knows nothing about the holiness and unity of the People of Israel, and is prepared to destroy the barriers between the holy, pure Jewish People and the other nations of the world. Assimilation and intermarriage are spreading throughout the country and there is almost no opposition to it. (Kotler 1986:202)

Less than three months after his election to the Knesset, Kahane tabled a private bill "for the prevention of assimilation between Jews and non-Jews and the holiness of the People of Israel." According to the bill, separate educational institutions and public beaches would be created, non-Jews would be prevented from residing in a Jewish neighborhood except with the consent of the majority of the Jewish dwellers, and it would be forbidden for Jewish citizens and residents of the state to marry or have sexual relations with non-Jews. These and other clauses were backed up by references to traditional Jewish sources. As Kahane pointed out in his notes to the bill:

The Jewish tradition is clear. . . . "And you shall be holy unto Me, for I the Lord am holy and have set you apart from the peoples that you should be Mine . . . not integration but separation into a holy nation . . . separated from the other nations of the world and their abominations." It is for this reason that the Torah commands "Neither shall you make marriages with them, your daughter you shall not give to his son, nor his daughter shall you take for your son." (Kotler 1986:202–203)

But it is not only marriage to non-Jews that constitutes a threat to the continued existence of the Jewish state. According to Kahane, their mere presence in the country does so. Israel, he argued, is endangered above all by the exceptionally high birth rate amongst the Arabs on both sides of the Green Line. This, together with a number of demographic trends amongst Israeli Jews (e.g., a much lower birth rate, a large number of abortions, the continuing decline in immigration, and a steady increase in emigration), constitutes a threat to even the most minimal conception of Zionism—a state with a Jewish majority. If these trends are not reversed, the Arabs will be able to "peacefully, quietly and non-violently become the majority in Israel, and then democratically vote the Jewish state out of existence" (Kahane 1981:129).

Kahane put forward many ideas as to how to deal with this threat. All of them, however, were designed to achieve two goals—a reduction in the number of Arabs living in Israel and the "political neutralization" of those who would remain. Kahane first called for the establishment of an Emigration Fund for Peace that would be used to provide Arabs with financial inducements to leave the country, and an exemption from national taxes for all residents of the occupied territories who opt for noncitizenship (Kahane 1974:46–50). However, both proposals subsequently became much more radical in nature. Thus, Kahane's private member's bill concerning "Israeli citizenship and a population transfer between Jews and Arabs" advocated the restriction of citizenship to members of the Jewish people. Non-Jews who wish to live in Israel would only be able to do so as "resident strangers" without the right to vote in elections to the Knesset or any other state and public body. According to the bill, those who were not prepared to accept this status would have the option of leaving the country willingly and receiving compensation for their property, or being forcibly removed.[1]

According to Kahane, this bill, like the one concerning assimilation, was "the embodiment of Jewish law." In addition, however, its implementation was considered as a necessary prerequisite for the final redemption. The Messiah, Kahane argued, will only come when the degradation of the Jews and, therefore, the desecration of God's name are brought to an end. Consequently, Arab attacks on the Jews must be eliminated, because "each stone is aimed at the Almighty." Sexual relationships with non-Jews must be outlawed because they "defile the seed of the Holy People, and strike at the God of Israel through the daughters of his people" (Kahane 1983:77–78). Even more important, the Arabs must be evicted from the land of Israel because their very presence represents a desecration of God's name. "Their rejection of sovereignty over the Land of Israel," Kahane argued, "constitutes a rejection of the sovereignty, and kingship of Lord God of Israel." Consequently,

their transfer from the land of Israel becomes more than a political issue. It is a religious issue, a religious obligation, a commandment to erase Hillul Hashem (desecration of God's name)—The great redemption can come immediately . . . if we do that which God demands. One of the great yardsticks of real Jewish faith . . . is our willingness to reject fear of man in favour of awe of God, and remove the Arabs from Israel and bring the redemption. They must go. (Kahane 1981:275–276)

Clearly, therefore, Kahane did not justify his policy of transfer and, for that matter, his general attitude toward the Arab ministry in Israel on pragmatic grounds; he also legitimated it in religious terms. He, and he alone, represented the "authentic Jewish idea."

DEFENSIVE DEMOCRACY

Meir Kahane's election to the Knesset sent shock waves through the Israeli body politic. The fact that he had managed to enter the Israeli Parliament after three unsuccessful attempts at doing so was not only regarded as being of great import in its own right; it was also seen as an omen of what was to come.[2] "When the time comes," the left-wing weekly *Koteret Rashit* warned, "we may well tell our grandchildren that it all began in 1984" (*Koteret Rashit,* 25 July 1984).

The furor that followed in the wake of Kahane's electoral success was mainly due to the feeling that he was the antithesis of "all the values both Western and Jewish that are dear to us." Thus, President Herzog explained his refusal to summon a representative of the Kach Party to consultations on the formation of a government in terms of Kahane's "abrogation of civil rights and his negation of the principles of the Torah of Israel."[3] And Yitzhak Zamir, then attorney general, attacked Kahanism on the grounds that it "contradicts the principle of international law and the standards of civilized nations" and "distorts Judaism by presenting a biased picture of the tradition and heritage of the Jewish people." As such, he argued, it also undermines the Declaration of Independence according to which the State of Israel grants complete social and political equality irrespective of race, nationality, or religion.[4]

It must be pointed out, however, that the opposition to Meir Kahane was also based on pragmatic grounds. His policies vis-à-vis the Arab minority in Israel were regarded as just a portent of what was to come. According to this way of thinking, hatred of the Arabs by no means guarantees love of Jews, and even if given the chance, Kahane would have gradually curtailed the rights of everybody who was not to his liking. To quote a widely distributed flier of the religious peace movements, Netivot Shalom (Paths to Peace) and Oz V'Shalom (Strength and Peace),

We would like the state to have a Jewish character, but not by compulsion. Kahane, on the other hand, would force you to observe the commandments. Under his government, you will be compelled to be religious, and let it be clear, that means religious according to his world-view. . . . Kahane will first attack the Arabs, then the Communists, then the leftists, and then the secularists. He will attack anyone who is not in complete agreement with his point of view. He wants to attack all of us. Perhaps you as well.

But Kahane's attitudes toward Arabs were not only regarded as a threat to the democratic nature of the State of Israel; they were often considered to be a danger to its very survival. According to this way of thinking, Kahane will transform the Arab-Israeli conflict into a religious war, and thereby both intensify the hatred and widen the front against Israel. A columnist of the independent daily *Ha'aretz* (15 August 1984) predicted that Kahane

is likely to become the Herzl, Balfour and Wingate of the Israeli Arabs . . . and to cause the establishment of a pan-Arab nationalist political movement, because extremism on one side generates extremism on the other; fanaticism on one side generates fanaticism on the other; and violence on one side generates violence on the other. . . . At first the Arabs will organize for purposes of self-defence, and at a later stage for counteroffensive actions. Kahane will be the person who transforms Arabs from a class into a nation.

It was these moral qualms and practical fears that convinced many politicians of the need to fight Kahane until the end and with every measure at their disposal. And a wide variety of measures were, in fact, taken, in order to put an end to "the growing menace of Kahanism." They ranged from legal reforms to educational programming; from media boycotts to street theater. Some were designed to prevent the dissemination of Kahane's message, others to propagate an alternative one. My analysis is concerned only with the former.

Administrative Measures

Immediately after Kahane's electoral success, politicians of all persuasions voiced their concern that it would provide him with a platform to expound his views within the Knesset and parliamentary immunity for his activities beyond its confines. Two events—Kahane's submission of the private bills described in the previous section and a series of provocative visits to Arab villages and towns—confirmed their worst fears. The Knesset therefore decided to take action on both fronts.

According to parliamentary procedure, a private member's bill can be given a preliminary reading only if it is approved by the speaker. However, he rejected Kahane's bills—the law for the prevention of assimilation and the law about Israeli citizenship and population transfer—on the grounds that they were racist. Kahane challenged the legality of this ruling in the Supreme Court, and his appeal was upheld. All three judges were of the opinion that the speaker had, in fact, overstepped his authority. He can only reject a bill on procedural grounds and "not because of a reservation, however powerful it may be, about its socio-political content."[5] In response to this decision the Knesset amended its standing orders. Henceforth, the speaker was vested with the power to deny a preliminary reading to any private member bill that is "essentially racist in character or negates the existence of the State of Israel as the State of the Jewish People."[6]

Immediately after entering the Knesset, Kahane made a series of visits to Arab villages and towns as part of his campaign to persuade the local inhabitants to voluntarily leave the country. This kind of provocation prompted the Knesset to revoke his parliamentary privilege to greater freedom of movement than ordinary citizens.[7] Henceforth, he could also be prevented from entering a public place, if his doing so was likely to lead to a breach of the peace. Nevertheless, Kahane's efforts to persuade the Arabs to seek their fortunes elsewhere continued unabated. In fact, he took advantage of his parliamentary right to send mail free of charge in order to campaign by post. It is not surprising, therefore, that this privilege was also abrogated.[8]

Although Kahane's electoral success posed particular problems for the Knesset, it was by no means the first public body to introduce preventive measures against him. At the very beginning of the school year, in September 1984, the Ministry of Education published a special circular calling for "a comprehensive and continuing educational effort to strengthen democracy." Schools were encouraged to present the different opinions that exist in Israeli society. However, activities likely to cause incitement, violence, or discrimination against "certain sections of the population" were for the first time explicitly forbidden.[9] The terminology may have been somewhat obscure; the message, though, was clear to all.

The Israeli Broadcasting Authority took equally swift action. The Board of Management was determined not to become "a tool in the hands of extremist elements." Within a week of the elections, therefore, it was decided to restrict coverage of Kahane and his supporters. Only "items of outstanding news value" or "front-page stories" were to be broadcast. Meir Kahane challenged the legality of this resolution on the grounds that it constituted an obstruction to the democratic process and was inconsistent with the Authority's statutory obligation to "ensure that room be given for appropriate expression of different opinions and views." In its reply the Board of Management argued that this particular duty was limited by another one—the furtherance of the aims of national education, which include "the striving for a society built on freedom, equality, tolerance, mutual help and love of one's fellow human being." In this case, however, Kahane's appeal was upheld. The resolution of the Authority was to be considered null and void.[10]

Parliamentary Legislation

In 1984 the Central Elections Committee decided to disqualify Meir Kahane's party, Kach, because "the implementation of the party's principles would constitute a threat to the maintenance of the democratic regime in Israel and is liable to lead to a breach of the public order."[11] However, its ruling was revised in the Supreme Court. All five judges were of the opinion that the Committee had overstepped its authority. According to the existing law it could only bar a party on procedural grounds and not on the basis of its political platform.

Kahane's electoral success and subsequent rise in popularity prompted the Knesset to extend the power of the Central Elections Committee. In

July 1985 it passed an amendment to the Basic Law: The Knesset, according to which

A list of candidates shall not participate in Knesset elections if any of the following is expressed or implied in its aims or actions:

(1) Denial of the existence of the State of Israel as the State of the Jewish People

(2) Denial of the democratic character of the State

(3) Incitement to racism.[12]

This enabled the committee to disqualify Kach in the 1988 elections. Once again Kahane turned to the Supreme Court. This time, however, it was to no avail. The Court had no hesitation in deciding that his disqualification was in accordance with the new law.[13] Kahane's parliamentary career came to an abrupt end.

Even before the amendment to the Basic Law it was an offense to promote feelings of ill-will and enmity between different sections of the population and publish material that may bring a person into disrepute because of his origin or religion.[14] However, not only was this legislation never used before Kahane's electoral success; few politicians suggested that it be implemented after his entry into the Knesset. They placed emphasis on the need to enact a new law dealing specifically with the problem of racial incitement. Only in this way, it was argued, would the severity of the offense be made clear to all.

After a lengthy and often acrimonious debate, the Knesset amended the Penal Law. The new enactment included the following provisions:

144B. (a) A person who publishes anything with the purpose of stirring up racism is liable to imprisonment for five years.

(b) For the purpose of this section, it shall be immaterial whether or not the publication leads to racism and whether or not it is true.

144C. (a) The publication of a correct and fair report of an action as referred to in section 144B shall not be regarded as an offense under that section, provided that it is not done with the purpose of inciting to racism.

(b) The publication of a quotation from religious writings and prayer books or the observance of a religious ritual shall not be regarded as an offense under section 144B, provided that it is not done with the purpose of bringing about racism.

144D. A person who has in his possession, for distribution, a publication prohibited by section 144B, with a view to stirring up racism, is liable for imprisonment of one year, and the publication shall be forfeited.[15]

Nobody has yet been indicted under the new law, and many legal experts believe that it is highly unlikely that anybody will be in the future. The need for direct proof of mens rea, or what is called specific intent, makes it almost impossible to secure a prosecution. The Knesset, they argue, may have to follow the British experience and dispense with this particular condition if the law is to be of instrumental as well as symbolic value.[16]

SPEAKING OUT

In Israel, as in other countries, the introduction of legislation against racial incitement was accompanied by a wide-ranging public debate. There were those who objected to restrictions placed on Kahane's right to express his ideas although they themselves were vehemently opposed to them. All points of view, they argued, however abhorrent they may be, have the right to be heard.

Freedom of expression does not only include the freedom to express pleasant, intelligent and beautiful points of view. It also includes the freedom to express stupid, false, insulting, upsetting, shocking and frightening ones. . . . The enunciation of racist ideas is no different from any other . . . and, therefore, it is necessary to defend the freedom to express them. (Beit-Halahmi 1984:2–3)

Restricting Kahane's freedom of speech may furnish a precedent for further limitations of free speech and thereby lead to the "destruction of democracy." Consequently, many of those in favor of legislation against racial incitement were at pains to point out that free speech is not, and for that matter cannot be, totally unrestricted. It has to be limited in order to guarantee other human rights (e.g., a fair trial, personal reputation, privacy) and basic societal needs (e.g., national security and democracy). The prohibition of racial incitement is therefore in no way unprecedented; it is simply an extension of existing legal limitations. The concept of defensive democracy was the one most frequently referred to in this respect. The amendment to the Basic Law, for instance, was explained in the following way:

Just as a man need not agree to his being killed, so the State need not agree to its being eradicated and erased from the map. Likewise any other organ of the State does not have to serve as a tool for those whose purpose is to undermine the very existence of the state.... [T]he proposed amendment gives expression to the idea of a defensive democracy and to provide a means for the defense of the State and its basic values against those who are trying to undermine it from within.[17]

These arguments are by no means unique. They are rooted in the western liberal tradition and are therefore used in every democratic country in which a similar debate occurs. It is not surprising, though, that the controversy surrounding Meir Kahane was also markedly different from those that took place elsewhere. The proponents of anti-hate laws often appealed to traditional Jewish values—and even more frequently to the lessons of Jewish history in general, and the holocaust in particular.

The appeal to Jewish values is clearly illustrated in the following quotation from the explanatory notes to the Penal Law Amendment.

The Jewish tradition considers the dignity of man who is created in the image of God and making peace between people as to the highest values ... and the degradation of man as a serious sin. ... In the Jewish tradition the dignity of man became a constitutional principle that overrode other laws. The sages introduced a number of injunctions according to which it was permissible to break certain rabbinical laws in order to prevent hatred between Jews and gentiles.[18]

Jewish history—or, to be more precise, the fact that the Jewish people have been the victims of racism throughout the generations—was also given as a reason for outlawing racial incitement. Thus, on several occasions Attorney General Yitzak Zamir drew attention to Justice Berenson's eloquent statement in the Supreme Court about the lessons to be learned from the Jewish experience in the diaspora.

When we were exiled from our country and banished from our land we were victims of the nations of the world among whom we dwelt, and in every generation we knew the bitter taste of persecution, repression and discrimination for no other reason than we were Jews whose religion differs from all others. Given these bitter and wretched experiences ... it was hoped that we would not follow the perverse ways of the Gentiles, and that when we gained our independence in the State of Israel, we would take care to avoid any form of discrimination against law-abiding non-Jews who wished to live according to their own faith and religion. (Zamir 1984)

Particular importance was attached to the holocaust in this respect.[19] "It is inconceivable," the Supreme Court argued concerning Meir Kahane's private member's bills, that "motions similar to the legislation and policies of the greatest antisemite will be presented to the parliament of the Jewish State just forty years after the remnants of the Jewish people were saved from the atrocities of the most terrible racial hatred and nationalist incitement."[20]

Politicians and publicists adopted a much more strident tone than their judicial counterparts. They referred to Kahane's policies toward the Arabs as "a Jewish variation of Nazism" or "a Judenreich in reverse." In a speech to the Knesset Rules Committee, Member of the Knesset Michael Eitan argued in favor of restricting Kahane's freedom of movement, by pointing out the resemblance between his bill for the prevention of assimilation and the infamous Nürnburg Laws of 1935. The main points of his speech were reported in tabular form in the afternoon daily, *Hadashot,* on 16 November 1984 (see table).

Invidious comparisons of this nature were often backed up by analyses of both the similarities between the political situation in Israel and Weimar Germany (e.g., galloping inflation, an unsuccessful war) and the failure to take effective action against the Nazis during the early stages of their rise to power (Peri 1984; Horowitz 1984). To quote Gideon Hausner, the former attorney general and government prosecutor at the Eichmann trial, "we have long accused the Germans of silence in the face of evil. We, of all people, must speak out. Each and every one of us. If we do not it will be a grave mistake" (*Jerusalem Post,* 2 August 1984).

WITCH HUNT

Meir Kahane's struggle against the preventive measures just described was, of course, grounded in his rendering of the Jewish tradition. In his appeals to the Supreme Court, for instance, he was at pains to point out that the policies criticized for being racist were, in fact, nothing of the sort. They were simply an attempt to ensure the separation of Jews and Gentiles in accordance with the Jewish tradition. It must be pointed out, however, that Kahane's campaign was by no means limited to this kind of argumentation. Two further claims were made—one was based on the liberal values he so bitterly opposed, the other on the irreconcilable conflict between the Jewish and Gentile worldviews.

The argument based on liberal values found its clearest expression in the case of the Israeli Broadcasting Authority. As has already been pointed out, Kahane's appeal to the Supreme Court was based on the grounds that

Subject	Kahane's Bill	Nazi Legislation
Residential restrictions	Non-Jews may not live within the Jerusalem city limits.	Apartments in Berlin and Munich rented to Jews may not be rented again to the Jew, his wife, or a Jewish undertaking without a special permit.
Prohibition of intermarriage	Male and female Jews, citizens and residents of the state, are forbidden to marry non-Jews both in and out of the country. Mixed marriages will not be recognized.	Marriage between Jews and citizens of German blood or related blood is forbidden. Marriages in violation of the law are invalid even if performed outside the country.
Separation of students	All educational institutions in Israel will be segregated between Jews and non-Jews.	It is forbidden for Jewish students to study in German schools. They are only allowed to study in Jewish schools.
Extra-marital relations	A. It is forbidden for male and female Jews who are citizens of the state to have full or partial sexual relations of any kind with non-Jews, including outside marriage. Violation of this provision is to be punished by two years' imprisonment. B. A non-Jew who has sexual relations with a Jewish prostitute or a Jewish male is to be punished by fifty years in prison. A Jewish prostitute or Jewish male who has sexual relations with a non-Jewish male is to be punished by five years in prison.	A. Extra-marital relations between Jews and subjects of the state of German blood or of related blood are forbidden. B. Jews are not permitted to employ in their households subjects of the state of Germany or related blood who are under the age of forty-five.
Prevention of meetings among youth	All summer camps, community centers, and other mixed institutions will be abolished. Visits by Jewish and Arab students in villages and homes, overseas trips in which Jewish students are guests in non-Jewish homes, and similar visits by non-Jews in Israel will be abolished.	It is forbidden to include non-Aryan students in visits to youth hostels. It is intolerable that Jewish students take part in school events in which they may come into contact with Aryan students.

the Authority's ruling was anti-democratic and inconsistent with the statutory obligations to provide airspace to all points of view. But the attack was not limited to the confines of the court of law. In a widely distributed flier Kahane argued as follows:

The television and radio decided that you have no right to know about the activities of M. K. Meir Kahane and his movement. Since we were elected to the Knesset they have engaged in a hate campaign against us. . . . Those who talk in the name of democratic principles have banned us completely. . . . You do not have to identify with the Kach movement in order to understand that the kinds of methods used in totalitarian communist countries like Russia are being used against us. Join us and fight against the fascism of the left and for free speech in Israel.

Kahane's argument regarding the conflict between traditional Jewish and contemporary western values played an important part in his appeal against being disqualified from the 1988 elections. In effect, he repeated the claim made in his widely quoted *Uncomfortable Questions for Comfortable Jews:*

The Declaration of Independence of Israel, of course, guarantees equal political rights for all citizens, Jews and Arabs. This is a *democracy.* The Declaration of Independence of Israel guarantees that Israel shall always be a Jewish State. That is *Zionism.* Under the first paragraph, of course, the Arabs have a right to democratically become a majority and create an Arab State just as Jews created a Jewish one in 1948. Under the second paragraph, of course, the Jews have a right to prevent the Arabs from ending the Jewish, Zionist State even though they become a majority through democracy. Which paragraph do you read? Does the Declaration of Independence of Israel create a State of Jews or a state of schizophrenia? (Kahane 1987:20)

Clearly, therefore, Kahane's argument was a threefold one. He referred to Jewish values, western values, and the irreconcilable conflict between them. It must be pointed out, however, that the latter claim was not only used vis-à-vis individual preventive measures; it also furnished the basis for a more general attack on the "hate campaign" waged against him. Sometimes Kahane attributed it to the fact that he posed a threat to the "privileges of the well-to-do." Expulsion of the Arabs, for instance, would destroy their source of cheap labor. Usually, however, he emphasized the less material aspects of the situation—the way in which he threatened the "ideological sanity" or what Berger and Luckmann (1967) so aptly called "the protective cocoon" of his opponents.

Kahane often referred to the conflict between Israel as a Jewish and a democratic state as the "ultimate contradiction" of secular Zionism. In actual fact, however, he regarded it as just a reflection of an even more basic clash between "the Torah of the Jews and the civilization of the Gentiles." The irreconcilability of these worldviews has led, Kahane argued, to a conspiracy of silence. Nobody besides himself is prepared to address the issue. Only he is not afraid to raise the question and give the authentic Jewish answer. The reaction is predictable.

As long as they were able to avoid facing reality they were safe. But when a Kahane came along and forced them to stare at the truth, at the contradiction between Judaism and their gentilized concepts, and choose, the pain and agony were too much. Rather than choose they condemned. . . . They revert to the McCarthy of 30 years ago and to the witch hunts of Salem 250 years before that. Defamation is the last refuge of non-thinkers and those for whom honest thought is too unbearingly painful. (Jewish Press, 24 August 1984)

It must be pointed out, however, that Kahane did not regard the "unprecedented campaign of hatred and abuse" as being directed solely against him. The fight against Kahanism, he argued, was only a cover for a much more comprehensive attack—or, to be more precise, an "unholy war" against traditional Judaism in general.

They hate and wish to destroy Kahanism, but only as a symbol of that which is the ultimate target of their hate. They hate Kahanism because they hate Judaism, and Jews, and themselves. And there is nothing they will not do in order to wipe out that Judaism they correctly see as true Judaism, a Judaism that brands their own life as fraudulent, empty and truly un-Jewish. Concerning these did the rabbis say "Greater is the hate that an ignoramus has for a scholar, than of a gentile for a Jew." (Kahane 1987:12)

Clearly, therefore, Kahane did not only try to nullify the measures taken against him; he also used them in his more general struggle for political legitimacy. The need to prevent the dissemination of his ideas was, Kahane argued, the surest sign of their veracity. After all, "Falsehood always recognizes pure truth, and out of fear and terror tries to destroy it" (Jewish Press, 24 August 1984).

CONCLUSIONS

The dichotomy between legal and educational responses to the problem of racial incitement is somewhat misleading. After all, even the most avid supporters of legislation tended to emphasize its pedagogic functions. Politicians and jurists alike were at pains to point out that the amendment to the Penal Law was meant to teach the public a lesson—that racial incitement is completely unacceptable, that it is taboo.[21] However, the fact that neither Kahane nor anybody else has been charged with (let alone found guilty of) the offense means that the legislation may have had exactly the opposite effect. As Mala Tabory pointed out,

Prior to the passage of legislation prohibiting incitement to racism the fact that a person could express ideas with impunity did not indicate official approval of them. Once the law was passed, any racist expression that is *not* now prosecuted can be construed as having the stamp of legitimacy, under the assumption that if such expression were truly racist, it would not be allowed. (Tabory 1987:297–298)

This argument seems to suggest that legislation would have had the desired effect if it were, in fact, implemented. However, this is not necessarily the case. Using the amendment to the Basic Law to disqualify the Kach Party from the 1988 elections lent a certain legitimacy to those on the extreme right of the political spectrum. After all, the exclusion of Kach implied that all other lists were in order. Even the newly founded Moledet Party that advocated the transfer of Arabs from the occupied territories was acceptable. Only Kahane was beyond the pale.

Kahane's entry into the Knesset gave a certain degree of "public legitimacy" to his policies and the ideology on which they are based. Politicians who had previously been wary about expressing such ideas in public, especially concerning the possibility of a population transfer, now felt free to do so. In August 1984, less than a month after Kahane's electoral success, a newspaper columnist claimed that

Kahane's strength is to be found in his lack of shame, in the legitimacy that he gives to other dark forces, in the breaches that he makes in the red line. . . . Kahane is the AIDS virus in the weary body of Israeli society . . . he undermines what remains of its immunity system. We will not die, it seems, from Kahane himself, but he makes it easier for the fatal illness to develop. *(Hadashot,* 24 August 1984)

The same argument could be made four years later. Only this time, it was Kahane's disqualification from the Knesset that "broke the barrier of shame."

The decision of the Central Elections Committee had a very detrimental effect on the fortunes of the Kach Party. And the situation worsened after the assassination of Meir Kahane in November 1990. Squabbling between different groups of activists as to which of them constituted the true standard bearer of his ideas led to the splintering of the party into a number of small factions. As a result, it may well be on the verge of extinction. However, the same cannot be said for Kahane's policies concerning the Arab minority in Israel. The Moledet Party gained two Knesset seats in the 1988 elections and subsequently joined the coalition government headed by the Likud. Although Kahane and his party are no longer a force to be reckoned with in Israeli politics, their policies most definitely are.

NOTES

1. The name of the bill is based on Kahane's contention that the removal of Arabs constitutes the second stage of the population transfer that began in 1948 with the "flight of the Jews from Arab and Moslem lands accompanied by a violent expulsion without compensation for confiscated property."

2. These fears were deepened by Kahane's increasing popularity. He received 1.2 percent of the votes cast for the Eleventh Knesset in July 1984. By August of the following year the public opinion polls predicted that as many as 9 percent of the electorate would vote Kach.

3. Statement concerning the decision not to invite a representative of Kach to the consultations on the formation of a government, 1 August 1984.

4. This quotation is taken from the unpublished protocol of the Knesset House Committee's deliberations on the question as to whether Meir Kahane's parliamentary immunity should be restricted.

5. *Kahane v. Speaker of the Knesset*, 39 (4) *Piskei Din* (1985): 88–89. *Piskei Din* is the Israeli Supreme Court reporter.

6. Knesset Standing Order Amendment 134 (c) 3271 *Yalkut Hapirsumim* (1986): 772. *Yalkut Hapirsumim* is the official digest of government notices.

7. *Divrei Knesset* 14 (1984): 885–904. *Divrei Knesset* is the Israeli parliamentary reporter.

8. *Divrei Knesset* 14 (1987): 1920–1925.

9. For further details, see *Special Circular of the Director General, Ministry of Education* (Jerusalem), No. 1, September 1984.

10. *Kahane v. Broadcasting Authority*, 41 (3) *Piskei Din* (1987): 225.

11. *Neiman v. Chairman of the Central Elections Committee*, 39 (2) *Piskei Din* (1984): 238.

12. Basic Law: The Knesset Amendment No. 9 1155 *Sefir Hahukim* (1985): 196. *Sefir Hahukim* is the official digest of Israeli laws.

13. *Neiman v. Chairman of the Central Elections Committee*, 42 (4) *Piskei Din* (1988): 177.

14. For further details of these laws, see Tabory (1987:271–272).

15. Penal Law Amendment No. 20 1191 *Sefir Hahukim* (1986): 219.

16. See, for example, Kretzmer (1988).

17. *Hatzaot Hok* No. 1728, 17 April 1985: 194. *Hatzaot Hok* is the official digest of draft parliamentary bills.

18. *Hatzaot Hok* No. 1728, 17 April 1985: 196.

19. For further details of this argument, see Cromer (1987, 1988).

20. *Kahane v. Speaker of the Knesset*, 39 (4) *Piskei Din* (1985): 88–89.

21. See, for instance, the comments of Moshe Nissim, the minister of justice, during the first reading of the amendment to the Penal Law (*Divrei Knesset* (24) 1985:2381).

7

Her Majesty The Queen v. James Keegstra: The Control of Racism in Canada, A Case Study

Bruce P. Elman

INTRODUCTION: CASE HISTORY

On 11 January 1984, James Keegstra, the former mayor of the town of Eckville, Alberta, and a teacher in its junior and senior high school, was charged with "the wilful promotion of hatred of an identifiable group, to wit the Jewish people," which was contrary to what was then section 281.2(2)[1] of the Criminal Code of Canada.[2] The subject matter of this charge involved statements made by Keegstra while teaching social studies to students in grades 9 and 12 at Eckville Junior and Senior High School between 1 September 1978 and 31 December 1982.

When this matter came to light in 1982, Jim Keegstra had been teaching at Eckville Junior and Senior High School for approximately fifteen years. He had begun his teaching career as an industrial arts teacher but had shown an interest in history, and he ultimately found himself teaching Social Studies 9 and 30 (Grade 9 and Grade 12 History, respectively). The curriculum of Social Studies 30 was an examination of world history since 1900.

Keegstra taught that all the major events of history were connected to one central theme: a Jewish conspiracy to take over the world and rule it through the mechanism of one world government. He taught that the Jews were responsible for World Wars I and II. He linked the Jewish conspiracy to the American, French, and Russian Revolutions. He taught that Jews formed secret societies—the Jacobins, the Illuminati, the Bolsheviks—to pursue their evil plan to rule the world. He taught that the Jews controlled the government, the banks, the courts, and the media. And he taught that the holocaust was a hoax. The Talmud, for Keegstra, was the "blueprint" for this one world government. To support his views, he cited from the New Testament.

What emerged from the evidence presented at trial was a sophisticated system of anti-Jewish dogma. There were, on the one hand, examples of classic anti-Semitism. In discussing the French Revolution, Keegstra taught that the Jews were responsible for the Reign of Terror—or, as one student's notes called it, the "Feast of Reason." This seems to have been a variant of the traditional "Blood Libel" anti-Semitism: "In it [the Feast of Reason] an innocent girl was slaughtered in the church of Notre Dame and her blood was poured over a naked prostitute. Then they would cook the girl and eat her" *(Edmonton Journal,* 7 June 1984; *Edmonton Sun,* 7 June 1984).

Material such as that found in the *Protocols of the Elders of Zion,* a notorious anti-Semitic diatribe fabricated by the czarist secret police (Cohn 1967) was also provided to the students. They were taught that the Jews controlled the banks, the media, the courts, and our political institutions.

There were also examples of what might be called the new anti-Semitism—attacking Jews by attacking Zionism and the State of Israel. There were two themes here. One attacked the historical entitlement of the Jewish people to the land of Israel. Keegstra taught his students that the Jews of today are not the descendants of Abraham and, therefore, not the heirs of his covenant. He suggested that the Jewish people are descended from a tribe of Mongol-Turks, known as the Khazzars, who existed in the eighth and ninth centuries in what is now Southern Russia and Turkey.

The second theme was an attack on the notion that Jews have been persecuted and need the State of Israel as a refuge. Keegstra taught that Jews have not been the persecuted but rather the persecutors, that they have been responsible for inflicting many hardships on others, and that the holocaust never happened.

A word must be said here about Keegstra's teaching methodology. Keegstra lectured, and students were instructed to take down what he said. Some statements were written on the blackboard and the students were instructed to copy them down. One student, when asked why she had written "Never trust a Jew!" in her notes, responded that "Mr. Keegstra said it and I thought it might be on the test" *(Edmonton Journal, 7 June 1984)*.

Evaluation was through essays, tests, and exams. Students were expected to use their class notes as the basis for their essays and examination answers. Outside sources, such as history books and encyclopedias, were proscribed by Keegstra. A true/false question perpetually posed on a test was: "Jews generally are good citizens." Only those answers indicating that the statement was "false" were marked correct.

The methodology employed by Keegstra is obvious. The target group, generally (but not exclusively) Jews, was routinely associated with what he alleged to be negative points of history. These negative pairings were reinforced in the students' minds by a system of evaluation that required them to rely heavily on the material provided by the teacher, which discouraged them from doing independent research and which rewarded them only when they correctly regurgitated the propaganda they had been taught. In short, the students were not receiving history education but, rather, anti-Semitic indoctrination.

THE CRIMINAL CODE PROVISIONS

At the epicenter of this case are controversial legislative provisions contained in the Criminal Code of Canada.[3] One of the earliest attempts at dealing with group defamation through the criminal law occurred in England in 1275. The law, known as De Scandalis Magnatum (3 Edward 1, c. 34), prohibited the spreading of false rumors that might sow discord between the King and the Noblemen of the Realm. This law is not only of historical interest. Its offspring, the crime of "Spreading False News," can be found in section 181 of the Criminal Code. It was upon this legislative provision that the prosecution of holocaust denier Ernst Zundel was based. The *Zundel* case (*Zundel v. The Queen* (1987), 35 D.L.R. (4th) 338, 31 C.C.C. (3d) 97 (Ont. C.A.)) will be discussed later in this chapter.

An early prosecution for promoting hatred against Jews occurred in 1732 in the case of *R. v. Osborn* ((1732), 2 Barn. K.B. 166, R.R. 425). The defendant in this case had published a false accusation that the Jews of London killed a Jewish woman and her illegitimate child because of her alleged promiscuity with a Christian. Riots occurred as a result of this libel, and Jews were attacked and beaten. Ultimately, Osborn was convicted of publishing a libel that occasioned a breach of the peace.

Prior to 1965, Canadian legislation seemed inadequate to deal with the problem of group defamation. First, the offense of defamatory libel applied only to the vilification of individuals and not to groups. Further, the offense of seditious libel was interpreted in a very narrow fashion by the Supreme Court of Canada. In the case of *Boucher v. The King* ((1951), S.C.R. 265), the Court ruled that the prosecution had to prove not only that ill-will had been promoted but also that the defendant had attempted to incite acts of violence or disturb the established order. The crime of spreading false news was interpreted in a similarly restrictive manner.[4] Criminal sanctions, then, appeared inadequate to resolve the problem of hate propaganda.

Race Hatred and the Criminal Law

Hitlerism and the horrors of the holocaust generated renewed calls for criminal sanctions for group defamation. Furthermore, Canada became a signatory to certain international instruments that unequivocally denounced racism in contemporary society. In 1965, the Honourable Guy Favreau, then minister of justice, established an advisory committee to examine the problem of hate propaganda. In its report, the committee, chaired by Dean Maxwell Cohen of the McGill Law School, concluded that the provisions of the Criminal Code of Canada were inadequate to deal with the problem of hate propaganda. In its *Report of the Special Committee on Hate Propaganda in Canada* (The Cohen Committee Report) issued in 1966, the Cohen Committee recommended amendments to the Criminal Code that would put into Canadian law a scheme of legislative sanctions to deal with the various aspects of group defamation.

In 1970, these recommendations became law. Consequently, the Criminal Code presently contains prohibitions against advocating genocide, public incitement of hatred, and willful promotion of hatred.

Section 318(1) of the Criminal Code prohibits the advocating or promotion of genocide. Anyone found guilty of this offense is subject to imprisonment for five years. "Genocide" is defined as:

any of the following acts committed with intent to destroy in whole or in part any identifiable group, namely,

(a) killing members of the group, or

(b) deliberately inflicting on the group conditions of life calculated to bring about its physical destruction.

"Identifiable group" is "any section of the public distinguished by colour, race, religion or ethnic origin" (Criminal Code, section 318(4)). This definition operates, as well, for other sections of the Code concerned with hate propaganda. Consent of the attorney general must be obtained prior to any prosecution under this section (Criminal Code, section 318(3)).

Section 319(1) of the Criminal Code, entitled "Public Incitement of Hatred," provides that:

Everyone who by communicating statements in any public place, incites hatred against any identifiable group where such incitement is likely to lead to a breach of peace is guilty of:

(a) an indictable offence and is liable to imprisonment for two years; and

(b) an offence punishable on summary conviction.[5]

"Public place" is "any place to which the public have access as of right or by invitation, expressed or implied." The essence, then, of this offense is the *public* incitement of hatred that is *likely to produce a breach of the peace*. Because of the requirement of proving, at least, the potentiality of a breach of the peace, this section has not been subject to extensive criticism.

From the outset, the most controversial of the Code provisions has been the prohibition against the "wilful promotion of hatred," which is found in section 319(2). The text of the provision is as follows:

Everyone who, by communicating statements, other than in private conversation, wilfully promotes hatred against any identifiable group is guilty of

(a) an indictable offence and is liable to imprisonment for two years; or

(b) an offence punishable on summary conviction.

Even in the years prior to the advent of the Canadian Charter of Rights and Freedoms, critics complained that this provision was a serious infringement of freedom of expression. The Cohen Committee had been sensitive to this criticism from the outset. In order to allay the fears of civil libertarians, the Committee made two suggestions: (1) that no prosecutions should be undertaken without the consent of the attorney general (Criminal Code, section 319(6)) and (2) that a set of defenses specifically designed to narrow the scope of the prohibition against the "wilful promotion of hatred" be included in the Criminal Code. These defenses are found in section 319(3):

No person shall be convicted of an offence under subsection (2)

(a) if he establishes that the statements communicated were true;

(b) if, in good faith, he expresses or attempts to establish by argument an opinion on a religious subject;

(c) if the statements were relevant to any subject of public interest, the discussion of which was for the public benefit, and if on reasonable grounds he believed them to be true; or

(d) if, in good faith, he intended to point out, for the purpose of removal, matters producing or tending to produce feelings of hatred towards an identifiable group in Canada.

Section 319(3) did not, in fact, alleviate the concerns of those civil libertarians who believed that the criminal prohibition against the willful promotion of hatred would have a chilling effect on public discussion. Not only was this provision unsatisfactory to civil libertarians, but it engendered a different type of criticism from those minority ethnic and religious groups who had lobbied so strenuously for the creation of the Cohen Committee in the first place. Their criticism was straightforward: The provisions were unworkable. The combined effect of sections 319(2) and (3) would make it impossible to convict anyone of this offense. This view was supported by many of the attorneys general across the country who were reluctant to commence prosecutions that they believed had little chance of success.

This view gained considerable support with the report of what was thought to be the first case prosecuted under what is now section 319(2). In the 1970 case of *Regina v. Buzzanga and Durocher* ((1979), 49 C.C.C. (2d) 369 (Ont. C.A.)), the defendants were charged with willfully promoting hatred against French Canadians. As it turned out, Buzzanga and Durocher were, in fact, French Canadian activists, who had launched a campaign to secure a French language high school for Essex County, Ontario. They were distressed, however, with the apathy of Francophones in Essex County and resolved to secure more support for their campaign. Consequently, they authored an anti–French Canadian leaflet and had it circulated among the residents, and particularly the Francophones, of Essex County in the hope of sparking the interest of their fellow French Canadians.

The case ultimately hinged on the meaning of the term "wilfully" in the phrase "wilfully promotes hatred" in section 319(2). If "wilfully" was synonymous with "intentionally" or "purposefully," then Buzzanga and Durocher would have to be acquitted because their purpose and intention, quite clearly, had not been to promote hatred of French Canadians. If the term "wilfully" were given a different meaning—one synonymous with recklessness or negligence—then Buzzanga and Durocher might be convicted in spite of their lack of intention to commit the crime. In the end, the Ontario Court of Appeal decided that "wilful" must be equated with "intentional" or "purposeful" and that Buzzanga and Durocher must be acquitted. This ruling, quite obviously, limited the potential scope of operation of the section.

Therefore, in order to gain a conviction for the "wilful promotion of hatred," the Crown must first prove beyond a reasonable doubt that the defendant *intended* to promote hatred. It is not sufficient for the Crown to show that hatred was promoted "accidentally," "negligently," or even "recklessly." The prosecution must show beyond a reasonable doubt that the accused's conscious purpose was to promote hatred.[6]

As a second requirement the Crown must prove, once again beyond a reasonable doubt, that the willful promotion of hatred was directed against an identifiable group, that is, a segment of the public distinguished by color, race, religion, or ethnic origin. Clearly, many groups who might be slandered will not be distinguishable by color, race, religion, or ethnic origin.[7] It is amazing that this issue arose during the course of the *Keegstra* trial. Although one might think it self-evident that Jews would be included in the definition of "identifiable group," and in spite of the fact that Jews were one group expressly identified by the Cohen Committee as being the subject of, and vulnerable to, hate propaganda, the defense sought to challenge the notion that Jews were an identifiable group according to the Code definition. In a special ruling, the trial judge ruled that the Jewish people were a segment of the public identified by their religion, namely, Judaism.

Third, the Code requires that the promotion of hatred occur "other than in private conversation." This further limits the scope of the intrusion into freedom of expression.

Should the prosecution be successful in proving that the promotion of hatred was willful, that it was directed against an identifiable group, and that it was not communicated in private, it is still open to the defendant to raise one of the defenses included in section 319(3) of the Criminal Code. Should the accused, as an example, raise the defense that he, in good faith, expressed or attempted to establish by argument an opinion on a religious subject, the onus will be on the Crown to negate that defense beyond a reasonable doubt. It should be noted here that the term "good faith" implies that the accused need not be acting reasonably when he expresses his opinion on a religious subject as long as he holds the opinion sincerely. This defense came into play in the trial—a matter that should be of some concern to Christians as well as Jews—as Keegstra claimed that what he taught about Jews was based, at least in part, on his interpretation of Christian theology.

The accused can also raise the defense that his statements were relevant to a subject of public interest, that the discussion was for the public benefit, and that he, on reasonable grounds, believed them to be true. Once again, if the Crown does not disprove this defense beyond a reasonable doubt, an acquittal must result. This defense might be characterized as the main one raised by Keegstra at his trial. He steadfastly claimed that he believed what he told the students about Jews, and he offered books and magazine and newspaper articles to show that his beliefs were based upon reasonable grounds.

A third defense could arise. The defendant might claim that he, in good faith, intended to point out matters producing or intending to produce feelings of hatred toward an identifiable group for the purpose of removing these matters as ones that produce feelings of hatred. This defense was originally thought to be the so-called media exception; that is, the media could publish a racist statement for the purpose of exposing it as such or refuting its contents. In the *Keegstra* trial, however, Justice MacKenzie, in his instructions to the jury, gave this defense a much broader, and arguably more tortured, meaning. The judge's directions to the jury imply that a person may promote hatred against one group (for example, Jewish people) if his purpose is to remove statements promoting hatred against other groups (for example, Germans or Arabs). Parliament could not have intended to exonerate racist incitement on the basis that it was in response to some other perceived racism. In this case at least, two wrongs do not make a right.

Finally, even if the Crown has proved all elements of the offense beyond a reasonable doubt and has disproved the foregoing defenses beyond a reasonable doubt, it is still open to the defendant to establish on the balance of probabilities that the statements he made were true. Although Keegstra never relied upon this defense at trial, the constitutionality of this so-called reverse onus clause was central to the decision of the Court of Appeal to acquit Keegstra.[8]

Once the Crown's task to gain a conviction is examined, one can readily see why minority groups and law enforcement officials were so pessimistic about the effectiveness of sections 319(2) and (3) in deterring group libel.

In this survey of legislative provisions it remains only for us to discuss the offense of publishing false news. This criminal provision, which was the basis of the prosecution of Ernst Zundel, was found in section 181 of the Criminal Code. It provided that:

Everyone who wilfully publishes a statement, tale or news that he knows is false and that causes or is likely to cause injury or mischief to a public interest is guilty of an indictable offence and is liable to imprisonment for two years.

The requirements of this provision are relatively straightforward. The defendant, in order to be convicted, must intentionally publish a statement that he knows is false. The effect of publishing the statement must be to cause, or to potentially cause, injury or mischief to the public interest. Section 181 has also been the subject of extensive criticism, to some extent more virulent in nature than that directed toward section 319(2). As will be explained later, section 181 has been declared unconstitutional.

PROVING A CASE OF RACIST INCITEMENT

Other potential problems in the detection, apprehension, and prosecution of racist incitement cases can be easily imagined. For example, problems of identifying the person promoting the hatred might occur if racist leaflets were left on a doorstep or arrived anonymously through the mail or if a swastika were painted on a synagogue in the middle of the night. But Jim Keegstra was a well-known and seasoned teacher in the local high school. Everyone knew him, knew his views, and whether they agreed with him or not, knew what had to be done to pass his courses. *Thus, in this case, the promoter of hatred was easily identifiable, and this presented no problem for the Crown.*

Further, the context in which the group defamation took place might be unclear. An individual might pass out defamatory leaflets on a street corner or speak to people in a park. In such a case the Crown might even have some difficulty proving that the defamation occurred "other than in private conversation," as required by section 319(2). In the *Keegstra* prosecution the promotion of hatred occurred in a high school classroom continuously for a period of years. *Thus, the context in which the promotion occurred was absolutely clear and discernible and presented no problems for a successful prosecution.*

In some cases, locating witnesses could prove to be difficult. The hate propagandist might make a speech on a street corner. Individuals passing by might catch only snippets of the speech. This presents at least three problems. Have these passers-by heard enough of the speech to testify as to what was being said by the offender? Can they remember what was said, when the event was so short and unimpressive? And most important, can the Crown find them? In the *Keegstra* case the audience was comprised of students who were compelled to be present in class. They were not only expected to pay attention to what was being said but to regurgitate it in essays and on assignments and exams. Thus, they were to participate in the group defamation themselves. *Thus, the audience was ascertainable with certainty and provided the Crown with an abundance of witnesses.*

Furthermore, differences in witnesses' accounts of the same event often create some difficulties for the Crown. No such problem arose in this case. Each student had kept a remarkably accurate record of what had transpired in the class. Indeed, Keegstra confirmed the substance of what had been taught in class in his own testimony. *Thus, there was no real controversy over what was said.*

Finally, in some cases, even though the person who commits the crime is identifiable, the Crown, in its discretion, chooses not to prosecute. This may occur when the offender is an emotionally unstable individual and when little or no deterrent effect, either specific to the individual or generally for the community, will be achieved by a prosecution. But Keegstra was an authority figure in Eckville. Indeed, he was the mayor of the town, a teacher in the high school, and a preacher in his church. A successful prosecution could well have had a deterrent effect in the community. *Thus, in this case, the defendant could not be dismissed out-of-hand as an admittedly unstable individual in regard to whom a prosecution would be neither necessary nor productive.*

This case, then, provided the ideal crucible to test the workability of the criminal prohibition against the willful promotion of hatred. In spite of the fact that identification of the perpetrator presented no problem, that the setting—the classroom—in which the promotion took place was anything but private, that plenty of witnesses were available to testify for the Crown, and that there was no real controversy over what the accused had said, the jury deliberated for three and one-half days before reaching a guilty verdict. This is a graphic illustration of the difficulty that a prosecution under this Code provision presents.

The trial of James Keegstra began on 9 April 1985 and lasted approximately three and one-half months. The jury, following three and one-half days of deliberations, found Keegstra guilty as charged. On 6 June 1988, James Keegstra's conviction was overturned by the Alberta Court of Appeal. The judgment of the Alberta Court of Appeal provided no vindication of Keegstra or his activities. Nor did it in any way suggest that what Keegstra taught was true. Rather, the Alberta Court of Appeal held that section 281.2(2)—now section 319(2)—of the Criminal Code was inconsistent with the provisions of the Canadian Charter of Rights and Freedoms and was, therefore, of no force or effect.

The attorney general of Alberta appealed the decision to the Supreme Court of Canada. On 13 December 1990, the Court, by a four to three majority, overturned the decision of the Alberta Court of Appeal and reinstated, at least temporarily, the conviction. The matter was sent back to the Court of Appeal, however, to resolve other issues related to the conduct of the trial. On 15 March 1991, the Alberta Court of Appeal ordered a new trial on the basis of an irregularity in the method of jury selection. On 25 April 1991, the attorney general of Alberta, in accordance with the order of the court, directed his department to pursue a new prosecution of James Keegstra. The second trial concluded on 10 July 1992 with another conviction. Keegstra was ordered to pay a $3,000.00 fine. He left the courtroom vowing to appeal again.

FREEDOM OF EXPRESSION

At the heart of the controversy surrounding attempts to deter racism through the use of criminal sanctions is the democratic principle of freedom of expression.[9] This principle was given constitutional protection in Canada on 17 April 1982 when the Canadian Charter of Rights and Freedoms came into force. Section 2(b) of the Charter provides that:

Everyone has the following fundamental freedoms:

(b) freedom of thought, belief, opinion and expression, including freedom of the press and other media of communication.

On the same date, the Constitution of Canada was made the supreme law of Canada. Section 52(1) provides that:

The Constitution of Canada is the supreme law of Canada, and any law that is inconsistent with the provisions of the Constitution is to the extent of the inconsistency, of no force or effect.

As a result of this declaration of supremacy, any law that is inconsistent with the Constitution is of no force or effect.

Consequently, in October 1984, well prior to any evidence being presented, Jim Keegstra applied to the Court of Queen's Bench to have what is now section 319(2) of the Criminal Code declared unconstitutional. The application, put simply, alleged that section 319(2) was inconsistent with the principle of freedom of expression as enshrined in the Canadian Charter of Rights and Freedoms and was, therefore, of no force or effect. A successful challenge to the constitutionality of section 319(2) would result in there being no section of the Code upon which to prosecute Keegstra. A stay of proceedings would have resulted.

The Alberta Court of Queen's Bench

Keegstra's application was heard by Justice Quigley of the Court of Queen's Bench. Justice Quigley, however, denied the accused's application to have the provision declared unconstitutional.

All instances of Charter review of legislative action involve a two-stage inquiry. In the first instance, the Court must address the question:

Does the legislation (in this case, the Criminal Code prohibition against the willful promotion of hatred) violate or infringe a guaranteed right under the Canadian Charter of Rights and Freedoms—in this case, freedom of expression under section 2(b)?

If a violation of the right is found, the court proceeds to the second stage. In this phase of the inquiry, the party seeking to justify the law in question—usually, the appropriate level of government—has an opportunity to justify the legislation.[10] The issue may be framed as follows:

Is the legislation (once again, the Criminal Code provision in section 319(2)) a reasonable limit prescribed by law that is demonstrably justified in a free and democratic society?

In answering the first question, Justice Quigley held that what is now section 319(2) of the Criminal Code was not an infringement of section 2(b) of the Canadian Charter of Rights and Freedoms. Although he answered the first question in the negative, Justice Quigley went on to hold that even if section 319(2) was an infringement, it was a reasonable one that was demonstrably justified in a free and democratic society.

On either branch of the test, Justice Quigley viewed section 319(2) as constitutionally valid.

The Alberta Court of Appeal

As part of his overall appeal from conviction, Keegstra challenged the correctness of Justice Quigley's ruling. The Alberta Court of Appeal overturned Justice Quigley's decision, declared section 319(2) to be unconstitutional, and entered an acquittal on behalf of Keegstra. Prior to the Alberta Court of Appeal's decision in the *Keegstra* case, only two other similar cases had reached the Court of Appeal level: the cases of *Zundel v. The Queen* (cited earlier) and *John Ross Taylor and the Western Guard Party v. The Canadian Human Rights Commission* ((1987), 37 D.L.R. (4th) 577 (Fed.C.A.)). The Alberta Court of Appeal gave little consideration to the judgment of the Ontario Court of Appeal in *Zundel v. The Queen.*

Zundel v. The Queen. No story of Canada's attempt to deal with anti-Semitism would be complete without some further discussion of the *Zundel* case.[11] This case began in 1984; its history parallels the *Keegstra* case and provides an interesting comparison with it.

Zundel, a citizen of West Germany, had been resident in Canada since 1958. He was born in the Black Forest region of Germany in 1939. His father served in the army of the Third Reich during World War II. Zundel testified that his father was rarely at home until 1948. He alleged that, as a boy, he had suffered great hardship during and after the war.

Zundel first came to public attention in 1979 when he organized a group, called Concerned Parents of German Descent, to protest alleged anti-German bias in the television mini-series, "Holocaust." He even picketed the local broadcaster of the show. Although he slipped back into obscurity, his samisdat publishing company continued to disseminate anti-Jewish material. In 1981, members of the German Bundestag denounced Zundel as a leading source of neo-Nazi propaganda. In November 1981, Canada Post suspended his mailing privileges but they were reinstated in October 1982.

Ernst Zundel was, in fact, charged with two violations of what was then section 177 of the Criminal Code (later section 181)—"publishing false news." One count was in relation to a publication entitled *The West, War and Islam,* which apparently was never distributed in Canada. The second count related to the more prominent publication, *Did Six Million Really Die?,* which had been circulated in Canada. This pamphlet was a classic example of revisionist, holocaust-denial hate propaganda. Brief excerpts give one a sense of the contents of the document. The introduction begins as follows:

In the following chapters the author has, he believes, brought together irrefutable evidence that the allegation that 6 million Jews died during the Second World War, as a direct result of official German policy of extermination, is utterly unfounded. This conclusion, admittedly an unpopular one, resulted from an inquiry which was begun with no pre-conceived opinions, beyond a general notion that the statistical possibility of such huge casualties was perhaps open to doubt, as well as the awareness that political capital was being made from the implications of this alleged atrocity. . . . The allegation is not merely an exaggeration but an invention of post-war propaganda. . . . It should be added, if one is to be honest, that this strength [of the State of Israel] has been much consolidated financially by the supposed massacre of the Six Million, undoubtedly the most profitable atrocity allegation of all time. To date, the staggering figure of six thousand million pounds has been paid out in compensation by the Federal Government of West Germany, mostly to the State of Israel (which did not even exist during the Second World War), as well as to individual claimants. (*Zundel v. The Queen*, 35 D.L.R. (4th) 338, at 350)

The pamphlet concludes in the following fashion:

Nothing could be more devastating proof of the brazen fantasy of the Six Million. Most of these claimants are Jews, so there can be no doubt that the majority of the 3 million Jews who experienced the Nazi occupation of Europe are, in fact, very much alive. It is resounding confirmation of the fact that Jewish casualties during the Second World War can only be estimated at a figure in the thousands. Surely this is enough grief for the Jewish people! Who has the right to compound it with vast imaginary slaughter, marking with eternal shame a great European nation, as well as wringing fraudulent monetary compensation from them? (*Zundel v. The Queen*, 35 D.L.R. (4th) 338, at 351)

The prosecution was originally commenced privately by the Canadian Holocaust Remembrance Association. The charges were laid under section 181 of the Code because section 319(2) requires consent of the attorney general to prosecute, a consent that was not forthcoming. It was the view of the Ontario Attorney General's Department that section 319(2) was weak and the prospects for conviction uncertain. Once the charges had been laid, however, the Attorney General's Department decided to take over responsibility for the prosecution.

On 28 February 1985, after ten hours of deliberations, the jury found Zundel not guilty on the first count of the indictment but guilty on the second count. One can only surmise that the acquittal on the first count resulted from the fact that the pamphlet, *The West, War and Islam*, had not been distributed in Canada and, therefore, could not cause injury or mischief to a public interest in Canada. For his conviction on the second count, Zundel was sentenced to fifteen months in jail. He was placed on three years' probation, during which time he was not to publish anything, directly or indirectly, on the holocaust or subjects related to the holocaust. Zundel appealed the criminal conviction and sentence.

Although the *Zundel* case dealt with a different section of the Criminal Code, the issues of freedom of expression are similar to those raised in the *Keegstra* case. Although the Ontario Court of Appeal allowed Zundel's appeal and ordered a retrial because of errors made in the conduct of the trial,[12] it is the court's decision on the constitutionality of what is now Criminal Code section 181 that is instructive for the *Keegstra* case. The court, at the outset, noted that "freedom of expression must necessarily have regard to the corresponding rights and freedoms of other persons" (*Zundel v. The Queen*, at 35 D.L.R. (4th) 338, at 356).

The court, then, explored the rationales that have been advanced for the protection of freedom of expression. Three specific rationales were identified:

1. The best way to obtain the truth is through the free exchange of ideas.

2. Freedom of expression is essential to the workings of a parliamentary democracy.

3. Freedom of expression is important for the "evolution, definition and proclamation of individual and group identity" (*Zundel v. The Queen*, 35 D.L.R. (4th) 338, at 357).

Analyzing section 181 in terms of these principles, the court held that no infringement of freedom of expression existed:

The nub of the offence in section 177 [later section 181] is the wilful publication of assertions of a fact or facts which are false to the knowledge of the person who publishes them, and which cause or are likely to cause injury or mischief to a public interest. It is difficult to see how such conduct would fall within any of the previously expressed *rationales* for guaranteeing freedom of expression. Spreading falsehoods knowingly is the antithesis of seeking truth through the free exchange of ideas. It would appear to have no social or moral value which would merit constitutional protection. Nor would it aid the working of parliamentary democracy or further self-fulfilment. In our opinion an offence falling within the ambit of section 177 [now section 181] lies within the permissibly regulated area which is not constitutionally protected. (*Zundel v. The Queen*, 35 D.L.R. (4th) 338, at 364–365)

Out of an abundance of caution, the court turned its attention to the question of justification. It noted that the activity proscribed by section 181 was the "very opposite of free public discussion" and asserted that "stopping such publication by prosecution would seem not only reasonable but important" (*Zundel v. The Queen,* 35 D.L.R. (4th) 338, at 356).

Further, the court held that the means employed in section 181 were "reasonable" and that any impairment was proportional to the objective to be achieved. On a final note, it held that section 181 was neither "vague" nor "overly broad."

The decision by the five-judge Ontario court, authored "By the Court," represented at the time an important statement on the principles underlying, and the extent of, the concept of "freedom of expression." Its failure to address these principles was a glaring omission in the Alberta Court of Appeal's reasoning.

John Ross Taylor and the Western Guard Party v. The Canadian Human Rights Commission. The case of *John Ross Taylor and the Western Guard Party v. The Canadian Human Rights Commission* (hereafter *Taylor*) was also relevant to the potential disposition of the *Keegstra* appeal. The Western Guard Party was a white supremacist, anti-Semitic organization; Taylor was its leader. A tribunal appointed under the Canadian Human Rights Act found that between 17 August 1977 and 8 May 1979 the Western Guard Party and Taylor had engaged in a discriminatory practice, as defined and prohibited by sections 3 and 13(1) of the Canadian Human Rights Act. Section 3 of the Act provides that "race" and "religion" are prohibited grounds of discrimination. Section 13(1) provides that:

It is a discriminatory practice for a person or a group of persons acting in concert to communicate telephonically or to cause to be so communicated, repeatedly, in whole or in part by means of the facilities of a telecommunication undertaking within the legislative authority of Parliament, any matter that is likely to expose a person or persons to hatred or contempt by reason of the fact that that person or those persons are identifiable on the basis of a prohibited ground of discrimination.

In a decision dated 20 July 1979, the tribunal found that Taylor and his group had "telephonically and repeatedly communicated hate messages respecting Jews" (*Taylor* (1987) 37 D.L.R. (4th) 577, at 578). The tribunal ordered them to "cease and desist" their discriminatory practice. Just over a month later, on 23 August, the tribunal's directive was made an order of the Federal Court of Canada.

However, Taylor and the Western Guard did not cease and desist. Consequently, on 21 February 1980, Justice Dube of the Federal Court found them in contempt of the order. He fined the party $5,000 and sentenced Taylor to one year of imprisonment. The Justice, nonetheless, suspended the sentence on the condition that the Western Guard and Taylor henceforth abide by the order of the tribunal. However, the Western Guard and Taylor continued to disobey the order and the suspension of sentence was vacated on 11 June. Taylor was committed to prison on 24 June. With remission, Taylor served a total of five months, from 17 October 1981 to 19 March 1982.

Taylor was either unchastened by his five months in prison or emboldened by the passage of the Charter, because he resumed his tape-recorded messages. The messages transmitted between 22 June 1982 and 20 April 1983 drew the renewed attention of the Human Rights Commission. For example, the message of 25 February included the following excerpt:

Without freedom of speech we'd perish. Few know what communism really is . . . to truly expose communism is the great no no. But moral decay, economic problems and war are all coming from the same source that produces communism. . . . The Fed's Kuhn-Loeb High Bank financed the Russian Revolution. December *Thunderbolt,* which is banned in Canada, states Andropov's real name is Lieberman. . . . *Toronto Star,* November 14, states of Andropov: "His mother's family is almost certainly Jewish." The founder of communism, Karl Marx, whose real name was Moses Mordecai Levy, was the grandson of Rabbi Mordecai. The founder of the Soviet Army was Trotsky whose real name is Bronstein. Help the Western Guard expose these bankers and their agents. Send funds and mail to . . . *(Taylor* (1987) 37 D.L.R. (4th) 577, at 583)

Justice Mahoney of the Federal Court of Appeal would, in due course, characterize these messages in the following manner:

The unequivocal message is: Jewry is the source of Communism; moral decay, economic problems and war all come from that same source. That might well expose Jews, individually and collectively, to the contempt or hatred of anyone who accepted it as true. *(Taylor* (1987) 37 D.L.R. (4th) 577, at 583)

It is not surprising, then, that the Human Rights Commission, once again, sought an order of committal for Taylor and a second $5,000 fine for the Western Guard Party. This time, however, Taylor and his party filed a notice challenging the constitutional validity of section 13(1) of the Canadian Human Rights Act on the basis that it violated freedom of expression as protected by section 2(b) of the Charter. The application for the order of committal was granted pending the outcome of any appeal, and the constitutional challenge was denied. Taylor and the Western Guard appealed to the Federal Court of Appeal. The major ground of appeal that concerns us contended that section 13(1) was *"ultra vires, inoperative, and of no force and effect because it is an unreasonable limit on freedom of expression"* (*Taylor* (1987) 37 D.L.R. (4th) 577, at 581).

It was common ground between the appellants and the Human Rights Commission that section 13(1) constituted a limitation on freedom of expression and that the case stood to be resolved under section 1 of the Charter.[13] In a relatively short but decisive judgment the court held that section 13(1) was a reasonable limit demonstratively justified in a free and democratic society. Justice Mahoney stated:

It seems to me that the concern of any free and democratic society to avoid the vilification of individuals or groups by reason of their race and/or religion is self-evident. Canada, specifically, is populated by immigrants and the descendants of immigrants of numerous races and religions and an indigenous population of races different from the vast majority of the immigrant population. Canada recognizes its multi-culturalism not only as a fact but as a positive characteristic of its national persona. (*Taylor* (1987) 37 D.L.R. (4th) 577, at 590).

Nor did Justice Mahoney require that the problem be serious or widespread:

It is not, in my opinion, necessary that vilification by reason of race and/or religion be rife or have become subject of active and general public interest to render pressing and substantial the concern to avoid it. We witness today the events in Ulster, the Punjab, Sri Lanka and Lebanon. The list is not exhaustive. All are struggling, in the teeth of violence fuelled by racial and/or religious hatred, to remain free and democratic societies or, within our ready memory, appear to have lost that struggle. I have no difficulty with the concept that the avoidance of the propagation of hatred on those grounds is, in itself, properly a pressing and substantial concern of a free and democratic society. (*Taylor* (1987) 37 D.L.R. (4th) 577, at 590)

Justice Mahoney further held that the means employed in section 13(1) were "narrowly drawn," rationally connected to the object, and "tailored precisely" to the problem of abusive use of the telephone. Finally, he noted that "the legislative scheme exemplifies restraint rather than severity" (*Taylor* (1987) 37 D.L.R. (4th) 577, at 590). Justice Mahoney concluded:

On balance, the interest of a free and democratic society to avoid the repeated telephonic communication of messages of hate based on race or religion clearly outweighs its interest to tolerate the exercise in that fashion of their freedom of expression by persons so inclined. (*Taylor* (1987) 37 D.L.R. (4th) 577, at 591)

The decision of the Federal Court of Appeal to uphold the law was delivered on 22 April 1987, more than a year before the *Keegstra* judgment, but it played no part in the Alberta Court of Appeal's decision.

The Supreme Court of Canada

The Supreme Court of Canada, by the narrowest of majorities, overturned the Alberta Court of Appeal decision and upheld the constitutional validity of the criminal prohibition against racist incitement. In their analysis, both the majority and the dissent followed the now-standard two-stage approach to Charter adjudication. First, each examined whether section 319(2) of the Criminal Code violated section 2(b) of the Charter.

The majority opinion, at the outset, noted that expression that "wilfully promotes hatred" does not fall outside the protection of section 2(b) of the Charter. Any activity that attempts to convey meaning through a nonviolent form of expression has expressive content and falls within the scope of section 2(b). Further, the majority held that hate propaganda was *not* analogous to violence and, consequently, that no exception for hate propaganda could be carved out of the protection afforded by section 2(b) of the Charter. Thus, the Court rejected the position taken by the Ontario Court of Appeal in the *Zundel* case and the subsequent case of *Andrews and Smith* ((1988) 65 O.R. (2d) 161 (Ont. C.A.))[14] that false news and hate propaganda fell outside the scope of the protection afforded by section 2(b) of the Charter.

The proposition that section 2(b) of the Charter had to be interpreted in light of sections 15 (equal protection) and 27 (preservation and enhancement of multiculturalism) of the Charter as well as our international agreements was similarly rejected. These latter constitutional provisions and international agreements could not be used to attenuate the scope of the protection afforded by freedom of expression under the Charter. These contextual values, in the Court's view, should be reserved for consideration during the second—or justification—phase of the inquiry. The dissent was in general agreement with the majority on this phase of the analysis.

In the second stage of the inquiry—the so-called section 1 or justification test—the Court examined whether section 319(2) was a reasonable limit that was demonstrably justified in a free and democratic society. The divergence of views between majority and dissenting factions of the Court rests, as it often does, on the result of this second-stage analysis: The majority found section 319(2) a reasonable and justifiable limitation; the dissent did not.

The majority began by noting that the objective—preventing pain to the target group and reducing racial, ethnic, and religious tension and, perhaps, violence—was of sufficient importance to warrant overriding a guaranteed right. Canada's international obligations and Charter sections 15 and 27 emphasize the importance of this objective. Furthermore, in the majority's opinion, section 319(2) was a reasonable and proportional response to secure that objective. During the course of his majority opinion, Chief Justice Dickson examined the relationship between the rationale supporting freedom of expression and the nature of hate propaganda. The Chief Justice identified three rationales supporting freedom of expression:

1. The need to ensure that truth and the common good are attained. Because truth and the common good are difficult to ascertain with absolute certainty, free expression cannot be prohibited without potentially impeding the free exchange of ideas necessary to achieve truth and the common good.

2. Free expression plays a vital role in ensuring that individuals achieve self-fulfilment by developing and articulating thoughts and ideas as they see fit.

3. Freedom of expression is central to the Canadian commitment to democracy because it ensures that the best policies are chosen from numerous possible opinions and because it allows full participation in the democratic process. (*The Queen v. James Keegstra* (1990) 61 C.C.C. (3d) 1, at 48–50)

In Justice Dickson's view, expression that is intended to promote hatred of identifiable groups is of limited importance when measured against the yardstick provided by the underlying rationales of free expression. The Chief Justice noted that speech can sometimes be a detriment in the search for truth. We should not "overplay the view that rationality will overcome all falsehoods in the unregulated market-place of ideas" (*The Queen v. James Keegstra* (1990) 61 C.C.C. (3d) 1, at 49). As there is very little likelihood that hate propaganda is true or that it will promote a better society, portraying such statements as being "crucial to truth and the betterment of the political and social milieu" is, in the Chief Justice's opinion, "misguided" (*The Queen v. James Keegstra* (1990) 61 C.C.C. (3d) 1, at 49). Similarly, hate propaganda works against the second rationale. Rather than encouraging the attainment of self-fulfilment, racist speech inhibits the ability of many members in our society to achieve the self-autonomy that will often stem from an individual's membership in a cultural, ethnic, or religious group.

Finally, hate propaganda is inimical to the enhancement of democratic expression and the democratic process. As Chief Justice Dickson stated:

Indeed, one may quite plausibly contend that it is through rejecting hate propaganda that the state can best encourage the protection of values central to freedom of expression, while simultaneously demonstrating dislike for the vision forwarded by hate-mongers. . . . I am very reluctant to attach anything but the highest importance to expression relevant to political matters. But given the unparalleled vigour with which hate propaganda repudiates and undermines democratic values, and in particular its condemnation of the view that all citizens need be treated with equal respect and dignity so as to make participation in the political process meaningful, I am unable to see the protection of such expression as integral to the democratic ideal so central to the s.2(b) rational. (*The Queen v. James Keegstra* (1990) 61 C.C.C. (3d) 1, at 50–51)

Justice Dickson concluded that the Code provision is rationally connected to the objective and does not unduly impair freedom of expression. On this latter point, the majority noted that section 319(2) was not vague or overly broad. Indeed, in the majority's view, the Code section was narrowly drawn. They pointed to many of the requirements for a successful prosecution to illustrate the narrow scope of the provision. Other methods, noncriminal in nature, may exist for combating racist incitement, but Parliament is not limited to only one of these methods. Occasionally, the majority noted, condemnation through the force of the criminal law will be necessary.

Finally, the majority held that the advantages of the prohibition against racist incitement outweigh any resulting harmful effects. Once again, the majority referred to the importance of the protection of equality, the preservation and enhancement of multiculturalism, and Canada's international obligations. They contrasted these with the fact that hate propaganda is only tenuously related to the values underlying freedom of expression: the search for truth, individual self-fulfillment, and the maintenance of a vibrant democracy. Thus, the majority upheld the constitutional validity of section 319(2) of the Criminal Code and reinstated Keegstra's conviction until such time as the Alberta Court of Appeal could adjudicate on other issues involving the conduct of the trial.

The dissent, while agreeing that the objective was an important one, disagreed on whether section 319(2) was a reasonable and proportional means of securing the objective. They were of the view that the Code section was not rationally connected to the objective: There was no evidence that criminalizing the dissemination of hate propaganda would, in fact, suppress it. Indeed, the dissent noted that criminalizing racist incitement might have the reverse effect of promoting racism by providing greater publicity and exposure for the racism and the propagandist. Further, the dissent held that section 319(2) was overly broad in that it could potentially catch more expression than was justifiable. Justice McLachlin, writing on behalf of the dissenters, noted:

The real answer to the debate about whether s.319(2) is overbroad is provided by the section's track record. Although the section is of relatively recent origin, it has provoked many questionable actions on the part of the authorities. There have been no reported convictions, other than the instant appeals. But the record amply demonstrates that intemperate statements about identifiable groups, particularly if they represent an unpopular viewpoint, may attract state involvement or calls for police action. Novels such as Leon Uris' pro-Zionist novel, *The Haj* (1984), face calls for banning. . . . Other works, such as Salman Rushdie's *Satanic Verses* (1988), are stopped at the border on the ground that they violate s.319(2). Films may be temporarily kept out, as happened to a film entitled "Nelson Mandela," ordered as an educational film by Ryerson Polytechnical Institute in 1986. . . . Arrests are even made for distributing pamphlets containing the words "Yankee Go Home." . . . Experience shows that many cases are winnowed out due to prosecutorial discretion and other factors. It shows equally, however, that initially quite a lot of speech is caught by s.319(2). (*The Queen v. James Keegstra* (1990) 61 C.C.C. (3d) 1, at 120)

In any event, according to the dissent, the provision has a chilling effect on legitimate public discourse. Justice McLachlin stated further:

The danger is rather that the legislation may have a chilling effect on legitimate activities important to our society by subjecting innocent persons to constraints born out of a fear of the criminal process. Given the vagueness of the prohibition of expression in s.319(2), one may ask how speakers are to know when their speech may be seen as encroaching on the forbidden area. The reaction is predictable. The combination of overbreadth and criminalization may well lead people desirous of avoiding even the slightest brush with the criminal law to protect themselves in the best way they can—by confining their expression to non-controversial matters. Novelists may steer clear of controversial characterizations or ethnic characteristics, such as Shakespeare's portrayal of Shylock in "The Merchant of Venice." Scientists may well think twice before researching and publishing results of research suggesting difference between ethnic or racial groups. Given the serious consequences of criminal prosecution, it is not entirely speculative to suppose that even political debate on crucial issues such as immigration, educational language rights, foreign ownership and trade may be tempered. These matters go to the heart of the traditional justifications for protecting freedom of expression. (*The Queen v. James Keegstra* (1990) 61 C.C.C. (3d) 1, at 121)

The dissent noted that alternative methods, less intrusive than prohibiting racist incitement, are available to Parliament. Given the serious potential damage to freedom of expression and the dubious benefit to be gained from prohibiting the dissemination of hate propaganda, the dissent held that section 319(2) was not a justifiable limit on freedom of expression and was of no force or effect.[15]

By a four-to-three majority, however, the Supreme Court of Canada upheld the constitutionality of Canada's hate propaganda laws.[16]

SOME CONCLUDING OBSERVATIONS

1. Majority support for the constitutional validity of section 319(2) is tenuous.

The debate concerning the criminalization of hate propaganda has raged for over two decades in Canada. The Supreme Court, for the time being at least, has decided that the criminal prohibition against the willful promotion of hatred is constitutionally acceptable. The validity of section 319(2) of the Criminal Code was supported only by the slimmest of majorities. Two of the four Supreme Court Justices who voted to support the provision and reinstate Keegstra's conviction have already retired from the Court. One, Chief Justice Dickson, was replaced by Justice Stevenson, who, as a member of the Alberta Court of Appeal, voted to strike down the hate propaganda law. Justice Stevenson has subsequently retired. A second, Justice Wilson, has been replaced by Justice Iacobucci, whose views on this subject are not known. On the other hand, Justice Cory took no part in the decision. While he was a member of the Ontario Court of Appeal, Justice Cory wrote a stirring judgment supporting the constitutionality of section 319(2) of the Code. Thus, we can be safe in asserting that he would have sided with the majority. Chief Justice Lamer also took no part in the decision. His vote on the subject may be crucial in any new challenge. Although he has often sided with Justices Dickson and Wilson, his precise views on this subject are unknown.

Nonetheless, it is unlikely that this change in Court personnel will result in the overturning of the *Keegstra* decision itself. The Supreme Court of Canada rarely changes its mind so quickly. But it was a forewarning of the eventual result in the *Zundel* appeal. In that case, as noted earlier, section 181 of the Code (publishing false news), upon which the *Zundel* conviction was based, has been declared unconstitutional.

2. The decision to uphold the criminal prohibition against hate propaganda is an important statement as to the values that are central to Canadian society.

There is important symbolic value in having a law prohibiting the dissemination of hate propaganda. Our society must make a clear statement as to the values that we deem of central importance. If we believe that equality, the protection of minorities, and the preservation of multiculturalism are values that are vitally important to Canadian society, we must be prepared to support these values with criminal sanctions, if necessary. As Justice Cory noted in his judgment in *Andrews and Smith,* we must heed the lessons of history:

I would have thought it sufficient to look back at the quintessence of evil manifested in the Third Reich and its hate propaganda to realize the destructive effects of the promotion of hatred. That dark history provides overwhelming evidence of the catastrophic results of expressions which promote hatred. The National Socialist Party was in the minority when it attained power. The repetition of the loathsome messages of Nazi propaganda led in cruel and rapid succession from the breaking of the shop windows of Jewish merchants to the dispossession of the Jews from their property and their professions, to the establishment of concentration camps and gas chambers. The genocidal horrors of the Holocaust were made possible by the deliberate incitement of hatred against the Jewish and other minority peoples. It would be a mistake to assume that Canada today is necessarily immune to the effects of Nazi and other hate literature. ((1988), 43 C.C.C. (3d) 193, at 211–212)

Indeed, although no causal connection can be demonstrated, there was an alarming increase in overt acts of racism and anti-Semitism in Alberta following the Court of Appeal's decision to strike down the hate propaganda law in 1988. People wore pins protesting the use of turbans by Sikh members of the Royal Canadian Mounted Police, skinheads attacked former broadcaster Keith Rutherford for having exposed a Nazi war criminal a number of years ago, and there was a cross-burning at Provost, Alberta, accompanied by chants of "Death to the Jews."[17]

The continuing availability of laws that prohibit racist incitement is important. But it is equally important that they be used in appropriate cases only. This leads to my third observation.

3. Even in the clearest of cases, such as *The Queen v. James Keegstra*, using the criminal process to deter racism is fraught with difficulties.

The criminal process is long, expensive, and, most important, unpredictable. It should not be casually invoked. We can see from *The Queen v. James Keegstra* that even in those cases where there is little doubt as to the adjudicative facts that constitute the crime, obtaining a conviction is not easy. Keegstra's second trial has been recently concluded. It has been ten years since the facts of this case first came to light, and it may still not be laid to rest.

The criminal process, quite properly, makes it difficult to convict any accused. The presumption of innocence—the Crown must prove the case against the accused beyond a reasonable doubt—is an important safeguard introduced into our criminal justice system to ensure that innocent people are not convicted. As was noted earlier, the text of section 319(2), itself, and the defenses contained in section 319(3) present other potential problems for the prosecution to overcome. Finally, we cannot deny the fact that a criminal prosecution provides the accused with an excellent opportunity to repeat, in front of members of the media, the racist speech that is the subject matter of the criminal prosecution in the first place. In some (perhaps many) instances, prosecuting an alleged hatemonger will be counterproductive.

Alternative legal means—perhaps human rights legislation—should be studied to determine if they might be effective in combating racism. Actions under human rights statutes such as the case of *Malcolm Ross* may point up new ways of deterring racist incitement.[18] It may turn out, however, that minority religious and ethnic groups will be forced to develop extra-judicial strategies to combat racist incitement or remain at the mercy of the hate propagandist.

4. We see an interesting dichotomy of philosophical perspectives disclosed in the *Keegstra* decision.

We often characterize Charter decisions as being either "conservative" or "liberal." Indeed, a decision to uphold a law that limited freedom of speech would generally be labeled conservative whereas a decision to strike down a government prohibition on speech would be recognized as classically "liberal." The *Keegstra* decision shows us that these labels may no longer be very useful, if they ever were.

The Canadian Charter of Rights and Freedoms is a unique document in that it attempts to combine the protection of individual rights with a recognition that groups also have rights that must be considered. The dissenting opinion might be classed as more "libertarian" than "liberal." It rejects government intervention to regulate the marketplace of expression and, in doing so, protects the right of the hatemonger at the expense of minority ethnic, racial, and religious groups. The majority, on the other hand, seems to be concerned with a particular subspecies of "communitarianism," namely, "minoritarian" values: the right of minority ethnic, racial, and religious groups to be free from defamatory speech that is potentially dangerous to them. The individual's right to engage in speech that is intended to promote hatred must yield to the greater community interest in the protection of minorities and the ensuring of racial, ethnic, and religious tolerance for all Canadians.

For the time being at least, the courts have ruled that Canada's hate propaganda laws are constitutionally valid. Whether the criminal law is the best vehicle for producing a truly tolerant and egalitarian society is a question with which we, as a nation, will continue to struggle.

NOTES

1. The sections of the Criminal Code of Canada were recently renumbered. Section 281.2(2) is now designated as section 319(2). In the Code, the crime is referred to as "the wilful promotion of hatred." It is found in a part of the Code referred to under the title "Hate Propaganda." The terms "racist incitement" and "group defamation" have no legal significance in Canadian law but are used interchangeably with "wilful promotion of hatred" and "hate propaganda."

2. See (1990), 61 C.C.C. (3d) 1 (S.C.C.) reversing (1988), 43 C.C.C. (3d) 150 (1988) 5 W.W.R. 211 (Alta. C.A.) reversing 19 C.C.C. (3d) 254 (A.C.Q.B.). Much has been written on the *Keegstra* case. See, for example, Bottos (1988), Elman (1989, 1990), Bercuson and Wertheimer (1985).

3. For a history of the Criminal Code provisions related to hate propaganda generally, see: Law Reform Commission of Canada, *Working Paper 50: Hate Propaganda* (Ottawa: Law Reform Commission of Canada, 1986); M. Cohen, "The Hate Propaganda Amendments: Reflections on a Controversy," *Alberta Law Review* 9 (1971): 103; M. Cohen, "Human Rights and Hate Propaganda: A Controversial Canadian Experiment," in S. Shoham, ed., *Of Law and Man: Essays in Honor of Haim H. Cohn* (New York: Sabra Books, 1971); S. S. Cohen, "Hate Propaganda—The Amendments to the Criminal Code," *McGill Law Journal* 17 (1971): 740; R. E. Hage, "The Hate Propaganda Amendment to the Criminal Code," *University of Toronto Faculty Law Review* 28 (1970): 63; B. G. Kayfetz, "The Story behind Canada's New Anti-Hate Law," *Patterns of Prejudice* 5 (May–June 1970); A. W. Mewett, "Some Reflections on the Report of the Special Committee on Hate Propaganda," *Criminal Law Quarterly* 9 (1966):16; M. R. McGuigan, "Hate Propaganda and Freedom of Assembly," *Saskatchewan Bar Review* 31 (1966): 232.

4. In *R. v. Carrier* (1951), 104 C.C.C. 75 (Que. K.B.) the Court held that the forerunner to section 181 required something in the nature of an intention to disobey openly or to act violently against the established order.

5.   There are essentially two types of criminal offenses. The more serious offenses are called indictable offenses. The less serious are referred to as summary conviction offenses. Different procedures and a different range of sentences coincide with each type of offense. Some offenses, such as section 319, are termed "hybrid" offenses. This is an offense in which the Crown may elect to proceed by indictment or summarily.

6.   Thus, they must prove the highest level of *mens rea* present in the criminal law. Most crimes are comprised of two elements: the physical element, known as *actus reus,* and the mental element, known as *mens rea.* In order to gain a conviction, the Crown must prove that the *actus reus* and the *mens rea* were simultaneously present. The *mens rea* of intention or conscious purpose is considered to be the most difficult mental state for the Crown to prove.

7.   As a simple example, if one wrote an anti-American diatribe, it is doubtful that a successful prosecution for willfully promoting hatred could result regardless of how scurrilous the attack might be. Americans are a group distinguishable by "national origin" but are not a segment of the public distinguished by "colour, race, religion, or ethnic origin."

8.   Reverse onus clauses have come under judicial review as potential violations of the presumption of innocence, which is guaranteed pursuant to section 11(d) of the Canadian Charter of Rights and Freedoms. The Court's responses to reverse onus provisions has not been uniform. In some cases the provision has been judged unconstitutional; in others its constitutional validity has been upheld.

9.   See, generally, Fish (1989), MacKay (1989), Regel (1985), Cotler (1985, 1991:249–257), Bessner (1988:183–218), Braun (1988:470–513, Borovoy (1985, 1991:243–248).

10.   The justificatory stage of Charter litigation is based upon section 1 of the Canadian Charter of Rights and Freedoms, which provides: "The Canadian Charter of Rights and Freedoms guarantees the rights and freedoms set out in it subject only to such reasonable limits prescribed by law as can be demonstrably justified in a free and democratic society."

11.   For discussion of the *Zundel* trial, see Troper (1985), Butovsky (1985), Singer-Ferris (1986), Fulford (1985), Adams (1985), Braun (1988).

12.   The matter was sent back for a retrial. On 11 May 1988, Ernst Zundel was convicted a second time in a trial before judge and jury. A second appeal to the Ontario Court of Appeal was unsuccessful but Zundel was granted leave to appeal by the Supreme Court of Canada. The Supreme Court declared section 181 unconstitutional.

13.   Such was not the view of the attorney general of Canada as intervenant. His contention was that section 13(1) did not constitute an infringement of section 2(b) of the Charter at all. The Federal Court of Appeal did not agree. Justice Mahoney noted that "there is nothing trivial, insubstantial, indirect, or unintentional in the impact of section 13(1) on freedom of expression," and thus the section "must be justified under section 1 of the Charter."

14.   Donald C. Andrews and Robert W. Smith were, respectively, the party leader and secretary of a white supremacist anti-Semitic group known as the Nationalist Party of Canada. They were charged under what is now section 319(2) of the Criminal Code with the willful promotion of hatred and were convicted in December 1985.

15.   The majority and dissent similarly differed on the validity of the reverse onus clause on the defense of "truth." The majority would have upheld it; the dissent would have found it to be an unjustifiable limitation on the presumption of innocence. The

decision in *R. v. Andrews and Smith* 61 C.C.C. (3d) 490 (S.C.C.) was identical to the *Keegstra* judgment except that the convictions were affirmed.

16.   The Supreme Court also upheld the Federal Court of Appeal decision in *Taylor and the Western Guard Party v. The Canadian Human Rights Commission* (1990) S.C.J. No. 129. Essentially, the reasoning in *Keegstra* was applied to section 13(1) of the Canadian Human Rights Act. For a comment, see D. Schneiderman, "A Review of the *Taylor* Case: Using Human Rights Legislation to Curb Racist Speech," *Constitutional Forum* 2 (1991): 90.

17.   On 1 May 1991 the minister of labour ordered an inquiry under the Individual Rights Protection Act into the cross-burning in Provost. That inquiry ordered that the Aryan Nations refrain from displaying swastikas and white power signs and from burning crosses.

18.   The New Brunswick Court of Appeal ruled that the Human Rights Commission hearing into *Ross* was lawful (*N.B. Dist. No. 15 v. N.B. Human Rights Board of Inquiry* (1989), 10 C.H.R.R. D/6426). The contention here was that the Moncton School Board, by continuing to employ Ross, engaged in a discriminatory practice even though Ross, unlike Keegstra, had not taught his anti-Semitic views in the classroom.

8

The Laws of Six Countries: An Analytical Comparison

Stephen J. Roth

The six preceding country studies have one common starting point: They all deal with countries deeply rooted in the western democratic tradition and ideology and respecting human rights and freedoms.[1] "Democratic tradition" can by now also apply to Germany: The past forty-five years were sufficient to make democracy the accepted form of social and political life in that country. The earlier, opposite experience may only have helped to strengthen an appreciation of the new ways; in any event, forty-five years is almost a matter of two generations. Absorbing the East Germans ideologically has caused some problems, but these will probably be short-lived and not beyond West Germany's political resilience to cope with.

But with the extremely significant label "western democracies"—which includes the notion of the state of law *(Rechtsstaat)* and the prevalence of the rule of law—the similarities pertinent to the subject of this volume end. In all other relevant respects the six countries display many dissimilarities.

DIFFERENCES IN LAW

Comparison of laws is always a difficult task and particularly so in regard to criminal laws (as has to be attempted in this instance). The more dissimilar the legal structures are, the more arduous the attempt. In regard to the six countries reviewed the differences are indeed powerful.

First, the six countries have different legal systems. The United Kingdom, the United States, and Canada are common law countries; Germany and France, however, are based on civil law. Israel is in a unique position of being a mixture of the two: The original basis of her legal system was common law, partly British, partly related to Ottoman law. Ottoman law has been repealed; the link with British law has been largely severed; and in their place there is now a modern statutory system, which, however, still leaves room for common law where gaps need to be filled. There is the additional influence of Jewish law, a separate legal system, some of it incorporated into modern Israeli law; how far it is also a source of interpretation of Israeli law in general is not fully resolved.

Second, four of the countries surveyed—the United States, Canada, Germany, and France—have a written constitution with normative superiority over other legal prescriptions, whereas the United Kingdom and Israel have none. All the constitutions mentioned clearly establish the freedom of expression. Other laws or judicial decisions that curtail such freedom can be challenged for their constitutionality.

A third difference arises out of the fact that three countries—Canada, Germany, and the United States—are based on a federal structure while the other three are not.[2]

Fourth, the laws curtailing freedom of speech on account of advocacy of racism are almost invariably criminal laws. Therefore, in their application it makes a difference whether the implementing criminal procedure is investigative, as in some of the countries, or accusatory, as in others.

A fifth disparity from the legal point of view is the attitude of the various countries toward international law. At issue in the present enquiry is the effect of international law on the freedom of expression. The degree to which international commitments in this regard are accepted and to which such commitments become part of domestic law has a fundamental impact on the countries' legal policies.[3] Two of these legal considerations—the constitutional and international legal aspects—will be discussed more fully in this chapter. But the short list already given shows that even from a purely legal point of view there are very considerable inherent limitations of comparison between these countries.

VARIATIONS IN POLITICAL CULTURES

Beyond the dissimilarities of the legal systems, there are historical and cultural differences between the six countries. These influence yet further their divergent response to the curbing of freedom of expression on the grounds of racist advocacy.

One of these differences is the relationship to the Nazi experience; in the countries' approach to laws against racism, this must count as probably the most potent factor. Two countries in our study, Germany and France, experienced the Nazi rule directly; this is still deeply ingrained in their national consciousness. But the impact of Nazism is even stronger in Israel, a country in which about half the population are survivors—or children of survivors—of the holocaust, while the other half completely identifies itself with that trauma. Indeed, this is so much the case that the memory of the holocaust could be described as "part of the rhythm and ritual" of Israel's public and private life and a "latent hysteria" of the nation, but one that causes "an existential sense of self-assertion in adversity" (Elon 1971:189–221). As to the other countries under review, it would appear that the memory of the holocaust plays a significant role particularly in Canada where a vocal group of survivors is bent on driving home the lessons of the past. Although they are smaller in numbers than people with similar backgrounds in the United States, they seem to be proportionately more influential.

The memory of the Nazi cataclysm is not the only burden of racism our societies have carried since the end of World War II. There emerged new developments; these, too, have appeared in different forms and with different strength in the six countries. This new manifestation of racism appears as the problem of blacks in the United States, of blacks and Asians in the United Kingdom, of North Africans in France, and of Turkish, Vietnamese, and other *Gastarbeiter* (foreign workers) and asylum-seekers in Germany. Nor has the principal motor of the holocaust, anti-Semitism, been relegated to a matter of the past; it played an important role in political awareness in the early 1960s following the worldwide campaign of swastika daubing in 1959–1960, which was the only phenomenon that affected all the countries we are surveying more or less equally—except, of course, Israel.[4] Anti-Semitism is now a problem again because of its visibly increased manifestations.

The reaction to the new racial problems is different in the various countries according to their varying political cultures. The United States regards the more conspicuous strength of ethnic groups as an expression of greater pluralism, an acceptance of being "beyond the melting pot," and feels that their greater strength makes laws for the protection of these racial groups unnecessary. In Europe, the contrary view prevails: Greater pluralism is seen as making protective laws imperative.

Indeed, in some European countries, particularly in France, racist agitation is seen as a potential threat to democracy. This is certainly not the case in the United States, not because democracy is more stable there but because of the full reliance on the power of the "free market of ideas" in which (it is held) the good is bound to win over the evil.

In his analysis of the Israeli scene in this volume, Gerald Cromer (Chapter 6) not only describes the racism of Meir Kahane as "a threat to the democratic nature of the State of Israel" but says it was "often considered to be a *danger to its very survival.*" In none of the other five countries would the issue of racism—serious though it is—be described in such terms of a threat to national existence. This view is undoubtedly exaggerated even for Israel; a more measured assessment is made by Ehud Sprinzak (1991:5), who believes that although the radical right does not pose an immediate threat to Israel's democratic system of government, "[i]t has made a significant contribution to the erosion of Israel's democratic culture and may be more damaging in the future." Both views demonstrate an extreme sensitivity in the Israeli public to the threat posed by racism to the moral basis of their state and society.

Another specific Israeli reaction is that racism is a negation of basic Jewish values.[5] It is interesting to note that similar religious considerations in regard to Christian values have hardly been voiced in the other five countries—except, of course, by church leaders. But then, these countries are politically more secular than Israel, which, although nowhere near to being a theocracy, is nevertheless strongly imbued by Jewish religious concepts (Lifshitz 1990:507–524), the more so as these are mostly indistinguishable from national concepts. The values that the other countries wish to protect against the onslaught of racist agitation are, therefore, expressed more in political or social rather than in religious terms.

THE SOCIAL AND POLITICAL BACKGROUND

Freedom of expression, more than most other rights, had a pendulum existence throughout the ages. It flourished in the democracy of ancient Greece, restricted though that democracy may have been. The *agora* and later in Rome the *forum romanum* were the original and literal "marketplace of ideas."

Subsequent periods saw freedom of expression suppressed by absolutist rulers, more than any other right—except perhaps freedom of religion (to which it is not unrelated). Parallel to the *cuius regio eius religio* system, there operated also (and for a long time) a less officially sanctioned *cuius regio eius opinio* state of affairs in which those in power imposed their standards as a rule of conduct for others.

It was the Enlightenment that challenged the rulers' monopoly on the truth. In the Anglo-American environment John Milton (through his *Aeropagitica* of 1644) and John Stuart Mill (through his essay *On Liberty* of 1859) are mainly regarded as the spiritual fathers of the new freedom of expression and particularly of the theory of the marketplace of ideas. Milton's ([1644] 1991:236, 269) declaration of faith:

For who knows not that truth is strong, next to the Almighty; she needs no policies, no stratagems, nor licensing to make her victorious. . . . Let her and Falsehood grapple; who ever knew Truth put to the worse in a free and open encounter.

and Mill's (1859:76) argument in favor of publishing even falsehood:

[T]he peculiar evil of silencing the expression of an opinion is, that it is robbing the human race . . . those who dissent from the opinion, still more than those who hold It. If the opinion is right, they are deprived of the opportunity of exchanging error for truth: if wrong, they lose the clear perception and livelier impression of truth, produced by the collision with error.

are constantly reverberating in Anglo-American theoretical writings and judicial pronouncements. But in French culture equal place will be accorded to Jean-Jacques Rousseau, the Encyclopaedists, or Voltaire; to the latter has been attributed the classic (but often misapplied) formulation of the freedom of speech: "I disapprove of what you say, but I will defend to the death your right to say it"[6] (Tallentyre 1907:199). German political thinking, on the other hand, will emphasize the pivotal role of Immanuel Kant in advancing the concept of free speech.[7]

Since Israel is one of the countries surveyed in this volume, it is appropriate to refer also to the Jewish tradition. As Judge Haim Cohn has pointed out in a masterly study, Jewish law "postulates a system of duties rather than a system of rights"; however, these duties usually imply a collateral right (Cohn 1984:18). Freedom of speech can be deduced from its restrictions in which "[t]he Bible abounds" (Cohn 1984:109). Dissenting voices were free; indeed, "the hallmark of the creation of the Oral Law [an important source of Jewish law] was doctrinal controversy" (Cohn 1984:115). Jewish sages believed in the truth-finding function of free speech long before John Milton pronounced this theory. Rabbi Judah Loew of Prague, known as the Maharal (1526–1609), said:

Even if his words spoken are directed against faith and religion, do not tell a man not to speak and suppress his words. Otherwise there will be no clarification in religious matters. On the contrary, one should tell a person to express whatever he wants . . . and he should never claim that he would have said more had he been given the opportunity. . . . Thus my opinion is contrary to what some people think. They think that when it is forbidden to speak against religion, religion is strengthened; but it is not so. The elimination of the opinions of those who are opposed to religion undermines religion and weakens it. (Cohn 1984:128)

Although their traditions and their philosophical underpinning were different, the various countries have arrived—sometimes independently, sometimes through interaction—at the same conclusion: that freedom of speech is a superior human value. It happened at different times in different countries depending on when they reached the state of democracy.

Basically, it was in the last years of the eighteenth century that the arguments of philosophers and political thinkers came to fruition. France proclaimed the freedom of speech in its "Declaration des droits de l'homme et du citoyen" (Declaration of the rights of man and citizen) in 1789.[8] The United States did it in the First Amendment to its Constitution, ratified on 15 December 1791.[9] It is significant that Britain's earlier Bill of Rights (1689) only stipulated the freedom of speech in Parliament (Article 9); in the absence of a more modern Bill of Rights (which is being increasingly demanded), the freedom of speech is not spelled out in law in Britain. It is residual; the British legal system has always operated on the principle that everything that is not specifically forbidden is free. In Germany, the republic's constitution of 1919 (the Weimar Constitution) laid down the right to freedom of expression, but it permitted restrictions by law on grounds of obscenity or protection of the youth (Article 118).[10]

Because the U.S. formulation in the First Amendment is the only one that is articulated in absolute terms, without reference to any possibility of a restriction of that right, the United States introduced restrictions through jurisprudence and did so at a relatively early stage. In 1919, when faced with the potential dangers emanating from the October Revolution in Russia and from anarchist agitation in the states, Justice Oliver Wendell Holmes, in the landmark case *Schenck v. United States* (249 U.S. 47 (1919)), developed the hallowed doctrine of "clear and present danger" as the basis on which limits on freedom of speech were permissible. A European interpretation often saw in this doctrine a serious restriction on restrictions: *Only* in the case of clear and present danger are restrictions applicable. An equally legitimate construction of the doctrine, however, is the following: *Despite* the absolute language of the First Amendment, in the right context restrictions *are* permissible. I find the second interpretation more in tune with the circumstances in which Justice Holmes's famous words were pronounced.

It is true that very soon, in a dissenting opinion in *Abrams v. United States* (250 U.S. 616 (1919)), Holmes changed his position somewhat and asserted the overwhelming benefit for society derived from the "free trade of ideas," the "competition of the market." Ever since, these doctrines have dominated American legal thinking on the issue of free speech. Yet, as we will see, it did not take long until a changing political climate made American judges more cautious about giving free range to any kind of speech.

These changes set in mainly with the rise of Nazism in Germany—not just with the actual *Machtergreifung* (seizure of power) by Hitler in 1933 but with the earlier years of insidious racist agitation on the part of the Nazis in Germany and their followers in other countries. Actually, freedom of speech was already threatened a few years before in the Soviet Union, but the world took a reasonably benevolent attitude to this "shortcoming" of the new order. Be that as it may, Nazism in Germany and the Communist tyrannical reign in the Soviet Union meant that the achievements of the Enlightenment in establishing man's right to speak his mind freely were destroyed in a large part of the world. The pendulum of freedom of speech swung again the opposite way. As Cyril Levitt demonstrates in Chapter 1 of this volume, even in pre-Hitler Germany a "legal distress" prevailed in the attempt to counteract this incipient threat to society by means of existing law; nor was there any possibility of obtaining new laws to relieve the situation, or even a favorable interpretation of the inadequate laws on the statute book.

The United Kingdom was one of the few countries that realized the need to adopt new measures against the increasing danger created by Mosley's Union of Fascists. Yet the United Kingdom acted only through the adoption of the Public Order Act 1936, which regulated mainly public meetings and processions, banning the wearing of uniforms with political connotations and the like. Words or behavior of a threatening, abusive, or insulting character were outlawed only if they were uttered at a public meeting and if they threatened a breach of the peace. (See Chapter 3 by Avrom Sherr on the United Kingdom.) Divorced of its motivation and objectives, the 1936 Act would appear as a run of the mill, public order law of no anti-racist nexus. The word "race" (or for that matter, "religion") does not appear in the law at all. During the debate in

Parliament, attempts to make it an offense to use insulting words or behavior to incite racial or religious prejudice, failed (Lester and Bindman 1972:359, n.32).

A few years later, in 1939, France introduced its first group libel law, which was clearly for the protection of persons belonging to a racial group. However, as Roger Errera explains in Chapter 2, it was an unsatisfactory law and, mainly, it came too late.

Otherwise, there hardly existed any anti-racist legislation anywhere during the entire period of the Nazis' racist agitation prior to coming to power and while in power.[11]

The events in Europe, with their echoes beyond the seas, must have conditioned the thinking of the U.S. Supreme Court when in 1942, in *Chaplinsky v. New Hampshire* (315 U.S. 568, 571–572 (1942)), it established the "fighting words" doctrine, by which "insulting or 'fighting' words—those which by their very utterances inflict injury or tend to incite an immediate breach of the peace" need not be protected because they are "of such slight social value" that they are "clearly outweighed by the social interest in order and morality." This kind of approach still prevailed ten years later in *Beauharnais v. Illinois* (343 U.S. 250 (1952)), in which the Supreme Court upheld an Illinois group libel statute that banned publication or exhibition of material which inter alia "exposes the citizens of any race, color, creed or religion to contempt, derision, or obloquy or which is productive of breach of the peace or riots" (Illinois Criminal Code, Ill. Rev. Stat., 2242, 1949, c. 38. Div. 1, 471). The Supreme Court has actually never overruled *Beauharnais,* yet a widely accepted view regards it as no longer good law (Kretzmer 1987:446, 449–450).

The subsequent change in the United States toward a much more liberal attitude to speech—even offensive, or defamatory or fighting speech—again coincided with new political and social events: the emergence of the civil rights movement and the anti–Vietnam War demonstrations. The Supreme Court became less and less willing to curb free expression[12] lest it lead to the "slippery slope."

Bollinger (1986:34) summarizes these arguments as they were advanced later in the Skokie case:[13] "to permit this [deeply offensive] speech to be restricted, would jeopardise the entire structure of free speech rights that had been erected . . . [t]o permit . . . to ban this speech because of its offensiveness would mean that Southern whites could ban civil rights marches by blacks." Skokie became the culmination point of the pro–free speech trend.

These developments are well described in Chapter 5 by Donald Downs in this volume. He, too, asserts that "the development of modern free speech doctrine in the United States is an offshoot of the civil rights movement itself."[14] What needs to be highlighted is the fact that Europe (and even Canada) remained unaffected by the civil rights movement and the Vietnam War. Their parallel experiences were the swastika-daubing epidemics in the winter of 1959–1960, the consequent realization that anti-Semitism had not died with Hitler, and the fact that a new race relations problem (not restricted to Jews) was *ante portas*.

The anti-racist laws surveyed in this volume—United Kingdom 1965, France 1972, amendments of the German Penal Code in 1960 and again in the 1970s, the Cohen Committee on Hate Propaganda in Canada in 1966 and the subsequent introduction of the hate speech crime into the Canadian Criminal Code in 1970—all show the concurrence of political events and legal developments. The picture is sharpened by the international scene, the adoption by the United Nations of the Covenant on Civil and Political Rights and of the Convention on Race Discrimination in 1966 and 1965 respectively, with their anti-racist provisions.

The only exception is Israel: It is a latecomer to the anti-racism legislation scene (1980s). But its specific problem of racist agitation is a consequence of the Arab-Israel conflict, from which the phenomenon of racism emerged only gradually after the 1967 war.

It is of course natural, and indeed expected, that *legislators* should respond to events (as well as make them happen). One feels less comfortable with the thought—as is the case in the United States—that the *judiciary* should be so much conditioned by the flow of outside developments. But in the particular case where the essence of the judge's decision is to establish the proper equilibrium between the value of free speech, on the one hand, and that of social harmony and protection of the rights and dignity of minorities, on the other, judicial decisions must also be influenced by societal conditions; this is because the relative value of the "values" changes as the mores and perceptions of society change. Thus, we see legal and sociopolitical issues developing on parallel lines, and one cannot evaluate and compare laws in different countries and at different times without having the social context and background in equally sharp focus.

A noteworthy feature of this picture is that the United States could remain relatively unaffected by the stirrings in other parts of the world and could react almost exclusively to domestic events. No doubt it requires the position of a dominating great power to be able largely to ignore the international process. This is manifested in the fact that out of the seventy-two universal and regional human rights instruments,[15] the United States has so far ratified only twelve, and some with very restrictive reservations. The most important one, the UN Covenant on Civil and

Political Rights,[16] was ratified only in June 1992, again with extensive reservations. The first of these relates to the provision on incitement to racial hatred.[17] Another ratified instrument that is relevant to this study is the UN Convention on the Prevention of Punishment of the Crime of Genocide.[18] But the United States has not ratified the UN Convention on the Elimination of All Forms of Racial Discrimination.[19] As a result we have, in regard to straight incitement or group libel laws, a situation of "United States v. the rest of the world,"[20] and this is not only true of the legal position but also of public opinion. Few things would illustrate this more than the fact that the American Civil Liberties Union supported the right of the American Nazi Party to march through the predominantly Jewish town of Skokie, while their opposite number in Britain, the National Council of Civil Liberties (NCCL), has refused to support the right of the racist British National Front to organize marches. The NCCL's Draft of Bill of Rights, released in 1991 under the title "A People's Charter," explicitly limits (under its Article 10) the freedom of information and expression "to prevent incitement to racial hatred."

Yet the American scene is not entirely blank. One of the merits of Donald Downs's chapter is that it shows that—particularly lately—the United States has increasingly adopted speech-related or racism-related measures in response to its own problem of racism. As he explains, some of these measures deal with "performative" speech (i.e., speech integrally involved in an illegal action), others with intimidation and harassment in a close target context (like the workplace or the campus), while some are "enhancement" statutes that make a racist or similar context or motivation an aggravating circumstance in conventional crimes.

These are useful but rather limited measures in attempting to curb racial incitement. They are not really on the same level as the laws existing in the other five countries. In turning now to a legal comparison of the laws, I therefore have to limit myself to a comparison between the other five countries.

THE IMPACT OF A CONSTITUTION

The oldest of the constitutional rules affecting freedom of expression is undoubtedly the First Amendment to the United States Constitution, ratified on 15 December 1791 (see Note 8). All legal norms must conform to the provisions of the Constitution, and the Supreme Court strikes down any legal enactment that does not comply with this test. The difficulties described earlier in curbing free speech in the United States on grounds of racist content are due to this constitutional bar or, more precisely, to its interpretation by the U.S. Supreme Court.

I have called the U.S. constitutional rule the oldest, but this is only due to the fact that the United States has not changed the First Amendment provision since its adoption. France's constitutional rule on freedom of speech, as entrenched in the Declaration of the Rights of Man and Citizen, is actually two years older (1789). However, since then France has changed its constitution repeatedly. Yet it reaffirmed the constitutional force of the "Declaration" by referring to it in the new constitutions.[21]

Germany's Basic Law of 23 May 1949 has four relevant provisions, of which one (Article 18) on the possible forfeiture of basic rights is paraphrased in Juliane Wetzel's chapter on Germany in this volume (Chapter 4). The other three are Article 5 on Freedom of Opinion, the prime focus of our study; Article 9 on associations; and Article 21 on parties.[22]

In Canada, the Charter of Rights and Freedoms, which has constitutional force, stipulates the freedom of expression, as reproduced in this volume in Bruce Elman's chapter on Canada (Chapter 7).

As mentioned, in countries with a constitution, legal provisions can usually be challenged for their conformity with the constitution.[23] However, to the best of my knowledge, in France the provisions outlawing racist incitement have never so been contested. But in Germany there were two instances. A member of the Action Front of the National Socialists (ANS), convicted for participating in neo-Nazi activities that were considered an incitement to race hatred, challenged the respective law before the Federal Constitutional Court in Karlsruhe. However, the Court's committee on preliminary examination denied admissibility of the complaint of unconstitutionality as having no prospect of success.[24] The same was the result of the complaint of the well-known right-radical leader Michael Kühnen regarding his conviction for distributing neo-Nazi literature.[25]

A more significant but also unsuccessful challenge was made in Canada in the *Keegstra* case; it is fully described in this volume's chapter on Canada. *Keegstra* must be regarded as a landmark case on the justification to curtail freedom of expression on account of racist agitation, with a significance far beyond Canadian jurisdiction, because of the brilliantly argued judgment by the (then) Chief Justice of Canada, Brian Dickson.

In the United States, the Supreme Court has, of course, consistently been seized with the question of the constitutionality or otherwise of free speech restrictions. All the cases quoted in this study were challenges to constitutionality.

In the United Kingdom, because of the absence of a constitution, laws cannot be challenged before or by the courts. The principle of the sovereignty of Parliament means that only the elected legislators can decide on the laws; and they do not authorize the unelected judiciary to overrule their decisions, as is the case in constitutional jurisdictions. On this point, Avrom Sherr makes an interesting comment in Chapter 3 on the United Kingdom: Because, in the absence of constitutional checks, it is possible to apply greater limitations on the freedom of speech, this may induce prosecution authorities to exercise checks through limiting the number of prosecutions. In fact, he suggests that this factor is "overplayed" in the United Kingdom.[26]

The position is more complicated in Israel. Unable to agree on a fully fledged constitutional document, the Israeli Knesset decided in 1950 on the drafting of a number of so-called Basic Laws that would become chapters of the constitution, if and when it will be drafted. Eleven such Basic Laws have since been enacted.[27] They have an entrenched status similar to a constitution, and primary legislation can be reviewed by the Supreme Court as to whether it is in conflict with a Basic Law. Of the Basic Laws that have been so far adopted, only one—"Basic Law: The Knesset"—is relevant to the subjects discussed in this volume. Its section 7A excludes from the right to participate in Knesset elections, inter alia, a list of candidates who in their aims or actions express or imply "incitement to racism." ("Basic Law: Human Dignity and Freedom" does not deal with the freedom of expression.)[28]

However, even where constitutions do exist and guarantee the freedom of speech, there can be significant differences. The Canadian, French, and German constitutional provisions, in postulating freedom of speech, also contain a balancing proviso: They *permit* restrictions, though at the same time they *restrict* the restrictions.[29] The First Amendment to the U.S. Constitution envisages no restrictions at all. It is not suggested that because the American formulation sounds like an absolute guarantee, the American courts treat it in that absolute sense. The American courts, too, have taken competing values into account and tried to balance them. Nevertheless, one cannot ignore the persuasive influence of language.

RELATIONS TO INTERNATIONAL LAW

Only two of the six country studies in this volume refer to this aspect—and only marginally (Roger Errera's Chapter 2 and Avrom Sherr's Chapter 3). Therefore, it seems essential to look, in this overview, into the commitments regarding hate-speech legislation accepted by the six countries through international instruments.

There are two principal international treaties relating to the subject: (1) the International Covenant on Civil and Political Rights (1966); its Article 20(2) outlaws advocacy of national, racial, and religious hatred that constitutes incitement to discrimination, hostility, or violence;[30] (2) the Convention on the Elimination of All Forms of Racial Discrimination (1965); its Article 4 prohibits dissemination of ideas based on racial superiority or hatred and incitement to racial discrimination or violence.[31]

All the surveyed countries have ratified the Civil and Political Rights Covenant, whereas the Race Discrimination Convention has been ratified by only five of them, the United States being the exception. However, some of these ratifications are practically meaningless in relation to the hate-speech clauses of the instruments in view of the reservations made on these clauses. The reservations mean, in other words, that the commitments in regard to hate-speech inherent in the respective instruments were not accepted, or not without qualification, by the nation-state making the reservation.

Reference was made earlier to the reservation that the United States has made to the Civil and Political Rights Covenant on its most recent ratification. Although it has not ratified the Race Discrimination Convention, nevertheless the United States has made the following declaration:

The Constitution of the United States contains provisions for the protection of individual rights, such as the right of free speech, and nothing in the Convention shall be deemed to require or authorize legislation or other action by the United States of America incompatible with the provisions of the Constitution of the United States of America.[32]

France and the United Kingdom similarly made reservations or declarations on both instruments.[33]

The position is more complicated with the European Convention on Human Rights,[34] to which three of the countries surveyed—the United Kingdom, Germany, and France—are parties. The Convention contains no explicit provision against racist propaganda, and consequently one has to rely on the general restriction clauses of the Convention.[35] Fortunately, the jurisprudence of the European Commission and Court of Human Rights comes to our aid; it made it abundantly clear that racist incitement is not protected by the freedom of information, because it conflicts with the rights and freedoms of others.

There are three relevant cases that were brought before the European organs in relation to the European countries included in our study.

In *X. v. Federal Republic of Germany*, the applicants complained against a judicial decision forbidding them to exhibit brochures alleging that the murder of millions of Jews under the Third Reich was a lie or a piece of Zionist trickery. The European Commission held that the protection of the reputation of others justified the German judicial restriction. It stated, inter alia: "The protection of these principles may be especially indicated vis-à-vis groups which have historically suffered from discrimination" (No. 9235/81, 16 July 1982, D. & R. 29, 194).

A second case, also relating to Germany, is *Michael Kühnen v. the Federal Republic of Germany*. Kühnen, a leader of the Action Front of the National Socialists (ANS), an organization attempting to reinstitute the National Socialist Party (NSDAP), complained about his conviction for preparing and disseminating publications which, in the finding of the German Court that had convicted him, "aimed at impairing the basic order of freedom and democracy" and "could revive antisemitic sentiments, inter alia, as they depreciated Zionism and emphasized pride of race." The Commission agreed with these findings, ruled that the applicant wanted to use the freedom of expression contrary to the democratic spirit of the European Convention, and, if permitted, would contribute to the destruction of the rights and freedoms of others; for these reasons, it declared the application inadmissible (No. 12194/86, 11 April 1986, decision 12 May 1988).

A third relevant case regarding a country surveyed in this study is *M. Lowes v. United Kingdom*, the application of a prisoner who saw his right to receive information violated because the prison authorities refused to let him receive an issue of "Gothic Ripples," an anti-Semitic publication, as it would present "a threat to good order and discipline." The European Commission agreed with the view of the British authorities and declared this application, too, inadmissible (No. 13214/87, 9 December 1989).

There are additional cases on the issue of racism relating to European countries not covered in this volume.[36] They are nevertheless pertinent to our study, as they establish the proper interpretation of the provisions of the European Convention.

The (UN) Human Rights Committee, which is established by the Civil and Political Rights Covenant for its implementation, has also considered two individual cases relating to racism; these were submitted to it under its procedure for individual petitions. One is highly relevant because it relates to one of the countries under review—Canada. The treatment of this case on the domestic level is mentioned in Chapter 7 of this volume, but the international follow-up is not described there. It is the case of John Ross Taylor and the Western Guard Party, an anti-Semitic group and its leader, who were engaged in a campaign of communicating hate messages by phone. Having been convicted by Canadian courts and having lost the challenge against the constitutionality of the domestic legal provisions, Taylor and the Party took the matter to the Human Rights Committee, claiming infringement by the Canadian authorities of their rights under the Covenant.[37] The Committee rejected the claim on procedural grounds but at the same time declared that "the opinions which Mr. T. seems to disseminate through the telephone system clearly constitute the advocacy of racial or religious hatred which Canada has an obligation under Article 20(2) of the Covenant to prohibit."[38]

The other case relates to Italy, a country not surveyed in this volume, yet it is important as an interpretation of the Covenant's general restriction clause on actions aimed at the destruction of human rights. The author of the complaint was convicted in Italy for involvement in reorganizing the dissolved Fascist Party. The Committee, which declared this communication also to be inadmissible, stated that "the acts of which M.A. was convicted . . . were of a kind which are removed from the protection of the Covenant by Article 5 thereof and which were in any event justifiably prohibited by Italian law.[39]

One has to consider as well the most recent international regulation of the subject, which, although not legally binding, has considerable political and moral force. It is contained in the agreement by the Conference on Security and Cooperation in Europe (CSCE, also known as the Helsinki Process); it is significant because in this instance the United States is also committed to it (as are all the other countries surveyed in this volume with the exception of Israel, which is not a participant in the CSCE). In June 1990, at its Copenhagen meeting, the CSCE strongly condemned racial and ethnic hatred, and the then thirty-five participating states committed themselves to take the necessary measures to provide protection against incitement to violence based on national, racial, ethnic, or religious grounds.[40] This was subsequently confirmed in the CSCE's Paris Charter in November 1990, a document signed by the heads of state or government of all the participating states[41] and in the Report of the CSCE Geneva Meeting in July 1991.[42]

A historic aspect of the CSCE provisions is that they specifically mention anti-Semitism—the first international instruments to do so.[43]

On the other hand, the CSCE provisions are weaker than those of the other international instruments; they speak only of incitement to violence, not of incitement to discrimination or hostility.[44] This is due to the fact that as the CSCE is operating by consensus, the provisions they adopt require the agreement of the United States as well, and as has been explained earlier, the Americans do not accept speech-crime, except when it is closely linked to an action like violence.

Let me sum up the international legal position: The preceding description clearly indicates that under certain conditions and with proper safeguards, the international community regards the restriction of freedom of expression on account of extremist racist speech as justified.[45] Most countries in the world, certainly those in Europe, follow that international approach. The laws in five countries discussed in this volume are telling proof. The United States, with its contrary view, stands virtually in splendid isolation. In the light of the widespread anti-restriction attitude in the United States—among politicians, the academic community, and the public at large—one must accept that this stand probably satisfies the needs of American society. The chilling effect of the American attitude— directly and via international law—on developments in other countries, where society still badly needs legislation against racist speech, is a different matter, however; it is one that, I feel, has not received sufficient consideration in the United States.

A COMPARISON OF PRESENT LEGISLATION

A meaningful comparison of legislation against incitement to racism can be made only in five of the six countries discussed in this volume. Even so, to compare among the five is not easy. We can approximate it best by breaking the norms on hate-speech offenses down to their individual elements, realizing full well that the comparison will inevitably be somewhat schematic and cannot deal with all the fine nuances.

Forms of Expression

The laws of all five countries cover oral and written expressions of racism, in the widest sense of the terms, including all sorts of pictorial representations by way of paintings, photographs, engravings, signs, posters, and the like—"all visible means," according to the Canadian definition.

Oral utterances must generally be made in public places or at public meetings. However, the Canadian law goes further by covering any communication "other than in private conversation" (provided that it is made with the intention to promote hatred); according to British law, utterances in private places (except in dwellings) may constitute an offense.

Written material must generally be sold or distributed to the public, but in Britain it suffices "to a section of the public" and in Israel "to a number of persons." In France, it must be sold or distributed at public places or meetings.

Pictorial representations, if displayed, must be "exposed to public view" (France) or generally accessible to the public.

Some of the laws cover explicitly the modern techniques of communication. In addition to "telephone, broadcasting, and other audible and visible means" (Canada), all "mechanical means" (Israel), and any other "oral medium" ("*support de la parole*") (France), the Canadian law adds the phrase, "recorded electronically or electromagnetically."

The British law extends the media of expression to performance of plays.

British and Canadian law go beyond "expressions" inasmuch as they also forbid objectionable "behaviour" (Britain) or "gestures" (Canada). U.S. jurisprudence regards "behavior" as a form of protected expression. German law has another useful provision: It specifically criminalizes the offering or making available or accessible of inciting material to youth under eighteen years of age.

Manner of Expression

British law alone stipulates the manner of expression as an essential element of the offense: It must be "threatening, abusive or insulting." This may be due to the fact that in the British concept the offense of racist incitement is as much a matter of "breach of the peace" as of racism. The addition of these words may mean that racist propaganda produced in more subtle and less strident style—for instance, in pseudoscientific or pseudo-intellectual terms—may escape prosecution. In a white paper of 1975, the British government had this to say:

[D]uring the past decade, probably largely as a result of Section 6 [of the Race Relations Act 1965], there has been a decided change in the style of racialist propaganda. It tends to be less blatantly bigoted, to disclaim any intention of stirring up racial hatred, and to purport to make a contribution to public education and debate. Whilst shift away from crudely racialist propaganda and abuse is welcome, it is not an unmixed benefit. The more apparently rational and moderate is the message, the greater is its probable impact on public opinion.[46]

Actually, the requirement of "threatening, abusive or insulting" words adds a qualification that goes beyond the international prescription laid down in Article 4(a) of the Race Discrimination Convention (see Note 31 at the end of this chapter) and was therefore criticized in the United Nations Committee on the Elimination of Racial Discrimination.[47]

Grounds of Incitement: The Target Groups

The grounds on which incitement to hatred is outlawed are usually color, race, religion, ethnic origin, and national origin. However, there are variations in the laws of the five countries. Some are of minor significance: Israel uses the combination "national-ethnic origin"; Canada does not include "national origin"; France omits "color"; Britain includes—in addition to "national origin"—"nationality (including citizenship)." French law specifies that not only the "belonging" to any such group but also "non-belonging" must not be grounds for incitement. A much more significant difference is, however, that Israel and Britain (but not Northern Ireland) exclude "religion" from the grounds of incitement. The reasons for this are obviously different in the two countries.

Gerald Cromer's chapter on Israel in this volume does not say much on this point. Other excellent studies on the Israeli law—by M. Tabory (1987), D. Kretzmer (1988; 1991), and A. Shapira (1986; 1987)—also fail to explain the reasons fully. However, they draw attention to the fact that a protection clause regarding religion exists in Israel's Defamation Law 1965 in regard to any person or group of persons brought "into disrepute because of his origin or *religion*" (emphasis added).[48] But the omission can be understood by the extreme sensitivity of Israel's public and body politic on the subject of religion. When the bill on incitement was originally introduced in April 1985, its definition of racism included "religion" (Tabory 1987:275–276; Shapira 1986:9–10), but "[v]arious religious groups voiced grave apprehension that the bill as drafted might be interpreted as attaching a stigma of criminality to certain religious teachings" (Shapira 1986:9–10).

Obviously, religion has been omitted from the relevant British law for other reasons. One is the different nature of the belonging to a racial or religious group that was referred to during the parliamentary debates. As stated by Lester and Bindman (1972:363),

Membership of a religious group involves personal choice, and religious beliefs and practices are as much the subject of public controversy as political opinions; membership of a racial group involves inherited and immutable physical characteristics, and is not directly relevant to controversial beliefs, ideas or behaviour. A racial attack is therefore a more fundamental assault upon a person's humanity than an attack upon his religion.

Yet the authors do not accept this distinction as justifying the exclusion of "propaganda deliberately disseminated so as to whip up religious hatred" (1972:363).

The main reason for the exclusion of religion from the British legislation on hate-speech was, however, the contention that there was no societal need for legislating against religious incitement (or, for that matter, discrimination). The Law Commission expressed this strongly in its Working Paper No. 79 when it advised against extending the grounds of protection to religion.

> We do not think that such an amendment would help in the present context. We have already stated that in our view there is no parallel in England and Wales between the social pressures on racial groups which gave rise to the necessity, as the Government saw it, of introducing section 5A [into the Public Order Act 1936], and the present situation in regard to religious worship. There seems to us to be little call for such an offence at present, and as we have pointed out, the creation of new offences of this kind for which there is no demonstrable need often focuses attention upon them and may even provoke unlooked for trouble.[49]

The Law Commission's view was shared by the British government. But this exclusion of religion does not apply to Northern Ireland where, it was felt, evidence exists of attempts to stir up hatred on the grounds of religion. Section 1 of the Prevention of Incitement to Hatred Act (Northern Ireland) 1970 establishes roughly the same offenses as the corresponding English Acts, except that they apply to incitement "on grounds of *religious belief*, colour, race or ethnic or national origins" (emphasis added).

The Prohibited Acts

The legislation of all countries surveyed makes it a punishable offense "to incite." British legislation uses the term "to stir up," and the Canadian law the equivalent term "promote" (or *fomenter* in the French version of the law). French and German law also cover "defamation";[50] German legislation identifies some other acts, notably those that are "insulting," "maliciously ridiculing," or "attacks on human dignity." German law also makes it an offense to "portray brutal or other inhuman acts of violence against people in such a way as to glorify [*Verherrlichung*] or seek to minimize [*Verharmlosung*] such acts of violence, or which represent brutal or inhuman events in a fashion which violates human dignity."[51]

The Effect of the Prohibited Acts

All the laws refer to actions that aim at or result in "hatred," but the French law also adds "discrimination" or "violence" as alternatives—thus following exactly the language of the Civil and Political Rights Covenant. Canadian legislation deals with incitement to discrimination not in the Criminal Code (where incitement to hatred is established) but in the Canadian Human Rights Act.[52] Israeli law lists a number of possible effects of the incriminating act: "persecution, humiliation, vilification, the display of enmity, hostility or violence, or the causing of animosity."

The nature of the "effect" is one of the aspects of the incitement issue on which the American approach differs so much from that of the other countries. The jurisprudence of the Supreme Court, as explained earlier, would only curtail incitement to a concrete (and unjustifiable) *action*, like violence, and not to creating a *state of mind*, like hatred or hostility.

The Subjective and the Objective Element

The only legislation that makes neither a specific subjective element (like intention or mens rea) nor a clearly defined objective element (like the result of "hatred" of "breach of the peace") a condition of the offense is that of France. Germany does not require the subjective "intent" either, but (in some instances) the incriminating act must have objective consequences, that is, be "liable . . . to disturb the public peace."

The Israeli law takes quite the opposite approach. The objective element is explicitly excluded from the conditions of the offense ("it shall be immaterial whether or not the publication leads to racism"), but it demands a high degree of mens rea: The act must have been committed "with the purpose . . ." Tabory points out that by using the term "purpose" (*matara*) rather than the more usual "intent" (*kavana*), the Israeli legislation may have demanded, or the courts may interpret it to have demanded, a "specially high level of mens rea," higher than is assumed with the general notion of intent.[53] It is paradoxical that although Jewish organizations in many countries urge that the condition of intent be dropped from anti-racist legislation (because the difficulty of proving intent often makes the laws unworkable), Israel has opted on this very subject for the requirement of such a high degree of intent. It is a strong indication of the innate dislike of Israeli society to curb free speech.

The most interesting is the situation in Canada and Great Britain. Here the subjective and objective requirements are *alternatives*: either the offending act must have been committed with intent (in the Canadian wording, "wilfully")[54]—in which case no further consequence is required—or the act must objectively "be likely" to lead to the stirring up of racial hatred (Britain) or to a breach of the peace (Canada)—in which case no subjective intention need be proved. In Britain this is clearly a compromise solution after legislators tried to make the subjective element a necessary ingredient of the offense (as in the Race Relations Act 1965) and then gave it up altogether (as in the Race Relations Act 1976). These changes in Britain—and their causes—are well described by Avrom Sherr in Chapter 3 of this volume. (See also Roth 1991b). Canadian legislators must have benefited from the British experience.

The objective criterion raises another problem: What is "likely"? Generally, it is assumed that likelihood means that more speaks for the occurrence of an event than against. But there are other issues. How *direct* must be the consequences, and how *immediate*? In the "clear and present danger" concept of the American jurisprudence, the word "present" surely suggests immediacy. The importance of immediacy in the American approach is best illustrated in the definition clause of the Genocide Convention Implementation Act 1988 (the Proxmire Act); paragraph 1093(3) uses it twice in one sentence: "the term 'incites' means to urge another to engage *imminently* in conduct in circumstances under which there is a substantial likelihood of *imminently* causing such conduct" (emphasis added) (see LeBlanc 1991:147–148).

The opposite extreme can be found in the Prevention of Incitement to Hatred Act (Northern Ireland) 1970 S.2 and the Public Order (Northern Ireland) Order 1981 S.14, where it is declared an offense to provoke, with intent, a breach of the peace "whether *immediately or at any time thereafter*" (emphasis added).

Another question: Does the "breach of the peace" requirement make the offense dependent on the audience's reaction? Does it create a "heckler's veto"? Does it mean that meek audiences, which do not fight back, are not afforded protection? These questions were left in each country for the judges to decide; none of the laws answer them unequivocally.

Procedures

An important procedural aspect of the legislation on the offense of incitement is the restriction in some countries on the right to initiate a prosecution. Such restrictions serve as a safeguard against oppressive, vexatious, or counterproductive prosecutions and are, at the same time, a concession to the libertarian opposition to the offense. Thus, the consent of the attorney general is required in Canada,[55] in Israel, and in Britain.

Critics of the present operation of the law (e.g., in Britain) claim that this procedural restriction impairs the effectiveness of the law. But one also hears an American view: The provision "is regarded as the greater protection to freedom of speech, since the Attorney General generally will be more sensitive to free speech than the police" (Delgado 1991:343, 366, n. 186).

The law in France and in Germany is much more complex. Here the power to institute proceedings for the offense of hate-mongering or allied offenses is specially extended. In France, certain anti-racist or human rights associations may start proceedings. (This power was extended further in 1983, 1985, and 1990 to specified types of associations and in regard to specific offenses; see Chapter 2 by Roger Errera). Moreover, the associations can assume the role of a civil party (*partie civile*) and can claim damages. In Germany, the position is in a sense the reverse: It is not the right of the aggrieved private parties that is extended, but that of the prosecution authorities, who are entitled, indeed enjoined, to start proceedings ex officio (*Strafantrag von Amts wegen*) in cases of defamation related to the Nazi past (see Chapter 4 by Juliane Wetzel).

It should further be added that in Israel, under the Defamation Law of 1965, which covers any material that "may bring a person into disrepute because of his origin or religion," any person or group of persons may sue and do not require the consent of the attorney general.

Defenses

In each jurisdiction defenses against the criminal charge are naturally available and in this, too, there are national differences. Although it is by no means unimportant, I will have to ignore this aspect of the comparative analysis owing to constraints of space.

Allied Offenses

Possession of Racially Inflammatory Material. This is an offense in Britain, in Israel, and in Germany ("keeps in stock" or "stores"), but not in the other countries.

Dissemination of Ideas Based on Racial Superiority. Based on the provision in Article 4 of the Race Discrimination Convention (see Note 31 at the end of this chapter), such dissemination ("propagation of ideas or theories") is made an offense in France (Article 9 of the Law of 1972). The other countries all fall short on this point.

Distribution of Racist Material to Youth. Special protective measures in regard to keeping racist material from youth are included in the French and German legislation. (It is allied to legislation regarding pornographic material or material glorifying violence.)

Group Libel: Defamation

Articles 3 and 4 of the French Law of 1972 make "defamation" or "insult when it has not been preceded by provocations" both a punishable offense and the basis of a civil rights claim for damages by the injured party or by appropriate anti-racist organizations.

In Germany, defamation is regulated by Article 185 of the Penal Code as a matter of criminal law; according to Article 194, special procedural rules apply if the defamation relates to the Nazi past.

In Israel, the general rules on defamation also apply to group libel; however, they were not considered adequate to meet the challenge of racism as presented by the Kahane phenomenon (Kretzmer 1991:5–6).

Revisionism: Denial of the Holocaust

As described in the various country chapters, the denial of the holocaust has become one of the most potent and most frequent manifestations of one form of racism—anti-Semitism. Yet legislation against it is sparse and weak.

Admittedly, this is a complex problem from a legal point of view whenever revisionism does not assume the form of direct incitement against Jews. (Such direct incitement must be seen, for instance, if denial statements not only allege that the holocaust is not true but add that it is a Jewish or Zionist swindle, invented for ulterior motives like extracting compensation money.) It is far beyond the confines of this chapter to discuss this problem. For studies on the legal aspect of holocaust denial, see Roth 1982 and Stein 1986:277–323.[56] I limit myself here to describing the legislation in the six countries surveyed.

Three countries have focused on holocaust denial in their legislation. France dealt with it in a fairly simple way: The contestation of the existence (*contester l'existence*) of clearly defined crimes against humanity is a punishable offense. The definition of the crimes is rather restrictive but the principle is clear.[57]

In Israel the "Denial of Holocaust (Prohibition) Law 5746-1986"[58] similarly outlaws the "denying or diminishing the proportion" of "crimes against the Jewish people or crimes against humanity," if done "with intent to defend the perpetrators of those acts or to express sympathy or identification with them." Also outlawed are statements that are positive toward such acts ("expressing praise or sympathy for or identification with . . .").

The German legal position is complex and unsatisfactory. Following a lengthy political debate, which is fully described in this volume's chapter on Germany, all that could be achieved was a provision (Article 194 of the Criminal Code) that makes "insult" an official delict if the insulted person or his descendant was a victim of persecution by Nazism (or by another terror regime) and the insult is connected with that persecution; this means that such a delict has to be prosecuted ex officio and not only on petition of the aggrieved party (see Chapter 4 by Juliane Wetzel in this volume and also Stein 1986).

The denial of the holocaust is sometimes attacked under provisions regarding spreading of falsehood with intention to cause injury or distress. This happened in the case against Ernst Zundel in Canada based on section 181 of the Criminal Code.[59] It is described in detail in Bruce Elman's chapter on Canada. The case is of considerable significance since Canada has lately become a proactive center of the production of holocaust-denial literature. On 27 August 1992 the Supreme Court of Canada, in a 4:3 decision, found that section 181 is too vague, possibly chilling legitimate forms of speech, and serves no objective of pressing and substantial concern. For all these reasons, the Court declared the provision unconstitutional. Zundel was acquitted.

In Britain a recent law—the Malicious Communications Act 1988 (which is not mentioned in Avrom Sherr's chapter)—may open some possibilities.[60] It has not yet been tested in regard to holocaust denial. Neither the Canadian nor the British provision refer to race, religion, and the like in any way. This makes their application to cases of holocaust denial more difficult. The Board of Deputies of British Jews has asked for an amendment to the British clause that would make it clear that the term "grossly offensive" also relates to material that is grossly offensive to the recipient on account of his belonging to a racial, ethnic, or similar group.

One must also bear in mind that any proceedings based on "false news" invite the defense of "truth." Although there is no danger that this defense could succeed in the case of a holocaust denial, the discussion and adjudication of historical facts in a public trial—for which judges are not qualified—is something that may not best serve the objectives such a law aims to attain. In his chapter on France—a country that has adopted an anti-revisionist provision—Roger Errera clearly expresses great doubts on this score.[61]

CONCLUDING REMARKS

The comparison of the laws is enlightening, but is it also instructive? Can we deduce from it which law, which formulation is better and more appropriate to curb racial incitement effectively without unduly harming that other important value, freedom of expression?

One would require a much more detailed analysis of the components of the various laws in order to make a definite assessment. Such an analysis could not be purely abstract; one would have to look at the data of the concrete number and the outcome of prosecutions. Even this would be of limited value, because the efficacy of the various laws is not dependent solely on their wording but much more on the sociopolitical conditions of the country in which the law operates.

Canadian Chief Justice Dickson correctly pointed out this limitation of comparisons in the judgment of the *Keegstra* case when, after analyzing U.S. jurisprudence, he added:

Canada and the United States are not alike in every way, nor have the documents entrenching human rights in our two countries arisen in the same context. It is only common sense to recognise that, just as the similarities will justify borrowing from the American experience, differences may require that Canada's constitutional vision depart from that endorsed in the United States.[62]

However, apart from the number of prosecutions and convictions, there is another, nonmeasurable aspect of the efficacy of the various laws: their educative and preventive force, their value in stigmatizing racist behavior. Would there be more racist agitation if the parliaments of the various countries had not declared racism to be beyond the pale? Would it, without such condemnation, be taken up also by more sober people (and not just the lunatic fringe) who might express their message in more moderate terms, thereby producing a more dangerous echo? It is impossible to tell.

Some of the country rapporteurs provide an insight into the reactions in their country, or at least their own personal reactions. They mostly emphasize the great difficulties of implementation, yet they all consider the availability of the law to fight racism—be it only for its symbolic value—

as important. For Germany, renewed objections by civil libertarians are reported. In Canada the scenario seems to be similar, although it is played out through or around a number of widely publicized court cases. In France, Israel, and Britain the debates are not on the question of *whether* there should be laws restricting dangerous speech but *how* to fashion the laws best. France has amended them as recently as 1990, and in Britain there are increasing demands for changes.[63]

The United States is, of course, a case of its own. The debate on the desirability or legitimacy of restrictive legislation has really never ceased there. Public and legal opinion overwhelmingly side with the protagonists of a strong First Amendment policy. But social realities increasingly force even the United States to consider employing legal instruments in the fight against racism, which, so far, it has done by applying subsidiary or ancillary solutions.

I myself have never entertained any doubts that the defense of democracy, of racial harmony, and of the rights and dignity of fellow human beings belonging to minority groups make it imperative to place some fetters on offensive and dangerous speech, as well as action. In the shadow of Weimar, and even more in the shadow of the holocaust, we must understand "clear and present danger" differently from before and must act on the realization that words in themselves can create danger, or certainly are the beginning of a danger. As to the conflicting values that are apparently hurt by speech restrictions, I can do no better in closing my contribution to this volume than by quoting once again the elegant words of the former Canadian Chief Justice Dickson. These words were expressed about Canadians, but they are true of all of us:

Indeed, one may plausibly contend that it is through rejecting hate propaganda that the state can best encourage the protection of values central to freedom of expression, while simultaneously demonstrating dislike for the vision forwarded by hate-mongers.

. . . [G]iven the unparalleled vigour with which hate propaganda repudiates and undermines democratic values, and in particular its condemnation of the view that all citizens need be treated with equal respect and dignity so as to make participation in the political process meaningful, I am unable to see the protection of such expression as integral to the democratic ideal.

I am of the opinion that hate propaganda contributes little to the aspirations of Canadians or Canada in either the quest for truth, the promotion of individual self-development or the protection and fostering of a vibrant democracy where the participation of all individuals is accepted and encouraged.[64]

NOTES

1. The United Nations Development Program (UNDP) lists five of the countries among the "high freedom ranking" countries; only Israel is in the second category of "medium freedom ranking." See *Human Rights Development Reports 1991*(1991:20), reprint in *14 HRI Reporter* 1 (1991): 84.

2. For an example of the impact, see Cohen and Bayefsky (1983:265, 279 n. 39, 292 n. 119). On nonfederal countries one should mention that in regard to those laws of concern to this study, there is a difference in the United Kingdom between those that are applicable in Great Britain and those in Northern Ireland.

3. On the issue of the acceptance of international commitments into domestic law, there are generally two approaches. One is adoption theory, which holds that international treaties accepted by a country are automatically part of its domestic law; the other is transformation theory, according to which international treaties have domestic force only if incorporated into domestic law by a special legislative act of the state concerned. The six countries surveyed in this analysis differ also in this respect. The position is highly complicated, therefore one can indicate it here only in the broadest terms and in a schematic way. It shows the following: In France, international treaties are generally part of domestic law. In the United States, they would be so only if they are self-executing treaties. The United Kingdom requires the incorporation of treaties. The position is similar in Canada, although the Canadian attitude to customary international law (as distinct to treaty law) seems to be more positive than in the United Kingdom. Germany and Israel also require incorporation, but the "general principles" of international law are considered part of domestic law. (Freedom of expression would probably be regarded as such a general principle; its restriction on account of racism would not.)

4. There were actually a few incidents in Israel also. However, their motive was not anti-Semitism, nor were they caused by Arabs. Rather, they were cases of sheer hooliganism, probably by mentally deranged people.

5. See Chapter 6 by Gerald Cromer. Israel's attorney general called racism " a distortion of Judaism." (Quoted by the Israel representative in the Committee on the Elimination of Racial Discrimination on 15 March 1985. See United Nations document CERD/C/SR.711,6.

6. Apparently this is not an actual quote from Voltaire but a "summary of his attitude." See Lee (1990:3).

7. A very useful collection of essays on the history and philosophy of the freedom of expression has been published as volume 6 of the series "Human Rights" of the University of Tübingen. See Schwartländer and Willoweit (1986). For a more general survey of the development of human rights (not specifically the freedom of expression), see Henkin (1978). Specifically on the European contribution, vol. 5 in the Tübingen series, see Dicke (1986).

8. Article 11 of the Declaration reads: "Free communication of ideas and opinions is one of the most precious of the rights of man. Consequently, every citizen may

speak, write, and print freely subject to responsibility for the abuse of such liberty in the cases determined by law."

9. It reads (in part): "Congress shall make no law . . . abridging the freedom of speech, or of the press." The earlier Declaration of Virginia (1776) was limited to safeguarding the freedom of the press (Article 12).

10. Earlier, only the freedom of the press was protected. See, for example, the constitutions of the Kingdom of Bavaria of 1918 and of Württemberg of 1819. The "Pauls-Church" Constitution of 28 March 1849 did include a guarantee for the freedom of expression (Article 143), but this constitution never became effective. The freedom was not included in the intervening constitutions, only in the Weimar Constitution of 11 August 1919 (Article 110). The post–World War II constitution of the Federal Republic of Germany (Grundgesetz—Fundamental Act) of 1949, in its Article 5, changed the grounds of restrictions on the freedom of expression to the protection of youth and of "personal honor."

11. My searches found only the Manitoba "Act to amend the 'Libel Act'," 24 George V 1934, which is a group libel law on ground of "race" or "creed"; the law of the State of New Jersey, introduced 28 January 1935, which bans the discrimination of written or pictorial material tending to create hatred, violence, or hostility by reason of "race, colour, religion or manner of worship"; the South West Africa Ordinance No. 13 of 1933 regarding promotion of hostility "between different races"; and provisions in some old laws such as the Penal Code of Finland of 1889 and the Penal Code of Norway of 1902.

12. See particularly *New York Times Co. v. Sullivan*, 376 U.S. 254 (1964); *Brandenburg v. Ohio*, 395 U.S. 444 (1969); *Cohen v. California*, 403 U.S. 15 (1971).

13. *Collin v. Smith*, 578 F. 2d 1197 (7th Cir. 1978), cert. denied, 439 U.S. 915 (1978); *Village of Skokie v. National Socialist Party of America*, 69 Ill. 2d 605, 373 N.E. 2d 21 (1978).

14. In my view the statement quoted goes somewhat too far—unless one strongly emphasizes the word "modern." I see the present attitude as a phase in a moving scenario.

15. As listed by J.-B. Marie in his annual survey—*Human Rights Law Journal* 12, no. 1–2 (1991): 27–44.

16. U.N.G.A. Res. 2200A (XXI), 999 U.N.T.S. 171 (1966).

17. The reservation reads: "I (1) That Article 20 does not authorize or require legislation or other action by the United States that would restrict the right of free speech and association protected by the Constitution and laws of the United States."

18. (U.N.T.S. Vol. 78, 277). Its Article III (c) makes "direct and public incitement to commit genocide" punishable—but this is incitement to commit a concrete act, not incitement to hatred, hostility, contempt, or similar "non-conduct" results. In modern American legal thinking, such "incitement to act illegally" may be subjected to constraints.

19. 600 U.N.T.S. 195 (1969). The other instruments ratified by the United States are: the 1926 Slavery Convention and its 1956 supplementary convention; the Protocol relating to the Status of Refugees 1967—but *not* the 1951 convention; the 1952 UN Convention on the Political Rights of Women and the Inter-American Convention on the same subject, as well as the OAS Convention on the Nationality of Women; and the four Geneva conventions on humanitarian law of 1949.

20. "[T]he United States stands virtually alone in the degree to which it has decided legally to tolerate racist rhetoric" (Bollinger 1986:38). Of course, not every country

outside the United States has adopted laws against racist expression; but I know of no country outside the United States that would have declared itself *unable in principle* to adopt such laws for constitutional or other reasons. Suffice it to mention that as of 1 January 1991, 128 states have ratified the Race Discrimination Convention that prescribes such laws, making this convention (next to the ILO Convention (no. 29) Concerning Forced Labour (1930)—with 128 ratifications—and the 1949 Geneva Conventions on humanitarian law—with 164 ratifications) one of the most widely accepted international documents.

21.   The French Constitution of 28 September 1946, in its preamble, "solemnly reaffirms the rights and freedoms of man and of the citizen consecrated by the Declaration of Rights of 1789." A similar statement appears in the preamble of the now effective Constitution of 4 October 1958.

22.   The relevant parts of these three articles read as follows:

Article 5(1)
Everyone shall have the right freely to express and disseminate his opinion by speech, writing and pictures and freely to inform himself from generally accepted sources. Freedom of the press and freedom of reporting by means of broadcasts and films are guaranteed. There shall be no censorship.
(2) The rights are limited by the provisions of the general laws, the provisions of law for the protection of youth, and by the right to inviolability of personal honour.

Article 9(2)
Associations whose aims or whose activities are contrary to the criminal law, or which are directed against the constitutional order or against the idea of understanding among people, are prohibited.

Article 21(2)
Parties, which through their aims or the behaviour of their followers seek to impair or to eliminate the free democratic order or to jeopardise the existence of the Federal German Republic, are unconstitutional. The question of unconstitutionality is decided by the Federal Constitutional Court.

23.   For details, see Zierlein (1991:301, 304–311, 319–321, 339). On France, see Errera (1990a:67–68).

24.   Decision of the Vorprüfungsauschuss of the Bundesverfassungsgericht, 27 April 1982 (*Neue Juristische Wochenschrift* 35 (1952): 1803).

25.   Judgment of the Bundesverfassungsgericht, 25 November 1985–2 BVR 1294/85.

26.   See Sherr's chapter on England in this volume (Chapter 3). I quote Sherr's view on the impact of the absence of a constitution on prosecution policy more for its originality than for agreeing with it.

27.   Basic Law: The Knesset (12 L.S.I. 85); Basic Law: Israel Lands (14 L.S.I. 48); Basic Law: The President of the State (18 L.S.I. 111); Basic Law: The Government (22 L.S.I. 257); Basic Law: State Economy (29 L.S.I. 273); Basic Law: The Army (30 L.S.I. 150); Basic Law: Jerusalem, Capital of Israel (34 L.S.I. 209); Basic Law: Judicature (38 L.S.I. 101); Basic Law: State Comptroller (S. H. no. 1237, p. 30); Basic Law: Human Dignity and Freedom (S. H. no. 1391, p. 150); Basic Law:

Government (S. H. no. 1396, p. 214); Basic Law: Freedom of Occupation (S. H. 1387, p. 60). Rubinstein (1966:201) called them "Israel's Piecemeal Constitution."

28. Israel's "Declaration of Independence" (1 L.S.I. 3) contains two phrases relevant to freedom of speech and racism: "The STATE OF ISRAEL will be based on freedom, justice and peace *as envisaged by the prophets of Israel*" and "it will ensure complete equality of social and political rights to all inhabitants, irrespective of *religion, race or sex*" (emphasis added). The Declaration is not a constitution, nor has it otherwise similar force; it is only a source of interpretation of the laws of Israel. See Shetreet (1990:368, 411–413). Freedom "as envisaged by the prophets of Israel" must be deemed to include speech freedom, in the light of Cohn's conclusion that "Prophecy is the classical manifestation of biblical freedom of speech." He quotes several examples as proof (Cohn 1984:110 n. 13).

29. In Canada, section 1 of the Charter guarantees rights "only to such reasonable limits prescribed by law as can be demonstrably justified in a free and democratic society." The German Basic Law Article 5(2) stipulates that the rights to freedom of expression "are limited by the provisions of general laws, by the provision of law for the protection of youth, and by the right to inviolability of personal honor." In France the Declaration speaks of "subject to responsibility for the abuse of such liberty in the cases determined by law."

30. U.N.G.A. Res. 2200 A(XXI), 999 U.N.T.S. 171 (1966). The exact text reads:

Article 20(2) Any advocacy of national, racial or religious hatred that constitutes incitement to discrimination, hostility or violence shall be prohibited by law.

Also relevant are:

Article 5(1) Nothing in the present Covenant may be interpreted as implying for any State, group or person, any right to engage in any activity or perform any act *aimed at the destruction of any of the rights and freedoms recognized herein* or at their limitation to a greater extent than is provided for in the present Covenant.

Article 19(3) The exercise of the rights provided for in paragraph 2 of this article [freedom of expression] carries with it special duties and responsibilities, but these shall only be such as are provided by law and are necessary:

(a) For *respect of the rights of reputations of others*:

(b) For the protection of national security or of public order (*ordre public*), or of public health or morals. (emphasis added)

On the freedom of expression and its restriction in the Civil and Political Rights Covenant, see Nowak (1989:355–393), Partsch (1981:209–245), Humphrey (1984:181–188), Roth (1983:108–125).

31. U.N.G.A. Res. 2106 AXX; 600 U.N.T.S. 195 (1969). The text reads:

Article (4) States Parties condemn all propaganda and all organisations which are based on ideas or theories of superiority of one race or group of persons of one colour or ethnic origin, or which attempt to justify or promote racial hatred and discrimination and, to this end, with due regard to the principles embodied in the Universal Declaration of Human Rights and the rights expressly set forth in Article 5 of this Convention, inter alia:

(a) Shall declare an offence punishable by law all dissemination based on racial superiority or hatred, incitement to racial discrimination, as well as all acts of violence or incitement to such acts against any race or group of persons of another colour or ethnic origin, and also the provision of any assistance of racist activities, including the financing thereof;

(b) Shall declare illegal and prohibit organizations, and also organized and all other propaganda activities, which promote and incite racial discrimination, and shall recognize participation in such organizations or activities as an offence punishable by law;

(c) Shall not permit public authorities or public institutions, national or local, to promote or incite racial discrimination.

On the Race Discrimination Convention, see Meron (1985, 1986:23–35), Lerner (1980, 1983:170–188).

32. UN Doc. ST/LEG/SER. E/7 114.

33. The French declaration regarding the Race Discrimination Convention reads (in part) as follows:

With regard to article 4, France wishes to make it clear that it interprets the reference made therein to the principles of the Universal Declaration of Human Rights and to the rights set forth in article 5 of the Convention as releasing the States Parties from the obligation to enact anti-discrimination legislation which is incompatible with the freedoms of opinion and expression and of peaceful assembly and association guaranteed by those texts.

The United Kingdom made the following statements:

Reservation to the Civil and Political Rights Covenant (in part):
The Government of the United Kingdom interpret article 20 consistently with the rights conferred by articles 19 and 21 of the Covenant and having legislated in matters of practical concern in the interests of public order (*ordre public*) reserves the right not to introduce any further legislation. The United Kingdom also reserves a similar right in regard to each of its dependent territories.

Interpretative Statement to the Race Discrimination Convention: Upon signature (in part):
[T]he United Kingdom wishes to state its understanding of certain articles in the Convention. It interprets article 4 as requiring a party to the Convention to adopt further legislative measures in the fields covered by subparagraphs (a), (b) and (c) of that article only in so far as it may consider with due regard to the principles embodied in the Universal Declaration of Human Rights and the rights expressly set forth in article 5 of the Convention (in

particular the right to freedom of opinion and expression and the right to freedom of peaceful assembly and association) that some legislative addition to or variation of existing law and practice in those fields is necessary for the attainment of the end specified in the earlier part of article 4.

Upon ratification (in part):
   First, the reservation and interpretative statements made by the United Kingdom at the time of signature of the Convention are maintained. (UN Doc. ST/LEG/SER. E/7, 109, 138, 113)
34.   213 U.N.T.S. 221 (1950).
35.   The relevant provisions of the European Convention are:

Article 10(2). The exercise of [the freedom of expression], since it carries with it duties and responsibilities, may be subject to such formalities, conditions and restrictions or penalties as are *prescribed by law and are necessary in a democratic society* in the interests of national security, territorial integrity or public safety, for the prevention of disorder or crime, for the protection of health or morals, for the *protection of the reputation or rights of others*, for preventing the disclosure of information received in confidence, or for maintaining the authority and impartiality of the judiciary.

Article 17. Nothing in this Convention may be interpreted as implying for any State, group or person any right to engage in any activity or perform any act *aimed at the destruction of any of the rights and freedoms set forth herein* or at the limitation to a greater extent than is provided for in the Convention. (emphasis added)

On the freedom of expression in the European Covenant, see: Frowein/Peukert (1985:223–241), Fawcett (1987:250–273), Cohen-Jonathan (1989), Nedjati (1978:176–183), Robertson (1977:84–107), Castberg (1974:149–152), Genn (1983:189–207).
   36.   *X. v. Italy* (6741/74, 21 May 1976, D. & R. 5, 83 (1976)) regarding activities aiming at the reconstitution of a Fascist Party; *Glimmerveen and Others v. Netherlands* (D. 8348/78 and 8406/78, 11 October 1979, D. & R. 18, 187 (1980, 4 E.H.R.R. 260 (1979)) regarding the racist propaganda of the Nederlandse Volks Unie; *T. v. Belgium* (9777/82, 14 July 83, D. & R. 34, 158 (1983)), the case of the publisher of a revisionist document by a former leader of the Belgian Rexist movement denying the reality of Auschwitz; *Felderer v. Sweden* (11001/84, 1986, 8 E.H.R.R. 91), the case of a journalist convicted for publishing literature denying the holocaust; and *H. W. P. and K. v. Austria* (12774/87 of 25 February 1987, decision of 12 October 1989), in which four activists of the right-wing Aktion Neue Rechte (ANR) and Nationalistischer Bund Nordland (NBN) complained about their convictions for having engaged in "activities inspired by National Socialist ideas." In all these cases the applications to the European Commission on Human Rights were considered inadmissible. Though the rejections were sometimes based on different grounds, the Commission invariably made it clear that it regarded the ban on racist activities as a legitimate restriction on the freedom of expression. The case *Jersild and Jencens v. Denmark* (application August 1990) about propaganda of a Danish racist group, the Green Jackets, is not yet decided.
   37.   *J. R. T. and the W. G. Party (names deleted) v. Canada*, Communication No. 104/1981 of 18 July 1981, declared inadmissible 6 April 1983. CCPR/C/OP/2, 25.

38. Ibid., 28.

39. *M. A. v. Italy*, Communication No. 117/1981 of 21 September 1981, declared inadmissible 10 April 1984, CCPR/C/OP/2, 31, 33.

40. Document of the Copenhagen Meeting of the Conference on the Human Dimension of the CSCE, 25 June 1990 (29 *I.L.M.* 1305, 1940). The most important parts of the relevant article read:

> Article (40). The participating States clearly and unequivocally *condemn* totalitarianism, *racial and ethnic hatred, anti-semitism*, xenophobia and discrimination against anyone as well as *persecution on religious and ideological grounds*. In this context, they also recognize the particular problems of Roma (Gypsies).
> They declare their firm intention to intensify the efforts to combat these phenomena in all their forms and therefore will

> (40.1)—take effective measures, including the adoption, *in conformity with their constitutional systems* and their international obligations, of such laws as may be necessary, to provide protection against any acts that constitute *incitement to violence* against persons or groups based on national, *racial, ethnic or religious discrimination, hostility or hatred*, including *anti-semitism*;

> (40.2)—commit themselves to take appropriate and proportionate measures to protect persons or groups who may be subject to threats, acts of *discrimination, hostility or violence* as a result of their *racial, ethnic, cultural*, linguistic or *religious* identity, and to protect their property. (emphasis added)

41. Charter of Paris for a New Europe, 21 November 1990 (30 *I.L.M.* 1991). The relevant clause is: "We express our determination to combat all forms of *racial and ethnic hatred, anti-semitism*, xenophobia and discrimination against anyone as well as *persecution on religious* and ideological *grounds*" (emphasis added).

42. Report of the CSCE Meeting of Experts on National Minorities, 19 July 1991. Text in *HRLJ* 12 (1991): 332. The language is almost identical with that of Copenhagen (see Note 33 above).

43. On this, see Roth (1990a), Lerner (1991:121, 125–126). On the Copenhagen, Paris, and Geneva CSCE meetings in general, see Buergenthal (1990:217–232), McGoldrick (1990:935–939), Tretter (1990:235–239), Roth (1990b:373–379; 1991:330–331; 1992).

44. See criticism of the CSCE provisions in Roth (1990a:8–9).

45. This emerges also from the recent (update) report of the Special Rapporteurs to the UN Sub-Commission on Prevention of Discrimination and Protection of Minorities, Danilo Turk and Louis Joinet, UN Document E/CN.4/Sub/2/1991/9 of 16 July 1991.

46. Racial Discrimination, Cmnd. 6234, para. 126, 30 (1975). See on this also "Report of a Sub-Committee of the Law and Parliamentary Committee of the Board of Deputies of British Jews on Group Defamation," p. 32 (adopted on 15 December 1991 but not yet published) (henceforward "Board Report"). I was a member of this subcommittee.

47. GAOR (XXXIII) Suppl. no. 18 (A/33/18), para. 339.

48. 19 Laws of the State of Israel, section 1(4). See Tabory (1987), Kretzmer (1987, 1988, 1991).

49. Law Commission, Working Paper No. 79, "Offenses against Religion and Public Worship," 119 para. 8.5 (1981).

50. I deal separately with the issue of group libel subsequently.

51. The latter point has become significant in relation to the problem of revisionism (denial of the holocaust), to which I will return.

52. The provision reads (in part): "Section 12. It is a discriminatory practice to publish or display before the public or to cause to be published or displayed before the public any notice, sign, symbol, emblem or other representation that . . . (b) incites or is established to incite others to discriminate."

53. Tabory (1987:278, 281–228). See also Shapira (1986:10), who writes: "[T]he highest possible level of mens rea was made a sine qua non of the conviction. (Such a high degree of criminal intent is expressly required in the Israeli Criminal Code only infrequently—for example, in the definition of the crimes of murder or treason)."

54. "Wilfully" was equated with "intentionally" by the Ontario Court of Appeal in *R. v. Buzzanga and Durocher* (1979) 49 C.C.C. (2d) 369 (Ont.A.). See Chapter 7 by Bruce Elman, and the judgment in *R. v. Keegstra* (1990) 61 C.C.C. (3d) 1 (S.C.C.) of 13 December 1990, 63–65 (and in *Western Weekly Reports* 2 (1991).

55. But only for charges of incitement, not for spreading false news. See Bruce Elman's Chapter 7 in this volume, and my comments on "Revisionism—Denial of the Holocaust" later in this chapter.

56. A detailed study by this author on the legal aspects of holocaust denial will appear in volume 23 of the *Israel Yearbook on Human Rights*.

57. See Roger Errera's chapter on France in this volume (Chapter 2). Errera also describes the administrative measures and case-law in considerable detail. But he concludes on a rather despondent note about the usefulness and the desirability of legal measures against revisionism.

58. *Sefer Ha-Chukkim* of 5710 p. 281. (This law is not mentioned in the chapter on Israel by Gerald Cromer.)

59. Section 181 reads: "Every one who wilfully publishes a statement, tale or news that he knows is false and that causes or is likely to cause injury or mischief to a public interest is guilty of an indictable offence and liable to imprisonment for a term not exceeding two years."

60. Its Section 1 reads:

S. 1—(1) Any person who sends another person
  (a) a letter or other article which conveys i) a message which is indecent or grossly offensive; ii) a threat; or iii) information which is false and known or believed to be false by the sender; or
  (b) any other article which is, in whole or part, of an indecent or grossly offensive nature,
is guilty of an offence if his purpose, or one of his purposes, in sending it is that it should, so far as falling within paragraph (a) or (b) above, cause distress or anxiety to the recipient or to any other person to whom he intends that it or its contents or nature should be communicated.

61. In some court cases, the judge has taken "judicial notice" of the truth of the holocaust. This obviates a lengthy historical investigation, which is so offensive to survivors.

62. *R. v. Keegstra* (1990) 61 C.C.C. (3) 1 (S.C.C.) and in *Western Weekly Reports* 2 (1991): 37.

63. They come from bodies like the Commission for Racial Equality; the Jewish community (see "Board Report," note 32, which proposes a number of amendments to strengthen the law); and the growing Moslem community, which wants the law to be extended to protect religious groups. See Roth (1991b) in which these "reform" proposals are fully described.

64. *R. v. Keegstra* (1990) 61 C.C.C. (3) 1 (S.C.C.) and in *Western Weekly Reports* 2 (1991): 56–57.

Bibliography

Adams, C. 1985. "Through the Fingers." *Canadian Lawyer* (April).

Anti-Defamation League. 1988. *Hate Crime Statutes: A Response to Anti-Semitism, Vandalism, and Violent Bigotry*. New York: Anti-Defamation League.

Arndt, I., and A. Schardt. 1989. "Zur Chronologie des Rechtsextremismus. Daten und Zahlen 1946–1989." In *Rechtsextremismus in der Bundesrepublik. Voraussetzungen, Zusammenhänge, Wirkungen*, edited by W. Benz. Frankfurt-am-Main: Fischer IB.

Bastole, D. M. Hanatiou, and O. Daurmont. 1991. "La Lutte contre le racisme et la xenophobie, mythe ou realité?" *Revue trimestrielle des droits de l'homme*.

Beer, U. 1986. *Die Juden, das Recht und die Republik*. Frankfurt-am-Main: Peter Lang.

Beer, Udo. 1988. "The Protection of Jewish Civil Rights in the Weimar Republic." In *Leo Baeck Institute Yearbook XXXIII*, edited by A. Paucker. London: Seclar Warburg.

Beit-Halahmi. 1984. "Against the Restriction of Racist Publications." *Civil Rights* 10 (November).

Bell, Derrick A. 1973. *Race, Racism and American Law*. Boston: Little, Brown and Co.

Bercuson, David J., and Douglas Wertheimer. 1985. *A Trust Betrayed: The Keegstra Affair*. New York: Doubleday.

Berger, P., and T. Luckmann. 1967. *The Social Construction of Reality: A Treatise in the Sociology of Knowledge*. New York: Anchor Books.

Bering, D. 1985. "Von der Notwendigkeit politischer Beleidigungsprozesse—Der Beginn der Auseinandersetzung zwischen Polizeipräsident Bernhard Weiss und der NSDAP." In *Die Juden in der Weimarer Republik*, edited by W. Grab and J. Schoeps. Stuttgart: Burg Verlag.

Bessner, R. 1988. "The Constitutionality of Group Libel Offences in the Criminal Code." *Manitoba Law Journal* 17: 183, 218.

Bickel, A. 1975. *The Morality of Consent*. New Haven: Yale University Press.

Bindman, G. 1982. *New Law Journal* (March 25): 299–302.

Böhme, J. 1985. "Die Lüge von der 'Auschwitz-Lüge' und kein Ende." *Zeichen. Mitteilungen der Aktion Sühnezeichen/Friedensdienste* 13, no. 2 (June).

Bollinger, L. C. 1986. *The Tolerant Society: Free Speech and Extremist Speech in America*. New York: Oxford University Press.

Bonnet, J. C. 1976. *Les pouvoirs publics français et l'immigration dans l'entre-deux guerres*. Lyon: N'ane.

Borovoy, A. A. 1985. "Freedom of Expression: Some Recurring Impediments." In *Justice beyond Orwell*, edited by R. Abella and M. Rothman. Montreal: Blais.

———. 1988. *When Freedoms Collide*. Toronto: Lester and Orpen Dennis.

———. 1991. "How Not to Fight Racial Hatred." In *Freedom of Expression and the Charter*, edited by D. Schneiderman. Toronto: Carswell, pp. 243–248.

Bottos, D. 1988. "*Keegstra* and *Andrews:* A Commentary of Hate Propaganda and the Freedom of Expression." *Alberta Law Review* 27: 461–475.

Bowes, S. 1966. *The Police and Civil Liberties*. London: Lawrence and Wishart.

Braun, S. 1988. "Social and Racial Tolerance and Freedom of Expression in a Democratic Society: Friends or Foes: *Regina v. Zundel*." *Dalhousie Law Journal* 11: 470–513.

Braunbehrens, V. 1984. "Die Vertreibung der Auschwitz-Lüge." *Vorgänge* 69.

Bredin, J. D. 1983. *L'Affaire*. Paris: Juilliard R.

———. 1984. "Le droit, le juge et l'historien." *Le Débat* (November).

Buergenthal, T. 1977. "Implementing the UN Racial Convention." *Texas International Law Journal* 12.

———. 1990. "The Copenhagen CSCE Meeting—A New Public Order for Europe." *Human Rights Law Journal* 11: 217–232.

Burgelin, C. 1990. "Lyon, capitale du négationnisme." *Esprit* (September).

Butovsky, M. 1985. "The Holocaust on Trial in Canada." *Patterns of Prejudice* 19, no. 3.

Byrnes, Robert R. 1969. *Antisemitism in Modern France: The Prologue to the Dreyfus Affair*. New York: H. Fertig.

Bytwerk, R. L. 1975. *Julius Streicher: The Rhetoric of an Anti-Semite*. Ph.D. diss., Northwestern University.

Castberg, F. 1974. *The European Convention on Human Rights*. Leiden: Sijthoff; Dobbs Ferry, N.Y.: Oceana.

Cohen, M. 1971a. "The Hate Propaganda Amendments: Reflections on a Controversy." *Alberta Law Review* 9: 103–117.

———. 1971b. "Human Rights and Hate Propaganda: A Controversial Canadian Experiment." In *Of Law and Man: Essays in Honor of Haim H. Cohn*, edited by S. Shoham. New York: Sabra Books, pp. 59–78.

Cohen, M., and A. F. Bayefsky. 1983. "The Canadian Charter of Rights and Freedoms and Public International Law." *Canadian Bar Review* 61: 265, 279 n.39, 292 n.119.

Cohen, S. S. 1971. "Hate Propaganda—The Amendments to the Criminal Code." *McGill Law Journal* 17: 740–791.

Cohen-Jonathan, G. 1989. *La Convention européenne des droits de l'homme*. Paris: Economica.

Cohn, H. 1984. *Human Rights in Jewish Law*. New York: Ktav Publishers.

Cohn, N. 1967. *Warrant for Genocide: The Myth of the Jewish World-Conspiracy and the Protocols of the Elders of Zion*. New York: Harper-Row.

Compte-rendu des travaux de la Commission de surveillance et de controle des publications destinées à l'enfance et à l'adolescence. 1965. Paris. Small brochure.

Costa-Lascoux, J. 1976. "La loi du 1er juillet 1972 et la protection pénale des immigrés contre la discrimination raciale." *Droit social* (May).

Cotler, I. 1985. "Hate Literature." In *Justice beyond Orwell*, edited by R. Abella and M. Rothman. Montreal: Blais.

———. 1991. "Racist Incitement: Giving Free Speech a Bad Name." In *Freedom of Expression and the Charter*, edited by D. Schneiderman. Toronto: Carswell, pp. 249–257.

Cromer, G. 1987. "Negotiating the Meaning of the Holocaust: An Observation on the Debate about Kahanism in Israeli Society." *Holocaust and Genocide Studies* 2, no. 2: 289–297.

———. 1988. *The Debate about Kahanism in Israeli Society 1984–1988*. New York: Harry and Frank Guggenheim Foundation.

de Comarmond, P., and C. Duchet, eds. 1960. *Racisme et société*. Paris.

Delgado, R. 1991. "Campus Antiracism Rules: Constitutional Narratives in Collision." *Northwestern University Law Review* 85.

Dicke, K. 1986. *Menschenrechte und europäische Integration*. Kehl am Rhein: N. P. Engel.

Downs, D. A. 1985. *Nazis in Skokie: Freedom, Community and the First Amendment*. Notre Dame, Ind.: University of Notre Dame Press.

Duraffour A., and C. Guittonneau. 1991. "Des mythes aux problèmes: l'argumentation xénophobe prise au mot." In *Face au racisme. I. Les moyens d'agir*, edited by P. A. Taguieff. Paris: Decouverte.

Elman, B. 1989. "The Promotion of Hatred and the Canadian Charter of Rights and Freedoms." *Canadian Public Policy* 15: 72–83.

———. 1990. "A Review of the *Keegstra* Case: The Supreme Court Upholds Hate Propaganda Law." *Constitutional Forum* 2: 86.

Elon, A. 1971. *The Israelis, Founders and Sons*. New York: Holt, Rinehart and Winston.

Errera, R. 1987. "Freedom of the Press: The U.S., France and Other European Countries." In *Constitutionalism and Rights: The Influence of the U.S. Constitution Abroad*, edited by L. Henkin and A. J. Rosenthal. New York: Columbia University Press.

———. 1989. "Recent Developments in Anti-Nazi and Anti-Discrimination Legislation." *Patterns of Prejudice* 23, no. 1.

———. 1990a. "Recent Developments in the French Law of the Press in Comparison with Britain." In *Economical with the Truth: The Law and the Media in a*

Democratic Society, edited by D. Kingsford-Smith and D. Oliver. Oxford: ESC Publishing.

————. 1990b. "Sur les justes limites de la liberté d'expression." *Esprit* (December).

European Parliament. 1985. *Enquiry into the Rise of Fascism and Racism in Europe.* Brussels: European Parliament.

Eyck, E. 1926. *Die Krisis der deutschen Rechtspflege.* Berlin: Verlag für Kulturpolitik.

Fawcett, J. E. S. 1987. *The Application of the European Convention on Human Rights.* Oxford: Clarendon Press; New York: Oxford University Press.

Fish, A. 1989. "Hate Propaganda and Freedom of Expression." *Canadian Journal of Law and Jurisprudence* 2: 111–137.

Foerder, L. 1924. *Antisemitismus und die Justiz.* Berlin: Philo Verlag.

Foulon-Piganiol, J. 1970a. "Réflexions sur la diffamation raciale: Eléments constituitifs du délit et imperfections du texte actuel." *Recueil Dalloz.*

————. 1970b. "Nouvelles réflexions sur la diffamation raciale (Critique des propositions de loi en instance devant le Parlement)." *Recueil Dalloz.*

————. 1972. "La lutte contre le racisme: Commentaire de la loi du 1er juillet 1972." *Recueil Dalloz.*

Frowein, F. A., and W. Peukert. 1985. *Europäische Menschenrechtskonvention: EMRK-Kommentar.* Kehl am Rhein: N. P. Engel.

Fulford, R. 1985. "Speak No Evil." *Saturday Night* (June).

Genn, R. 1983. "Beyond the Pale—Council of Europe Measures against Incitement of Hatred." *Israel Yearbook of Human Rights* 13: 189–207.

Greenawalt, Kent. 1989. *Speech Crime and the Uses of Language.* New York: Oxford University Press.

Guillaumin, C. 1972. *L'idéologie raciste: Genèse et langage actuel.* The Hague and Paris.

Hage, R. E. 1970. "The Hate Propaganda Amendment to the Criminal Code." *University of Toronto Faculty Law Review* 28: 63–73.

Haiman, F. 1981. *Speech and Law in a Free Society.* Chicago: University of Chicago Press.

Hearst, A. 1960. "When Justice Was Not Done: Judges in the Weimar Republic." *The Wiener Library Bulletin* 14, no. 1.

Henkin, L. 1975. *Foreign Affairs and the Constitution.* New York: W. W. Norton.

————. 1978. *The Rights of Man Today.* Boulder, Colo.: Westview Press.

Hirschberg, A. 1926a. "Münchmeyer-Prozess auf Borkum." *C.V. Zeitung,* 14 May, pp. 271–272.

————. 1926b. "Disziplinverfahren gegen Münchmeyer?" *C.V. Zeitung,* 21 May, p. 283.

————. 1929. *Kollektiv-Ehre und Kollektiv-Beleidigung.* Berlin: Philo Verlag.

Holländer, L. 1923. "Lehren Politischer Prozesse." *C.V. Zeitung,* 11 October, p. 1.

Horowitz, D. 1984. "Israel Is Ripe for Fascism." *Davar,* 7 December.

Horowitz, D. C. 1985. *Ethnic Groups in Conflict.* Berkeley: University of California Press.

Human Development Reports. 1991. Reprint in *14 HRI Reporter* 1.

Humphrey, J. P. 1984. "Political and Related Rights." In *Human Rights in International Law: Legal and Policy Issues,* edited by T. Meron. Oxford: Clarendon Press; Toronto: Oxford University Press, pp. 181–188.

Kahane, M. 1974. *Our Challenge: The Chosen Land.* Radnor, Pa.: Chilton Book Co.

————. 1981. *They Must Go.* New York: Grosset and Dunlop.

———. 1983. *Forty Years*. Jerusalem: Institute of the Jewish Idea.

———. 1987. *Uncomfortable Questions for Comfortable Jews*. Secaucus, N.J.: Lyle Stuart Inc.

Kalinowsky, H. 1985. *Rechtsextremismus und Strafrechtspflege: Eine Analyse von Strafverfahren wegen mutmaßlicher rechtsextremistischer Aktivitäten und Erscheinungen*. Bonn: Bundesministerium der Justiz.

Kalven, H., Jr. 1965. *The Negro and the First Amendment*. Chicago: University of Chicago Press.

Kaplan, K. 1990. *Report on the Murder of the General Secretary*. Columbus: Ohio State University Press.

Kayfetz, B. G. 1970. "The Story behind Canada's New Anti-Hate Law." *Patterns of Prejudice* 5 (May–June).

Kayser, P. 1989. "Les pouvoirs du juge des référés civiles à l'égard de la liberté de communication et d'expression," *D*. II.

Kidd, R. 1940. *British Liberty in Danger: An Introduction to the Study of Civil Rights*. London: Lawrence and Wishart.

Kiejman, G. 1984. "L'histoire devant ses juges." *Le Débat* (November).

Klein, S. 1984. "Von den Schwierigkeiten der Justiz im Umgang mit KZ-Schergen und Neonazis in der Bundesrepublik." In *Rechtsextremismus in der Bundesrepublik. Voraussetzungen, Zusammenhänge, Wirkungen*, edited by W. Benz. Frankfurt-am-Main: Fischer.

Kotler, Y. 1986. *Heil Kahane!* New York: Adama Books.

Kretzmer, D. 1987. "Freedom of Speech and Racism." *Cardozo Law Review* 8, no. 3.

———. 1988. "Racial Incitement in Israel." Paper presented at Israel-Canada Conference on Racial Incitement and the Law, Jerusalem, December.

———. 1991. "Racial Incitement in Israel." Paper presented to a conference on Racial and Religious Hatred and Group Libel, Tel Aviv University, 28–31 December.

Kuntzemüller, A. 1926. "Um die Frage der Kollektivbeleidigung: Eine wichtige Gerichtsentscheidung." *C.V. Zeitung*, 19 February, p. 88.

Langlois, B. 1991. "Clés pour un débat." *Le Nouveau Politis*, 25 April.

LeBlanc, L. J. 1991. *The United States and the Genocide Convention*. Durham, N.C.: Duke University Press.

Lee, S. 1990. *The Cost of Free Speech*. London: Faber.

Lerner, N. 1980. *The UN Convention on the Elimination of All Forms of Racial Discrimination*, 2d ed. Alphen an den Rijn: Sitjhoff and Noordhoff.

———. 1983. "Curbing Racial Discrimination—Fifteen Years CERD." *Israel Yearbook on Human Rights* 13: 170–188.

———. 1991. *Group Rights and Discrimination in International Law*. Dordrecht: Martinus Nijhoff.

Lester, A. 1984. "Fundamental Rights: The U.K. Isolated?" *Public Law* 46.

Lester, A., and G. Bindman. 1972. *Race and Law*. Harmondsworth: Penguin.

Levitt, C. 1991a. "The Prosecution of Antisemites by the Courts in the Weimar Republic: Was Justice Served?" *Leo Baeck Yearbook* 36: 151–167.

———. 1991b. "Racial Incitement and the Law: The Case of the Weimar Republic." In *Freedom of Expression and the Charter*, edited by D. Schneiderman. Toronto: Carswell.

Lifshitz, B. 1990. "Israel and Jewish Law—Interaction and Independence." *Israeli Law Review*, nos. 3–4.

Loebe, P. 1954. *Der Weg war lang*. Berlin: Arani.

Low, P. W., and J. C. Jeffries, Jr. 1988. *Civil Rights Actions: Section 1983 and Related Statutes.* Foundation Press.

Lustgarten, L. 1986. *The Governance of the Police.* London: Sweet and Maxwell.

MacKay, A. W. 1989. "Freedom of Expression: Is It All Just Talk?" *Canadian Bar Review* 68: 713–764.

Marrus, Michael R. 1971. *The Politics of Assimilation: A Study of the French Jewish Community at the Time of the Dreyfus Affair.* Oxford. French translation: *Les Juifs de France à l'époque de l'affaire Dreyfus: L'assimilation à l'épreuve.* Preface by P. Vidal-Naquet. Paris: Complexe, 1972.

———. *Vichy France and the Jews.* New York: Basic.

Marrus, Michael R., and Robert O. Paxton. 1981. *Vichy et les Juifs.* Paris: Calmann-Levy, Diaspora.

Mason, J. D., and J. A. Thomson. 1985. "Racial and Religious Harassment: Idaho's Response to a Growing Problem." *Idaho Law Review* 21.

McGoldrick, D. 1990. "Human Rights Developments in the Helsinki Process." *International and Comparative Law Quarterly* 39: 935–939.

McGuigan, M. R. 1966. "Hate Propaganda and Freedom of Assembly." *Saskatchewan Bar Review* 31: 232–250.

Meron, T. 1985. "The Meaning and Reach of the International Convention on the Elimination of All Forms of Racial Discrimination." *American Journal of International Law* 79.

———. 1986. *Human Rights Law Making in the United Nations: A Critique of Instruments and Processes.* Oxford: Clarendon Press, pp. 283–318.

Mesnil, J. 1966. "Quelques opinions et attitudes des Français à l'égard des travailleurs africains." *Esprit* (April).

Mewett, A. W. 1966. "Some Reflections on the Report of the Special Committee on Hate Propaganda." *Criminal Law Quarterly* 9: 16–20.

Mill, J. S. [1859] 1987. "Of the Liberty of Thought and Discussion." *On Liberty.* Harmondsworth: Penguin.

Milton, J. 1991. "Aeropagitica—A Speech for the Liberty of Unlicensed Printing (1644)." In *John Milton,* edited by S. Orgel and J. Goldberg. Oxford and New York: Oxford University Press.

Milza, O. 1988. *Les Français devant l'immigration.* Brussels: Complexe.

Morgenthaler, S. 1991. "Countering the Pre-1933 Nazi Boycott against the Jews." *Leo Baeck Institute Yearbook* 36: 127–149.

Müller, I. 1991. *Hitler's Justice: The Courts of the Third Reich.* Cambridge, Mass.: Harvard University Press.

Nedjati, Z. M. 1978. *Human Rights under the European Convention.* Amsterdam and New York: North Holland Publishers.

Neier, A. 1979. *Defending My Enemy: American Nazis, the Skokie Case, and the Risks of Freedom.* New York: Dutton.

Niewyk, D. L. 1975. "Jews and the Courts in Weimar Germany." *Jewish Social Studies* 37.

Notin, B. 1989. "Le rôle des mediats [*sic*] dans la vassalisation nationale: omnipotence ou impuissance." *Economies et sociétés,* série "Hors série," no. 8.

Nowak, M. 1989. *UNO Pakt über bürgerlische und politische Rechte und Fakultativprotokoll: CCPR-Kommentar.* Kehl am Rhein: N. P. Engel.

Partsch, K. J. 1981. "Freedom of Conscience and Expression and Political Freedoms."
In *The International Bill of Rights: The Covenant on Civil and Political Rights*,
edited by L. Henkin. New York: Columbia University Press.

Paucker, A. 1966. "Der jüdische Abwehrkampf." In *Entscheidungsjahr 1932. Zur
Judenfrage in der Endphase der Weimarer Republik*, edited by W. E. Mosse.
Tübingen: J. C. B. Mohr, pp. 405–499.

———. 1968. *Der jüdische Abwehrkampf gegen Antisemitismus und Nationalsozial-
ismus in den letzten Jahren der Weimarer Republik*. Hamburg: Leibnitz-Verlag,
pp. 74–84.

———. 1986. "Jewish Self-Defence." In *Die Juden in Nationalsozialistischen Deutsch-
land*, edited by A. Paucker with S. Gilchrist and B. Suchy. Schriftenreihe wis-
senschaftlicher Abhandlungen des Leo Baeck Instituts. Tübingen: J. C. B. Mohr,
pp. 55–65.

Peri, Y. 1984. "The Road to Weimar." *Davar*, 25 July.

Perrineau, P., and N. Mayer, eds. 1989. *Le Front national à découvert*. Paris: Presse
Fond. Nat. Science PO.

Perrot, R. 1989. *Institutions judiciaires*, 3d ed. Paris: Montchrestien.

Petersen, K. 1988. *Literatur und Justiz in der Weimarer Republik*. Stuttgart: J. B. Met-
zlersche Verlagsbuchhandlung.

Picard, J. 1926. "Die Strafgesetzreform." *C.V. Zeitung*, 23 July, pp. 393–395.

Rasehorn, T. 1985. *Justizkritik in der Weimarer Republik: das Beispiel der Zeitschrift
"Die Justiz."* Frankfurt-am-Main: Campus Verlag.

Ratz, M. 1979. *Die Justiz und die Nazis. Zur Strafverfolgung von Nazismus und Neo-
nazismus seit 1945*. Frankfurt-am-Main: Roderberg.

Ravitsky, A. 1986. "Roots of Kahanism: Consciousness and Political Reality."
Jerusalem Quarterly 39.

Rebérioux, M. 1990. "Le génocide, le juge et l'historien." *L'Histoire* (November).

Regel, A. 1985. "Hate Propaganda: A Reason to Limit Freedom of Speech."
Saskatchewan Law Review 49: 303–318.

Robertson, A. H. 1977. *Human Rights in Europe*, 2d ed. Manchester: Manchester
University Press.

Roth, S. J. 1982. "Making the Denial of the Holocaust a Crime in Law." *IJA Research
Reports*, no. 1.

———. 1983. "Anti-Semitism and International Law." *Israel Yearbook of Human
Rights* 13: 108–125.

———. 1990a. "CSCE Outlaws Antisemitism—The Copenhagen Meeting of the
Helsinki Process." *IJA Research Reports*, no. 6.

———. 1990b. "The CSCE 'Charter of Paris for a New Europe': A New Chapter in
the Helsinki Process," *Human Rights Law Journal* 11, nos. 3–4.

———. 1991a. "Comments on the CSCE Meeting of Experts on National
Minorities and the Concluding Document." *Human Rights Law Journal* 12, nos.
8–9.

———. 1991b. "Curbing Racial Incitement in Britain by Law: Four Times Tried—
Still Not Succeeded." Paper presented to a conference on Racial and Religious
Hatred and Group Libel, Tel Aviv University, 28–31 December.

———. 1992. "Setting the Human Rights Standards: Developments in the Helsinki
Process 1991." *IJA Research Reports*, no. 1.

Rubinstein, A. 1966. "Israel's Piecemeal Constitution." *Scripta Hierosolymina* 16: 201–218.

Schneiderman, D. 1991. "A Review of the *Taylor* Case: Using Human Rights Legislation to Curb Racist Speech." *Constitutional Forum* 2: 90.

Schor, R. 1985. *L'opinion française et les étrangers, 1914–1939*. Paris: Publications de la Sorbonne.

Schwartländer, J., and D. Willoweit, eds. 1986. *Meinungsfreiheit—Grundgedanken und Geschichte in Europa und USA*. Tübingen: Tübi. Univ. Schriften.

Schwelb, E. 1966. "The International Convention on the Elimination of All Forms of Racial Discrimination." *International and Comparative Law Quarterly* 15.

Shapira, A. 1986. "Fighting Racism by Law in Israel." *IJA Research Reports*, no. 14 (December).

———. 1987. "Confronting Racism by Law in Israel—Promises and Pitfalls." *Cardozo Law Review* 8, no. 3, p. 585.

Sherr, A. H. 1989. *Freedom of Protest, Public Order and the Law*. Oxford: Blackwell.

Shetreet, S. 1990. "Developments in Constitutional Law." *Israel Law Review* 24, nos. 3–4.

Singer-Ferris. 1986. "Theatre of Hate: How Zundel Played to the Weaknesses of the Press." *Ryerson Review of Journalism* (Winter).

Smith, A. T. H. 1987. *Offences against Public Order, Including the Public Order Act 1986*. London: Sweet and Maxwell.

Sohn, Louis B., and Thomas Burgenthal. 1973. *International Protection of Human Rights*. New York: Bobbs-Merrill.

Southern Poverty Law Center. 1991. *Terror in Our Neighborhoods: A Klanwatch Report on Housing Violence in America*. Klanwatch Project of the Southern Poverty Law Center, April.

Sprinzak, E. 1991. *The Ascendance of Israel's Radical Right*. New York: Oxford University Press.

Stein, E. 1986. "History against Free Speech: The New German Law against the 'Auschwitz'—and Other—'Lies'." *Michigan Law Review* 85 (November).

Strauss, L. 1965. *Spinoza's Critique of Religion*, trans. E. M. Sinclair. New York: Schocken, 1965.

Strossen, N. 1990. "Regulating Racist Speech on Campus: A Modest Proposal?" *Duke Law Journal*.

Tabory, M. 1987. "Legislation against Incitement to Racism in Israel." *Israel Yearbook on Human Rights* 17: 270–299.

Taguieff, P. A. 1987. *La force du préjugé. Essai sur le racisme et ses doubles*. Paris: Gallimard.

Tallentyre, S. G. 1907. *The Friends of Voltaire*. London: Smith Eldad.

Tarnero, J. 1986. "Henri Roques: mention très bien." *CERAC* (June).

Tretter, H. 1990. "Das Kopenhagener Abschlussdokument Über die menschliche Dimension der KSZE." *Europäische Crundrechte Zeitschrift* 17, nos. 9–10.

Tribe, L. 1988. *American Constitutional Law*, 2d. ed. New York: Foundation Press.

Troper, H. 1985. "*The Queen v. Zundel: Holocaust Trial in Toronto*." *Congress Monthly* (July/August).

Varet, G. 1973. *Racisme et philosophie. Essai sur une limite de la pensée*. Paris: Denoël.

Verdès-Leroux, J. 1969. *Scandale financier et antisémitisme catholique. Le Krach de l'Union générale*. Paris.

Vernon, M. 1990. "Le renforcement du dispositif répressif contre la discrimination et le racisme." *Droit pénal*, no. 10 (October).

Vidal-Naquet, P. 1981. "Un Eichmann de papier. Anatomie d'un messonge." In *Les Juifs, la mémoire et le présent*. Paris: Decouverte.

———. 1987. *Les assassins de la mémoire. "Un Eichmann de papier" et autres essais sur le révisionnisme*. Paris: Decouverte.

———. 1991. *Les juifs, la mémoire et le présent*, vol. 2. Paris: Decouverte.

Weil, Bruno. 1926. "Borkum." *C.V. Zeitung*, 28 May, pp. 297–298.

Weinberg, D. 1974. *Les Juifs à Paris de 1933 à 1939*. Paris: Diaspora.

Wiener, A. 1919. "Die Pogromhetze." *Im deutschen Reich* 25 (July/August), pp. 289–299.

Williams, D. 1967. *Keeping the Peace: The Police and Public Order*. London: Hutchinson.

Wilson, N. 1978. *Antisemitism and the Problem of Jewish Identity in Late Nineteenth Century France*. Cambridge: BKS. Demand UMI.

Wilson, S. 1989. *Ideology and Experience: Antisemitism in France at the Time of the Dreyfus Affair*. London and Toronto.

Zamir, Y. 1984. "Cracking Down on Kahane." *Jerusalem Post*, 14 December.

Zierlein, K-G. 1991. "Die Bedeutung der Verfassungsrechtssprechung für die Bewahrung und Durchsetzung der Staatsverfassung." *Europäische Grundrechte Zeitschrift* 18, nos. 14–15.

Index

About the Editors and Contributors

GERALD CHAPPLE is Associate Professor of German in the Modern Languages Department at McMaster University, where has has taught since completing his Ph.D. at Harvard University in 1967. He was an editor and translator of Heinrich Zimmer's *Artistic Form and Yoga* (1984), an editor of *The Romantic Tradition: German Literature and Music in the Nineteenth Century* (1992), and a co-translator of Barbara Frischmuth's novel *The Convent School* (to appear in 1993).

GERALD CROMER is Senior Lecturer in the Department of Criminology at Bar Ilan University. He has published widely in the sociology of deviance and is currently working on a study of the rhetoric of violence in Israel.

DONALD A. DOWNS is Associate Professor of Political Science at the University of Wisconsin, Madison. He is the author of *Nazis in Skokie: Freedom, Community, and the First Amendment* (1985), and *The New*

Politics of Pornography (1989). Each book won a national award. He is the author of many articles on free speech issues, and he has discussed free speech and civil liberty issues in lectures and in print and broadcast media nationwide. He is currently working on two books on new psychological defenses in criminal law.

BRUCE P. ELMAN is Professor of Law and Chair of the Management Board of the Centre for Constitutional Studies at the University of Alberta. He has published numerous articles, including "Altering the Judicial Mind and the Process of Constitution Making in Canada," and "The Promotion of Hatred and the Canadian Charter of Rights and Freedoms."

ROGER ERRERA is a member of the Conseil d'Etat, France's highest court of administrative law. He is a member of the Board of Governors of the Ecole nationale de la magistrature, where most French judges are trained. He has been Visiting Professor of French Law at University College, London (1983–1984) and British Council Senior Research Fellow at the Institute of Advanced Legal Studies, London (1987 and 1988). He is a member of the editorial committee of *Public Law* and has published numerous articles and studies on EEC law, judicial review, privacy, and the law of the press. Errera has been a member of the United Nations Human Rights Committee from 1982 to 1985.

LOUIS GREENSPAN is Associate Professor of Religious Studies and Managing Editor of the Bertrand Russell Editorial Project at McMaster University. He is the author of *The Incompatible Prophecies* (1987) and co-editor of *Fackenheim: German Philosophy and Jewish Thought* (1992).

CYRIL LEVITT is Professor of Sociology at McMaster University, Fellow of the Alexander von Humboldt Foundation (1985), and Lady Davis Visiting Professor, Hebrew University of Jerusalem. He is the author of several books on law, social theory, and ethnic conflicts, including *Children of Privilege* (1984) and *The Riot at Christie Pits* (with W. Shaffir, 1987).

STEPHEN J. ROTH is an international lawyer specializing in human rights law. He was Director of the Institute of Jewish Affairs in London, a research institute on contemporary Jewish affairs, from 1966 to 1988, and is now the Institute's Consultant on International Law. He has written a number of articles and book chapters on international law and on current

Jewish problems. He has edited the volume *The Impact of the Six-Day War: A Twenty-Year Assessment.*

AVROM SHERR is Alsop Wilkinson Professor of Law at Liverpool University and Director of the Centre for Business and Professional Law there. He is a member of the English Law Society Race Relations Committee and the Ethnic Minorities Advisory Committee of the Judicial Studies Board. He has written articles on freedom of speech and demonstrations and has published *Freedom of Speech, Public Order and the Law* (1989). His other research includes the legal profession, legal skills, and legal services; in these areas he has won a number of publishing and research awards.

JULIANE WETZEL is Research Associate at the Center for Research on Antisemitism, Berlin. She is the author of *Jüdisches Leben in München: Durchgangsstation oder Wiederaufbau?* (1987), as well as numerous articles on the postwar history of the Jews and on right-wing extremism.